Nadine Gordimer's
Burger's Daughter

A CASEBOOK

DATE DUE FOR RETURN

CASEBOOKS IN CRITICISM

General Editor, William L. Andrews

NADINE GORDIMER'S
Burger's Daughter

◆ ◆ ◆

A CASEBOOK

Edited by
Judie Newman

OXFORD
UNIVERSITY PRESS

2003

OXFORD

UNIVERSITY PRESS

Oxford   New York
Auckland   Bangkok   Buenos Aires   Cape Town   Chennai
Dar es Salaam   Delhi   Hong Kong   Istanbul   Karachi   Kolkata
Kuala Lumpur   Madrid   Melbourne   Mexico City   Mumbai
Nairobi   São Paulo   Shanghai   Taipei   Tokyo   Toronto

Published by Oxford University Press, Inc.
198 Madison Avenue, New York, New York 10016

www.oup.com

Oxford is a registered trademark of Oxford University Press

Library of Congress Cataloging-in-Publication Data
Nadine Gordimer's Burger's daughter : a casebook / Edited by Judie Newman.
p. cm. — (Casebooks in criticism)
Includes bibliographical references.
ISBN 0-19-514716-2; 0-19-514717-0 (pbk.)
1. Gordimer, Nadine. Burger's daughter. 2. Fathers and daughters in
literature. 3. South Africa—In literature.   I. Newman, Judie.   II. Series.
PR9369.3.G6 B834   2003
823'.914—dc21   2002003639

T1003667932

1 3 5 7 9 8 6 4 2

Printed in the United States of America
on acid-free paper

Acknowledgments

I am grateful to my colleagues at the School of American and Canadian Studies, University of Nottingham, for their collegiate support on a project remote from their own research interests; to the staff of the Hallward Library, University of Nottingham, especially the interlibrary loans staff for assistance in pursuing elusive material; and to James Revie, for keeping me supplied with cheese on toast and jokes.

Credits

The editor and publisher are grateful to the authors and publishers listed below for permission to publish the essays that follow.

Stephen Clingman, *The Novels of Nadine Gordimer: History from the Inside*, 2d ed. (Amherst: University of Massachusetts Press, 1992). Reprinted by permission. First published in London: Allen and Unwin, 1986; reprinted by permission of Bloomsbury Press, London.

John Cooke, *The Novels of Nadine Gordimer: Private Lives/Public Landscapes* (Baton Rouge: Louisiana State University Press, 1985). Reprinted by permission of Louisiana State University Press. Copyright © 1985 by Louisiana State University Press.

Susan Gardner, "'A Story for This Place and Time': An Interview with Nadine Gordimer about *Burger's Daughter*," *Kunapipi* 3, no. 2 (1981): 99–112.

Susan Gardner, "Still Waiting for the Great Feminist Novel," *Hecate* (Brisbane) 8 (1982): 61–76.

Nadine Gordimer, John Dugard, and Richard Smith, *What Happened to Burger's Daughter; or, How South African Censorship Works* (Johannesburg, South Africa: Taurus, 1980). Reprinted by permission of Russell and Volkening as agents for the author. Copyright © 1980 by Nadine Gordimer.

Margot Heinemann, "*Burger's Daughter*: The Synthesis of Revelation," in *The Uses of Fiction: Essays on the Modern Novel in Honour of Arnold Kettle*, edited by

Contents

Nadine Gordimer's
Burger's Daughter

A CASEBOOK

Introduction

JUDIE NEWMAN

◆ ◆ ◆

W̶HEN NADINE GORDIMER was awarded the Nobel Prize for literature in 1991, she also achieved the unimaginable; she got the African National Congress (ANC), led by Nelson Mandela, and the South African government to agree. Both Prime Minister F. W. de Klerk and the ANC issued official statements congratulating her. De Klerk claimed the prize as also an honor for South Africa and described Gordimer as one of his "countrymen." Archbishop Desmond Tutu declared himself "over the moon for Nadine," while André Brink, her fellow South African novelist, saw the prize as the coming of age of South African writing.[1] Gordimer was the seventh woman to win the prize and the first South African.

In the judgment of the Swedish Academy of Letters, Gordimer won the prize for her great epic writings centering on the effects of race relations in her society, which are "of very great benefit to humanity."[2] The committee praised in particular the great works of Gordimer's middle period, *A Guest of Honour* (1970), *The Conservationist* (1974), *Burger's Daughter* (1979), and *July's People* (1981). Although Sture Ahlen, the permanent secretary of the academy that selects the prize winner, said that the award had nothing to do with political relations in South Africa, the citation also said, "Her continual involvement on behalf of literature and free speech in a police state where

3

censorship and persecution of books and people exist have made her the doyenne of South African letters."[3]

In contrast to the tendency of critics and journalists to portray Gordimer as a representative of South African society (the press reports of the Nobel award headlined her variously as "Nelson's Columnist," "ANC Author," "Muscular South African Liberal," and "A Thorn in the Side of Apartheid"), Gordimer always places her activity as a creative writer absolutely first. In conversation with Susan Sontag, she asserted:

> The day when it's more important for me to be more than a writer in the public sense, in the sense of being answerable to some political or social problem, in which I may be very involved as a citizen, the day that that becomes more important than being a writer, I think I'm discounted in the world. I've got no use and no place, because I believe that you must do the thing you do best, and if you're a writer it's a mistake then to become a politician.[4]

In her life, the two spheres of intense personal and imaginative creativity and of social responsibility and historical witness approach and retreat across the world of her fiction.

Nadine Gordimer was born on 20 November 1923 in Springs, a small gold-mining town of about twenty thousand people on Johannesburg's East Rand, the main mining area of the country, the daughter of Isidore Gordimer, a Latvian Jewish jeweler, and Nan Myers Gordimer, who was of British descent. she has described her father as lacking a strong personality, almost as if burnt out by his experience of persecution and by the effort involved in bringing his nine sisters out of Europe to safety. For Gordimer, there was something timid and arrested about him. His life is still something of a mystery to her, in many respects. She believed for many years that he was Lithuanian (like many South African Jewish immigrants) and only discovered later in life that he was Latvian.

Isidore Gordimer came from an area near Riga, where the first Jewish communities were later liquidated by the Nazis. Since secondary education was not available to Jews, he boarded a boat at the age of thirteen and joined his elder brother Marcus in South Africa. He became an itinerant watchmaker and later a small shopkeeper, selling such items as commemorative sets of knives and forks for presentation to retiring miners. He arrived with only his bag of watchmaking tools and traveled around to the mines on a bicycle, mending watches. As a Jew, he was largely unobservant, though Gordimer remembers sitting in the car in shorts outside the synagogue, waiting for him, on the Day of Atonement. Although her parents married in the Great Synagogue in Johannesburg, that was the last time Gordimer's mother set foot in it or in any other place of worship. She was scornful of all organized religion, and when she sent her two daughters to be educated to a Catholic convent, they were excused from all religious instruction.

Gordimer's mother, Nan Myers, had immigrated at the age of six from a much more secure background. Gordimer's maternal grandparents were originally from England and had gone to South Africa before Nan's birth. Her grandfather went prospecting for diamonds and then became what was then known as a "tickey-snatcher" on the stock exchange, a small-time dealer in stocks and shares. In South Africa, pregnant and alone in the house while her husband was at a poker game, Gordimer's grandmother Phoebe was taken aback when she opened the door to find a Chinese man with his throat cut from ear to ear, who dragged himself under her kitchen table and immediately died. Phoebe promptly packed her bags and caught the next train to Cape Town and the boat to England, returning only years later to a country that she clearly saw as uncivilized.

The society in which Nadine Gordimer grew up, however, was conventionally colonial and English-identified, with limited expectations for its daughters. Gordimer remembers celebrating the twenty-fifth anniversary of the ascension to the throne of King George V, decorating the house with bunches of leaves, feeling very patriotic. The family laid claim to Britain as "home" and the town of Springs related to British traditions, even though the province in which Gordimer was born had been a Boer republic. Most girls left school at fifteen or even before, did a short commercial course at a local college, and then worked as secretaries or clerks until marriage. In Spirings, the Mine Manager was like an English squire, whose annual garden party had considerable social importance. The environment was that of a company town. Situated on a great windy plateau, it had a man-made landscape of mountains of white sand from the underground mines, lakes of waste mine water, and plantations of eucalyptus trees (used as pit props).

Gordimer's cultural background was not at all literary. People in Springs read the U.S. Book of the Month and *Reader's Digest*. Gordimer, however, haunted the local library. Her mother broke with convention to some extent, sending her daughters to the local Catholic convent for a good education, in defiance of both her husband's origins and the general anti-Catholic prejudice of the town. Gordimer has described her mother as well-meaning toward blacks and humanistic. She was apolitical but carried out acts of individual charity, as opposed to Gordimer's father's frankly prejudiced attitude. She organized a daycare center and clinic for black children in the area. Gordimer herself only visited a black township for the first time as a young adult, incongruously as a member of an amateur dramatic troupe putting on a performance of *The Importance of Being Earnest.* Gordimer, playing Gwendolen in a bustle and a false bosom, was horrified by the filth and poverty of the township and recognized in consternation that she was displaying European culture to an audience of whose own culture she knew nothing at all. Gordimer was also educated by her reading and considers herself to have been decisively influenced by Upton Sinclair's *The Jungle* (1906), when she realized that black mine workers lived similar lives to those of Sinclair's exploited meat packers in Chicago. She had always thought that the miners, often in native dress, were exotic, and it was a shock to realize that in fact she was the exotic outsider in Africa.

In contrast to her father's shadowy presence, Gordimer's mother's influence was a dominating one, in one vital respect at least. At the age of ten, a sudden faint on Gordimer's part led to the diagnosis of heart trouble, a ban on all physical activity, removal from school, and an adolescence passed in isolation, writing and reading. Gordimer was prevented from dancing, which she passionately enjoyed. (Dancing is often a marker of freedom for the women of her novels.) She spent her time with her mother's generation, at tea parties and social events for adults, becoming a jester for the grown-ups and an accomplished mimic. Later, Gordimer discovered that the heart problem was a fiction, fostered by her unhappily married mother for obscure emotional reasons. As a result of having a "delicate" daughter, Nan gained a constant companion and sustained a friendly relationship with the local doctor, who became a regular visitor. Gordimer has described her mother's action as decisive in shaping her life: "I retreated into myself. I became very introspective. She changed my whole character. . . . It was such incredible loneliness—it's a terrible thing to do to a child."[5] Her mother arranged for private tutoring, but Gordimer had absolutely no contact with other children and became, in her own description, "a little old woman."[6] Before her mother's death, in 1976, Gordimer suppressed these facts in early autobiographical writings, portraying herself as an independent truant, voluntarily absenting herself from formal education. Interviewed in 1983, she commented, "It's only in the last decade of my life that I've been able to face all this."[7]

Critics of Gordimer's writing have seized upon this personal story to suggest that Gordimer went on to endow her private history with public associations and that her enforced dependency on the protective-oppressive mother gave her a sharp insight into the psychology of colonial dependencies, both of race and of gender. As Gordimer commented, "First, you know, you leave your mother's house. Later you leave the house of the white race."[8] But psychological analysis is as much Gordimer's own subject as a process to which she might be naively subjected. Her work demonstrates that she is well read in the literature of psychoanalysis, particularly the work of Freud and Reich, and her own fictional treatment of the heart problem (in *Occasion for Loving*) challenges the Freudian paradigm directly, construing it as an ahistorical explanation of the individual. The suspicion lingers nevertheless that it was this experience that made Gordimer into a writer. The years spent in solitude, reading and writing, gave extra impetus to a writing career initiated at the age of nine, somewhat improbably, with a poem written as a school exercise, which eulogized the Boer republic's president, Paul Kruger, an Afrikaner Nationalist symbol. By the age of ten she was creating whole newspapers, inventing details of weddings and funerals, advertisements, and book reviews, with the format modeled on the Johannesburg paper the *Star*. Real publications followed swiftly, first in 1937 as a child writing for children in the Sunday supplement of the Johannesburg newspaper the *Sunday Express*, and then, when she was fifteen, publishing her first short story, "Come Again Tomorrow," anonymously in the *Forum*, a liberal periodical. From then on, she became a regular contributor to local journals and magazines in South Africa.

If the false heart condition offers one way of defining Gordimer, her involvement in South African history offers another. For some critics, the life stealer was not so much her mother as her mother country. Stephen Clingman (*The Novels of Nadine Gordimer: History from the Inside*) reads Gordimer's work largely in terms of the conditioning force of social and ideological codes as if the writer were formed by South Africa itself, deprived of any individual agency. But history can be as much of an overarching master narrative as psychology, and Gordimer herself has always argued that she would have been a writer even if she had not been a South African. Although Sharpeville and Soweto are events in the personal life of every South African of her age, some political developments are nonetheless of particular biographical significance. The two events are notorious. On 21 March 1960 one word—Sharpeville—rang out around the world, when a PAC (Pan Africanist Congress) campaign against the pass laws ended in a massacre, with 67 unarmed protesters shot dead and 186 injured by the police. On 16 June 1976 the Soweto Revolt took place after 15,000 schoolchildren protested against the compulsory use of Afrikaans as the medium of instruction, and the police opened fire on demonstrators, killing two children. Gordimer recognized in 1965 that apartheid had been the crucial experience of her life. In this connection, two of her often reiterated comments speak for themselves: "If you write honestly about life in South Africa, apartheid damns itself."[9] "People like myself have two births, and the second one comes when you break out of the colour bar."[10]

Gordimer's own second birth appears to have taken place in the 1950s. As a young woman, Gordimer had only a year of formal education at the University of the Witwatersrand. She had no high school diploma and could not therefore undertake a degree program. But she began to move in Johannesburg's artistic circles and to meet blacks socially. In the 1950s Gordimer's involvement with *Drum* magazine brought her into contact with a large group of black writers and artists, in the brief golden age of multiracialism associated with Sophiatown, the mixed-race area of Johannesburg, and fostered by the Congress Alliance of the 1950s. Es'kia Mpahlele was her first black friend; both were struggling young writers. Mpahlele was a regular contributor to *Fighting Talk* and was highly politicized. Gordimer worked on the *Classic*, a magazine started by Nat Nkasa. Black musicians were leading the cultural drive in the 1950s, and it was a time of tremendous, memorable parties, with people dancing all night, visiting shebeens (illicit drinking dens), and going on pub crawls. (Gordimer found the shebeens, with their emphasis on solid, dogged drinking, rather boring.)

In the 1960s, the massacre of unarmed demonstrators at Sharpeville, the 1960 Treason Trial in which many ANC activists were condemned to jail, the state of emergency that imposed a form of martial law on the country, the arrest and imprisonment of Nelson Mandela, and the Rivonia Trial of 1963, which condemned almost all of the remaining leaders of the ANC to jail, resulted in unprecedented repression of both liberal and radical protest The Treason Trial was of major importance in Gordimer's life. Chief Luthuli (president general of the ANC) was staying in her house at the time. When Nelson Mandela was sent to prison for life for sabotage, she did not recoil from the ANC as many white liberals did, and became a close friend of Mandela's lawyer, George Bizos. (There was at one time a plan for her to write Mandela's memoirs.) Sharpeville also had momentous effects on her group of friends: it was "an incredible time when . . . almost everyone I knew was in jail or fleeing."[11] Sophiatown had been bulldozed and been replaced by a white suburb, unashamedly named Triomf. By the mid-1960s, Gordimer's friends from the previous decade—Es'kia Mpahlele, Lewis Nkosi, Can Themba, Nat Nkasa—had all left South Africa.

In reaction to the silencing of an entire generation of black artists, Gordimer began a concerted campaign against censorship, linking political and cultural repression in a battery of essays and speeches. *The Black Interpreters*, a study of indigenous African writing, was a product of her championship of black writers. As a vice president of PEN (International Association of Poets, Playwrights, Editors, Essayists, and Novelists) and a patron and regional representative of the largely black Congress of South African Writers, Gordimer has been tireless in the struggle against censorship worldwide. The 1970s were a painful period for white writers as the growth of Black Consciousness tended to silence and marginalize them, and black activists increasingly perceived them as irrelevant. The multiracial writers' association to which Gordimer belonged was dissolved, as black writers formed their own group. Although Gordimer had had attachments to the ANC while it was an underground organization, it was only in 1983 that the founding of the United Democratic Front offered her a left-wing organization with which she could identify. She had become more involved in the cultural wing of the ANC, with frequent contacts with Wally Serote, then staffing the ANC cultural desk in London, and she became a member of the ANC the moment that it was legal in February 1990. She remains committed to the Left, despite past history. As she explained, "We need to love truth enough, to pick up the blood-dirtied, shamed cause of the Left, and attempt to recreate it in terms of what it was meant to be, not what sixty-five years of human power perversion have made of it."[12] Twice married, to Gerald Gavron and Reinhold Cassirer, with a daughter, a son, and four grandchildren, she remains resident in South Africa.

From the weave of this biography, several threads emerge that are particularly relevant to the concerns of *Burger's Daughter*: the negotiation of freedom from parents; the nature of dependency; political conditioning; the problems of white responsibility; the relationship between the novel and state censorship: the relationship between the creative writer and history; and the place of gender politics in relation to immediate political and racial issues.

To understand the context in which Gordimer began writing it is important to recognize the peculiar history of South Africa, a history fought over and continuously rewritten by the different groups within the country's boundaries. During the apartheid era, South African historical propaganda tended to advance the view (entirely erroneous) that the whites reached South Africa before the black inhabitants or, more moderately, that the two groups arrived together. Many histories of South Africa need to be treated with great caution. Useful accounts include Charles Van

Onselen, *Studies in the Social and Economic History of the Witwatersrand* (which is particularly relevant to the area in which Gordimer grew up), Leonard Thompson, *A History of South Africa*, and John Laurence, *The Seeds of Disaster*, which provides an excellent discussion of Afrikaner propaganda and doublespeak. Heidi Holland, *The Struggle: A History of the African National Congress*, offers a readable account based on interviews with ANC spokespeople. The distortion or suppression of historical fact was one of the weapons of apartheid. In 1978, when Floors van Jaarsveld, a Pretoria professor of history, questioned the view that divine intervention was responsible for the victory of the Boers over the Zulus at Blood River, a group of men burst into the University of South Africa's lecture hall and tarred and feathered him. Because of the shortage of educational materials in South African schools, black children are still being taught, in the twenty-first century, from apartheid-era history books, one of which devotes precisely three pages to black South African history.

History is particularly vital to an understanding of *Burger's Daughter*. The novel is a historical and cultural document, both in its content and in its own history of censorship, which make it crucial to the understanding of South Africa in the 1970s. One of the anonymous reviewers for the current volume described it as a portrait, even a kind of sourcebook, of South Africa on the eve of democracy. As the epigraph to the novel suggests, Rosa's identity is both affirmed ("I am") as individual and yet constructed as passive to locality ("the place in which something has occurred"). Stephen Clingman is the best source for the historical context of the novel, which focuses in particular on the events culminating in the Soweto revolt, as the leadership of the struggle against apartheid passed from a coalition of mixed-race, often Communist-inspired activists to indigenous black leaders. In 1968, Steve Biko founded the black South African Students Organization, which promoted the Black Consciousness movement, which gained steadily in influence and culminated in the founding in 1975 of the Black People's Convention, with Biko as its president. On 16 June 1976 the Soweto revolt took place after fifteen thousand schoolchildren protested against the compulsory use of Afrikaans as the medium of instruction, and the police opened fire on the demonstrators, killing two children. Violence swept the country, and it took the police and army the better part of a year to regain control. The revolt was widespread and spontaneous, and it cost black South Africa dear. By 1977 the official toll (a gross underestimate) was 575 dead and thousands injured. In 1977 Biko was arrested and died from brutal treatment in police custody. He had been in custody for twenty-six days, kept naked and manacled.

By 1979, when Gordimer published the novel, P. W. Botha, who had become prime minister in 1978, was facing a much-strengthened ANC, which, although in exile, had attracted increased support after Soweto and was pressing for international isolation of South Africa by boycotts, sanctions, and embargoes. Victory was in the air, but it was to be hard won. The South African forces attacked alleged ANC bases in Zimbabwe, Botswana, and Zambia in 1986, and an indefinite, nationwide state of emergency was declared. Under the state of emergency it is estimated that thirteen thousand people, many of them children, were detained and tortured. In 1989 F. W. de Klerk succeeded Botha as state president, supported by reform-seeking whites, and immediately began consultations with the ANC leadership. In 1990 Nelson Mandela was unconditionally released, and the ANC and other outlawed organizations were unbanned. In 1994 the ANC was elected with 62 percent of the vote in the first free elections, and on 9 May, Mandela was elected president of the Republic of South Africa.

In *Burger's Daughter*, the correspondences between fiction and history are close. Lionel Burger is based to a large extent on Bram Fischer, a leader of the South African Communist Party, about whom Gordimer had written two articles at the time of his arrest and trial, clearly admiring his heroism.[13] Fischer was a lawyer and Lionel is a doctor, but the shape of their political careers is extremely similar. Fischer took a black child into his house, just as Lionel takes in Baasie. When the Communist Party was outlawed and dissolved, he continued to pursue its activities underground, while maintaining his career as a lawyer, defending the accused in political trials. It was reputedly Fischer who oversaw the security committee entrusted with the details of Mandela's movements when he was underground. A traditional Marxist, he saw the solution to human problems in social terms, and he was personally warm and sociable, maintaining an open house around his pool, just as Lionel does. Fischer was eventually uncovered and lived in hiding for nine months. Betrayed, he received a life sentence. Before being sentenced, he made a moving speech describing how he, as a lawyer, had been brought to defy the law by the evils of South African society. Unlike Lionel, who dies in prison, he was released from jail to die (of cancer) with his family. Fischer remains a hero. In June 1995 Mandela gave the first Bram Fischer Memorial Lecture in Johannesburg and in 1996 opened the Bram Fischer Memorial Library.

Stephen Clingman's recent biography of Fischer makes illuminating reading alongside *Burger's Daughter*, itself premised on the presence of a biographer whose questions to Rosa stir her memories of her father.[14] Clingman's account of the childhood of the Fischer children (Ruth, Ilse, and

Paul) reveals just how much the political struggle predominated. Ilse's first language was Zulu, because she was so often in the care of a servant. A Communist Party pamphlet of September 1945 shows Ruth and Ilse (ages six and two, respectively) looking fair and angelic and gazing at a soap bubble with the slogan "Safeguard Their Future." Their mother, Molly, was a Communist candidate in the local elections. As Clingman notes, all those in opposition to apartheid worried that they were sacrificing or exploiting their children. In the Fischers' case, it was a particularly acute anxiety, since Paul Fischer was terminally ill with cystic fibrosis and diabetes. The conflict between political belief in a utopian future and the human realities of suffering and death becomes a similar concern in Gordimer's novel, especially in several key scenes in Rosa's evolution: the death of a tramp in a city park, the beating of a donkey, an old woman found wandering. When Molly Fischer was arrested in 1960, Ilse kept the domestic machinery running at home. When a group of political detainees went on a hunger strike, Ilse was one of thirty children who demonstrated on the steps of the city hall in Johannesburg. (The children were promptly arrested.) When the Fischer family took in Nora Mlambo, a black child who had lost her mother, Nora and Ilse shared a room (though they attended different segregated schools). Later, at convent school, Nora became pregnant, and the girls' lives diverged. Gordimer transforms the adopted motherless black girl into Baasie, Rosa's adopted brother, replacing a young mother (Nora gave birth to a son) with a male child. Molly Fischer drowned in an accident, despite her husband's repeated attempts to bring her up to the surface of the pool into which their car had crashed. Gordimer transfers the details of family deaths, so that Rosa's brother Tony drowns in a pool despite the mother's attempts to save him; Rosa's mother suffers a lingering death from multiple sclerosis. Given the facts of Gordimer's own relationship to illness and to her mother, it is tempting to see a personal rather than a political intent here. The roles of child and mother are reversed; the mother becomes arrested, dependent, ultimately paralyzed. As a result of exchanging Nora for Baasie, the "you" to whom Rosa's monologues are addressed is not a mother or a sister but a father, brother, or lover. And Gordimer gives Lionel her own birthdate, 20 November.

Fiction is not history, but the truths of fiction are sometimes more revealing than fact. Personal relationships nonetheless have to be approached with historical understanding. Like Rosa, Ilse had also posed as the fiancée of not one political prisoner, but two (one in jail in Johannesburg, the other in Cape Town) in order to relay messages. One of them became her boyfriend for a time. Detainees were allowed to discuss "family matters" with their visitors. The reader who analyzes the references to family relationships in *Burger's Daughter* without knowing that "the family" was code for the banned South African Communist Party will not appreciate the full ironies. The party operated on a cell system with a pyramid structure, in which one member of a small group communicated upward, another down, with little lateral communication, a model not unlike the Western nuclear family. Yet close personal friendships were the basis of its links to the ANC, and the aim was to extend the nuclear model to a much-enlarged, inclusive, South African family, cross-racial and uniting Afrikaners and English speakers.

Richard Martin has argued that the novel may be representative and concern actual events, but resists the illusion of direct access to the real by emphasizing the mediating role of language and ideology, themselves historically determined.[15] In *Writing and Being*, a book-length meditation on the relationship between fiction and (auto)biography, Gordimer commented that although Lionel is like Fischer, with a similar background, she did not know Fischer or his family at all well. She purposely did not approach either of Fischer's daughters while writing the novel and allowed what little contact she had with the family to lapse. When the novel was complete, however, she sent it to one of them who was resident in South Africa. After a delay of some weeks, she walked in through Gordimer's gate with the novel. Gordimer takes up the story:

> She said, "This was our life." And nothing more. I knew this was the best response I should ever have to that novel. Perhaps the best I should ever have in respect of any of my fictions. Something I should never receive again. No critic's laudation could match it; no critic's damning could destroy it. For she was not speaking of verisimilitude, she was not matching mugshots, she knew that facts, events, sequences were not so; she was conceding that while no one can have total access to the lives of others—not even through means of the analyst's casebook, the biographer's research, the subjectively-composed revelations of diaries and letters—by contrast, on her or his vision the novelist may receive, from the ethos those lives give off, a vapour of the truth condensed, in which, a finger tracing upon a window-pane, the story may be written.[16]

Fiction could nevertheless become a direct form of political action, particularly in relation to state censorship. In *Burger's Daughter*, when Duma Dhladhla says that black liberation cannot be divorced from Black Consciousness "because we cannot be conscious of ourselves and at the same time remain slaves," he is quoting directly from Steve Biko, who was quoting Hegel.[17] Bram Fischer's speech at his trial is reprised in the mouth of Lionel Burger, and quotations from the writings of Joe Slovo are spoken by other characters. Most obviously, a handbill from the Soweto Students Representative Council is reproduced verbatim in the text. This ill-spelled, poorly expressed product of black children denied access to decent education makes a statement in itself. Biko, Slovo, Fischer, and the SSRC had little chance of being heard in the official world of South Africa, a world of bannings, embargoes, brutal repression, and official censorship. But in the novel they found expression.

A dominant feature of the apartheid era was censorship. Three of Gordimer's novels (*A World of Strangers, The Late Bourgeois World,* and *Burger's Daughter*) were banned. The censorship bureau was active in every province, and only three censors needed to agree in order for a book to be banned. The judges concerned generally had no literary qualifications but were loyal to the ruling National Party bureaucrats. They were paid for their services. There were ninety-seven definitions of what is undesirable in literature. In the period between the first censorship act in 1955 (which was followed by a more comprehensive act in 1963) and 1970, eleven thousand books were banned, including pornography and political propaganda, works of political analysis (Eldridge Cleaver, Frantz Fanon), sexually explicit novels (John Updike's *Couples* and *Rabbit Is Rich*), and such subversive texts as *Uncle Tom's Cabin* and Pascal's *Pensées*. The writer was not informed that the book was banned; it was merely mentioned in the *Government Gazette* in the weekly list of bannings (which included also records, posters, art works, and even T-shirts, if they bore a political slogan). Writers had to become ingenious to get around the problem of banning. Books were sometimes banned for sale and distribution, but not for possession. If the reader had already bought the book, she could keep it (but, officially, was not permitted to lend it to anybody else). Some documents were, however, also banned for possession, as was the case with the SSRC handbill in *Burger's Daughter*. As a result, possession of the novel was also a criminal offense. Getting the book into the country disguised as other merchandise was one solution. *Burger's Daughter* came into South Africa in unlabeled parcels (the sight of Gordimer's name would have been enough to ensure that it was embargoed) and a couple of thousand copies got around before the censors caught up with it. A banned book published abroad could not be brought into the country but, once established abroad, the banning of a book created bad publicity for the South African government, as in the case of *Burger's Daughter*, where protests from John Fowles, Heinrich Böll, and a host of others created a storm of negative international press coverage.

Gordimer made the most of the situation. When André Brink's publisher had refused to publish his novel *'n Oomblik in die Wind* in 1975, because his previous novel had been banned, a small group of academics had decided to begin *samizdat* publishing as Taurus, publishing clandestinely and distributing through mail order. (*Samizdat* in Russian means "circulating underground," as opposed to *tamizdat*, "publishing abroad.") Gordimer heard of this and approached Taurus to publish the text on the history of the banning of *Burger's Daughter, What Happened to Burger's Daughter; or, How South African Censorship Works* (1980), after which, in partnership with her South African publishers, Taurus published several of her works. She wanted to be associated with its owners' active protest; they were glad to have the support of a figure of her standing. In the volume, Gordimer reproduces the comments of the Publications Control Board on the reasons for banning the novel and systematically rebuts them.

History has moved on. Johannesburg now has an Apartheid Museum, located next to an amusement park and a casino and built only as a condition of the casino gaining a license.[18] *Burger's Daughter*, however, is no museum piece but a novel that tackles enduring issues of politics and gender, literary technique and critical theory. Different schools of thought—Marxist existentialist, feminist—have claimed the novel for their own, both inside and outside of academia. The essays reprinted here offer a variety of approaches to central topics of criticism, including censorship, psychoanalysis, colonialism, politics, history, feminism, the family, narrative structure, and style.

In her interview with Susan Gardner, Gordimer describes the germ of the novel and its development in her mind as she attended a series of political trials. She discusses the role of women in the resistance movements, her views on feminism, and the problems of the white writer who writes about black characters, while she also reasserts the absolute primacy of the imagination. Gordimer's description of Rosa as wanting to become embattled with suffering, to avoid a passive existence, resonates with the views expressed by Conor Cruise O'Brien in a contemporary review. O'Brien reads the novel not as a political work but as profoundly religious, even specifically Christian, invoking redemption through suffering. As a former representative of the United Nations' secretary general in Katanga, who was writing when he was editor in chief of the London *Observer*, O'Brien was prescient in 1979, describing the future of black South Africa with its different, tough, determined groups disputing the seat of power.

The next two essays provide insights into the crucial theme of the relationship between public and private in South Africa. Stephen Clingman, in a piece extracted from his critical monograph *The Novels of Nadine Gordimer: History from the Inside*, argues that the novel is deeply concerned with the climactic historical moment of revolution in South Africa, a subject that it approaches through scrutiny of its effect on the individual. Clingman offers an indispensable account of social and historical context and of political history, but is also acute in his ability to relate apparently formal literary devices to that context. He highlights, for example, the use value of quotations. Gordimer is a highly intertextual writer, but the process of quotation is designed less in terms of the "purchase" of textual attribution than as a challenge to white cultural property. Clingman also summarizes one essay that could not be included here for reasons of space in which Robert Green offers a cogent, formal analysis of the fashion in which certain narrative techniques replace the author, in the context of a discussion of the possible variations in the relationship between the author and the text.[19]

In opposition to Clingman, John Cooke reads the novel in terms of Gordimer's personal history, particularly her "lost childhood." Just as Gordimer's adolescence was interrupted by the fictitious heart complaint, so Cathy Burger preempts Rosa's adolescence for political ends. Rosa's decision to follow her animal instincts to run from pain and suffering, the treatment of her by the other radicals (after her father's imprisonment) as a convalescent, even the opening of the novel with its juxtaposition of adolescent suffering (menarche) subordinated to political purpose, take on fresh resonance in Cooke's analysis. At the close of her visit to Europe, as Rosa recognizes that her father only seemed to offer a safe place but could not nullify the existential miseries of sex and death, Cooke notes the moral that although love cannot cast out fear, the experience of love, the belated adolescence that Rosa enjoys in Europe, allows her to let her feelings go and to escape from the repression of her past.

This implicitly psychological approach is also that of the next essay (by Judie Newman), which examines the psychoanalytic politics of the novel, drawing on cultural and psychoanalytic theorists of colonialism, especially Mannoni and Fanon. The essay focuses in particular on the role of the tapestries of the Museum of Cluny, which Rosa's lover offers to show her in France and which are a focus for the questions of representation and visual politics that run throughout the novel. Rosa is under surveillance (political), and the complex narrative method with its first- and third-person narrators and its different implied audiences is carefully designed to short-circuit the connection often critically perceived between the realist novel's detailed cataloging of the world and the surveillance central to repressive power in the modern world. Seeing is all too readily connected with policing, with placing the entire world of the text under scrutiny. To the modern reader, familiar with Michel Foucault's *Discipline and Punish* (1975), the disciplinary and repressive effect of being the object of the gaze—as a woman, as a postcolonial subject—throws fresh light on the displayed image of the tapestry lady, admiring in the hand-held mirror only the reflection of the nonexistent unicorn. Where Newman's essay concentrates on the need to correct the errors of the eye in relation to racial and gender stereotypes, readers coming fresh to the novel today may broaden the scope of interpretation to understand the different ways in which the novel questions the dominance of the visual, of representation, in the modern world, whether the damage to the individual is the result of being the object of the gaze (Rosa in South Africa) or of becoming the self-indulgent gazer (Rosa in front of a series of art works in France). Rilke, whose account of the tapestries inspires the scene, wrote a poem, "Turning Point," which begins:

> There is a limit to what can be achieved by gazing
> And the world that has been won by more intense gazing
> Wants to come to fruition in love.
>
> Work of the eye has been done.
> Perform now the work of the heart.[20]

At a turning point in her life, Rosa disappears from the reader's sight as she disappears from the ever-present surveillance of state security to take up the work of the heart.

Rilke's chosen epitaph invoked "Rose, oh reiner Widerspruch" (Rose, oh, pure contradiction[21]) and it is the contradictions of Rosa Burger's position that occupy several other essayists. The oscillation in the novel among thesis (Communism, political life, society), antithesis (individual existence), and synthesis (recommitment to the political struggle, with a renewed sense of self) has produced different interpretations. For the South African authorities, the novel was clearly a defense of Communism. On the other side of the fence, a review by "Z. N." in the *African Communist* in 1980 began by arguing that *Burger's Daughter* was welcome as a discussion of the relationship between the Communist Party and the ANC, the mine workers strike of 1946 and the Comintern, but went on to regret the readability of the novel, which eclipsed any revolutionary content and sullied its doctrinal purity.[22] Richard Peck has analyzed the debates over the novel's dialectic method, concluding that Gordimer is influenced more by liberalism and existentialism than by Marxism.[23] Margaret Daymond argues against synthesis, maintaining that Rosa's imprisonment simply cuts off access to her story. She is sidelined rather than emerging as a new Rosa, the product of thesis (Communism) and antithesis (the personal life).[24] Paradoxically, where some critics object to political involvement, a more frequent criticism has concerned the nature of Gordimer's detachment. As early as 1969, Dennis Brutus argued that Gordimer lacked warmth and feeling and merely observed in a dehumanized fashion entirely typical of South African society.[25] Ursula Laredo agreed, but saw this detachment as a strength, reading the work from an essentially liberal viewpoint.[26] In 1989, David Ward returned to the question and argued that the nature of Gordimer's detachment hinges upon her ability to produce a narrator as other, quite distinct from any possibility of being perceived as the author's mouthpiece, so that it is essentially a technical virtue.[27]

Critics who have focused on Gordimer's ironic effects and her ability to set up a dialectic in her fiction have applauded the multivocality and variety of viewpoints for which a degree of detachment is a prerequisite. In a piece extracted from a landmark study of postcolonial writing, Abdul R. JanMohamed argues in the volume that the novel offers a trenchant critique of the liberal position. JanMohamed considers Gordimer's writing in the context of colonialist society's Manichean structure, but ultimately defends her against the charge of being a colonial writer. In the essay that follows, Margot Heinemann, one-time leader of the Communist Party in Great Britain, a poet and novelist, and a distinguished scholar of the Renaissance, argues (in contrast to other essays) that Rosa Burger's commitment does become that of her Communist father. Heinemann reads the novel both in the context of modern political fictions and in terms of the socially created nature of what we familiarly call the self. In contrast to the deterministic tendency of both historicist and psychoanalytical critics, Heinemann sees in Rosa the power of reason, arguing that the political, activist has to both experience oppression and analyze it rationally. Rosa's conversion to political action is not the product of a blind faith, but of a reasoned one. In "What the Book Is About," which systematically rebuts the comments of the Publications Control Board on the reasons for banning the novel, Gordimer is similarly reasoned. The sense of drama, of what it was actually like to be a writer under these conditions, emerges all the more forcefully for the terse and understated manner in which the author allows apartheid to damn itself.

As the immediacy of the South African political debate has diminished, gender politics have emerged as a major interest for critics. Battle has also been joined, perhaps predictably, over Gordimer's relationship to feminism, as her credentials as a woman writer have become a focus for concern, with her representation of women occasionally seen as fixed in outmoded and sexist paradigms. In some cases, there is a lack of understanding of the intellectual roots of Gordimer's discussions of gender which are based on Freudian and Marxist analyses of the family by Wilhelm Reich and Frantz Fanon. Unrepressed sexuality has always played a major part in Gordimer's writing, often as a force for radical individual and political change. For Gordimer, sexuality is clearly not restricting or oppressive but liberating, the way out from the white family into social freedom. Given her childhood experiences, she was never likely to idealize maternal love or any essentialist form of feminism. Although Gordimer famously described feminism in South Africa as "piffling," Karen Lazar makes it clear that what Gordimer was targeting was the type of "liberal feminism" that separates issues of gender from those of race.[28] In the context of apartheid, attempts by white women to insist on being allowed entry to white male clubs did not seem a high priority. Andrew V. Ettin goes some way toward meeting the antifeminist accusation.[29] Gordimer's denunciation of Olive Schreiner is persuasively read by Ettin as the product of her firm socioeconomic grasp, her sense that Schreiner's wronged sense of herself as a woman was a secondary matter given her historical situation. In consequence, Gordimer envisages feminism as elitist, arising from the bourgeois white intellectual's refusal to face up to her true position of power. Feminism becomes a surrogate protest; the racial situation is the real.

In relation to this debate, three essays are reproduced here. Susan Gardner argues for the relevance of *Burger's Daughter* to the understanding of feminism in South Africa and to Gordimer's own position. As Gardner admits, the novel is an irritating as well as an inspirational novel for feminist readers, as Rosa differentiates herself from her patriarchal identity and begins to evolve a language (inventing her own metaphors) to represent her reality more adequately than the inherited codes allow. Lorraine Liscio also relates the novel to European feminist theory and draws out intertextual links to Conrad and to Colette, via close analyses of the different voices and narrators of the novel. In an essay informed by Cixous, Irigaray, and a sophisticated understanding of recent discussions of the nature of women's writing, Liscio considers the possibility that Cathy Burger is the real revolutionary, the silenced, lost mother figure in the text. Rosa, in her desire for psychic wholeness, seeks out a surrogate mother in Katya, in order to move inward and backward through the mother, to be nurtured and thus enabled to reach out more fully to others. In an interesting approach, Louise Yelin argues that there is a sense in which Gordimer contributes to dialogical criticism, exposing the terms *race* and *class*, which are occluded in Bakhtin's writings. In the work of contemporary critics, the earlier straightforward opposition between art and politics is becoming a much more sophisticated and interesting account of the various intersections of race, class, and gender which operate in Gordimer's work. Because South African society offers such binary oppositions of black and white, body and mind, art and politics, Europe and Africa, male and female, Gordimer's fiction has to avoid playing into the same sorts of divisions and categorizations. Debates over the dialectical nature of her fiction have now moved on, toward a criticism more concerned with hybridity, border states, and transitionality. Yelin's account of Bakhtinian dialogism is sharply developed as it reflects on Gordimer and on Bakhtin. Her analysis of the language world of the novel underlines the fashion in which changes in Rosa's life are marked by changes in the person to whom she addresses her tale. Identity, like discourse, is constructed in and by the relation between speaker and addressee. At the same time, Yelin uses theory against theory, cautioning that Bakhtinian concepts such as polyphony, dialogue, and carnival may elide the masculine and European with the universal. In the novel, Brandt Vermeulen offers an ersatz version of "dialogue" between "people and nations" (p. 194) as a justification for the homelands policy of the Afrikaner government, which banished blacks to nations and places that had no existence except in the language of the state. As Lionel Burger understood, Brandt's long words are a justificatory jargon: "he won't scruple to invoke Kierkegaard's Either/Or against Hegel's dialectic to demonstrate the justice of segregated lavatories" (p. 193).

The essays reprinted here span the decades of the 1970s and 1980s. Later writers, however, have not neglected the novel. A particular emerging concern is the body. Gordimer was attracted to Barthes's definition of writing as the writer's essential *gesture*. Critics have highlighted the role of the physical and sensuous in the fiction, calling attention to Lawrence and Whitman as influences. Barbara Temple-Thurston has highlighted Gordimer's ability to catch the implications of even the smallest gesture or nuance and to trace its connections to broader social and political arenas, offering a kind of Freudian psychopathology of the everyday.[30] Similarly, for Andrew V. Ettin, Gordimer sings the body electric, with sexuality the route to liberation.

Rose Pettersson understands the fiction as growing out of two warring imperatives: the deep abhorrence of apartheid and the resistance to an orthodoxy of opposition.[31] Pettersson operates comparatively, making a persuasive case for close resemblances between *Burger's Daughter* and *My Son's Story* (similar revolutionary but silent and absent mother figures) thus undercutting ideas of development across the writing career. Kathrin Wagner's study of Nadine Gordimer is avowedly revisionary, setting out to examine the survival in the novels of cultural and ethnic stereotypes of a conservative, Eurocentric, or settler nature, stereotypes that conflict with the intended ideological message and therefore qualify Gordimer's commitment.[32] Along the way, Gordimer is accused of antifeminism, liberalism, idealization of blacks, ignoring class realities, emotional coldness, and various forms of thought crime. Gordimer may well be compromised in many ways by her South African upbringing (as she has candidly admitted herself), but who is not? What Wagner says of Gordimer is true only as far as it is true of all novelists who have lived through interesting times and kept on writing. Wagner seems to be measuring Gordimer against some impossible ideal of uncontaminated literary purity. Dominic Head offers a useful corrective to Wagner in his emphasis on the politics of textuality and the "literariness" of Gordimer's writing, which he envisages as a quest for a hybridized cultural expression, fusing African and European literary forms.[33] Throughout, there is a useful focus on ideas of space and of the body and on continuities of theme and method, which underlie the fiction. In his monograph (*White on Black in South Africa*, unfinished at his death in exile), Michael Wade explores the tendency of the white South African community to discover its own identity in relation to the Other, whether Afrikaner or African.[34] Gordimer's writings over a thirty-year period mark a major change in the psychic functioning of white South Africa, demonstrating a clearer understanding of its own identity. For Wade, there is an unwritten, repressed Jewish theme in Gordimer's writing, which also affects her construction of the Other.

Four collections are worthy of note. Rowland Smith offers a spectrum of the most useful scholarship by major critics.[35] The essays cover the period from 1953 to 1986, with contributors from four continents and very different critical perspectives. Dorothy Driver's essay on the politicization of women in Gordimer's work deserves to be singled out as of special interest. The editor's introduction is a first-rate account of Gordimer's historical and artistic development. Bruce King has brought together fifteen essays that usefully discuss the later fiction.[36] Again, it is worth singling out Karen Lazar's essay on the ambiguities of Gordimer's feminism, Graham Huggan on commitment, and Lars Engle on the political uncanny. Nancy Topping Bazin and Marilyn Dallman Seymour have edited *Conversations with*

Nadine Gordimer, which gathers together almost all of Gordimer's major literary interviews from 1958 to 1989, arranged chronologically.[37] Most recently, when Gordimer's seventy-fifth birthday became the occasion for a celebratory volume, tributes spanned the range of her career.[38] Albie Sachs described how reading *The Lying Days* had made him feel like the discoverer of his own continent, its familiarity stripped away by her prose. Günter Grass wrote of his admiration and enthusiasm for *The House Gun*. Seamus Heaney offered an image from Beowulf in her honor and introduced twenty more poetic tributes, followed by fictional pieces and a play, from both well-established writers and younger talents.

The events of the 1990s have provided a compelling context for new readings of Gordimer's work. Almost simultaneously the world has witnessed the end of apartheid in South Africa and the concomitant rise of new dangers in the politics of nationalism and ethnicity, both on the white Right and in black neo-tribal groupings. For the South African writer, the question of the future or of the many possible futures has developed from the imaginary realm to that of daily activity. As the writer comes out of battle dress into purely literary commitments, problems previously subordinated to single-issue politics have also surfaced anew. Has the South African novelist lost her essential subject? Can the white novelist survive the end of apartheid? Or has the artists' inspiration disappeared together with the tools previously employed? In a series of essays collected in *Rediscovery of the Ordinary*, Njabulo Ndebele has highlighted the dangers of the notion of literature as merely a weapon in the political struggle and of the tendency in South Africa to produce a quasi-journalistic literature of indictment, characterized by the psychology of the slogan. Such literature may inform but cannot transform. Ndebele argues for the ordinary as an antidote to the visual spectacle of modern life, as a site where culture and politics can encounter each other as realities, not through the meshes of constructed concepts, slogans, or symbols. There is a need, in his view, to see ordinary human lives as the direct focus of political interest. In addition, for Ndebele, there is a danger in emptying out interiority to the benefit of exterior signs. Richness of character is not simply the product of bourgeois escapism into an ethos of individualism. Interiority can be a way in which the individual steps out of the network of exchange relations and values, away from the performance principle and the profit motive and toward passion, imagination, conscience. For Ndebele, "the greatest challenge of the South African revolution is in the search for ways of thinking, ways of perception, that will help us break down the closed epistemological structures of South African oppression."[39]

At the close of *Burger's Daughter*, Rosa Burger has learned the necessity—even the revolutionary potential—of that inner life, lived beyond the reach of the forces of surveillance, outside the systems of symbolic representation in which, as her father's daughter, she had been entrapped. Throughout the novel, one phrase recurs like a mantra, the desire to live "like anyone else." At the last point in the novel at which the reader hears Rosa's own voice, she repeats the phrase five times in a half page, reflecting on the process by which she has decided to return to South Africa and ending with the comment, "Like anyone else, I do what I can" (p. 332). No longer a hero, now merely one political prisoner among others, Rosa has become ordinary, richly and passionately ordinary. Unusually, she is one of Gordimer's few characters to enjoy a literary future. Eight years later, Rosa makes a cameo appearance in *A Sport of Nature* (1987), a novel that ends with the imagined proclamation of a new African state, which used to be South Africa.[40]

Notes

1. John Carlin, "Gordimer Unites Old Foes with the Write Stuff," *Independent*, 4 Oct. 1991, 11.
2. "South African Author Wins the Nobel Prize," *Scotsman*, 4 Oct. 1991, 3.
3. "ANC Author Gordimer's Nobel Prize," *Glasgow Herald*, 4 Oct. 1991, 13.
4. "Nadine Gordimer and Susan Sontag: In Conversation," *Listener*, 23 May 1985, 16.
5. Jannika Hurwitt, "The Art of Fiction LXXVII: Nadine Gordimer," *Paris Review* 88 (1983). 90.
6. Ibid., 90.
7. Ibid., 89.
8. John Barkham, "South Africa, Perplexities, Brutalities, Absurdities: The Author," *Saturday Review*, 21 Jan. 1963, 63.
9. Pat Schwartz, "Pat Schwartz Talks to Nadine Gordimer," in *New South African Writing* (Johannesburg, South Africa: Lorton, 1977), 81.
10. Studs Terkel, "Nadine Gordimer," *Perspective on Ideas and the Arts* 12, no. 5 (1963): 44.
11. Stephen R. Clingman, *The Novels of Nadine Gordimer: History from the Inside* (London: Allen and Unwin, 1986), 75.
12. Nadine Gordimer, *The Essential Gesture: Writing, Politics and Places*, edited by Stephen R. Clingman (London: Cape, 1988), 283.
13. See the suggested readings at the end of this volume. In her essay

for *London Magazine*, Gordimer makes the point that the Fischer trial was a double trial, aiming both to convict Fischer and to nail organizations (the Defence and Aid Fund, Christian Action) that had funneled money into South Africa to provide lawyers for political prisoners, to help their families to buy school uniforms, and to travel on prison visits.

14. See Stephen R. Clingman, *Bram Fischer: Afrikaner Revolutionary* (Amherst: University of Massachusetts Press, 1998). The only biography of Fischer written prior to the publication of *Burger's Daughter* is Naomi Mitchison, *A Life for Africa: The Story of Bram Fischer* (London: Merlin, 1973).

15. Richard G. Martin, "Narrative, History, Ideology: A Study of *Waiting for the Barbarians and Burger's Daughter,*" *Ariel* 17, no. 3 (1986): 3–21.

16. Nadine Gordimer, *Writing and Being* (Cambridge, Mass.: Harvard University Press, 1995), 12.

17. Nadine Gordimer, *Burger's Daughter* (London and New York: Penguin, 1980), 164. Subsequent references follow quotations in the text.

18. Chris McGreal, "Inside Story," *Guardian*, 12 Dec. 2001, 6–7.

19. Robert Green, "Nadine Gordimer's *Burger's Daughter*: Censors and Authors, Narrators and Narratees," an unpublished paper presented at the Conference on Literature and Society in Southern Africa, University of York, England, 1981.

20. Rainer Maria Rilke, *Sämtliche Werke* (Wiesbaden: Insel-Verlag, 1955–1966), 82. See also Eudo C. Mason, *Rilke* (London: Oliver and Boyd), 95.

21. H. F. Peters, *Rainer Maria Rilke: Masks and the Man* (Seattle: University of Washington Press, 1960).

22. Z. N., "The Politics of Commitment," *African Communist* 80 (1980): 100–101.

23. Richard Peck, "One Foot before the Other into an Unknown Future: The Dialectic in Nadine Gordimer's *Burger's Daughter*," *World Literature Written in English* 29, no. 1 (1989): 26–43.

24. M. J. Daymond, J. U. Jacobs, and M. Lenta, eds., *Momentum: On Recent South African Writing* (Pietermaritzburg, South Africa: University of Natal Press, 1984).

25. Dennis Brutus, "Protest against Apartheid," in *Protest and Conflict in African Literature*, edited by Cosmo Pieterse and Donald Munro, 93–100 (London: Heinemann, 1969).

26. Ursula Laredo, "African Mosaic: The Novels of Nadine Gordimer," *Journal of Commonwealth Literature* 8, no. 1 (1973): 42–53.

27. David Ward, *Chronicles of Darkness* (London: Routledge, 1989).

28. Karen Lazar, "Feminism as 'Piffling': Ambiguities in Gordimer's

Short Stories," in *The Later Fiction of Nadine Gordimer*, edited by Bruce King, 213–27 (London: Macmillan, 1993).

29. Andrew V. Ettin, *Betrayals of the Body Politic: The Literary Commitments of Nadine Gordimer* (Charlottesville: University Press of Virginia, 1993).

30. Barbara Temple-Thurston, *Nadine Gordimer Revisited* (New York: Twayne, 1999).

31. Rose Pettersson, *Nadine Gordimer's One Story of a State Apart* (Stockholm, Sweden: Almqvist and Wiksell, 1995).

32. Kathrin Wagner, *Re-reading Nadine Gordimer. Text and Subtext in the Novels* (Bloomington: Indiana University Press, 1994).

33. Dominic Head, *Nadine Gordimer* (Cambridge: Cambridge University Press, 1994).

34. Michael Wade, *White on Black in South Africa: A Study of English-Language Inscriptions of Skin Color* (New York: St. Martin's, 1993).

35. Rowland Smith, ed., *Critical Essays on Nadine Gordimer* (Boston: Hall, 1990).

36. Bruce King, ed., *The Later Fiction of Nadine Gordimer* (London: Macmillan, 1993).

37. Nancy Topping Bazin and Marilyn Dallman Seymour, eds., *Conversations with Nadine Gordimer* (Jackson: University of Mississippi Press, 1990), 258.

38. Andries Walter Oliphant, ed., *A Writing Life: Celebrating Nadine Gordimer* (New York: Viking, 1998).

39. Njabulo Ndebele, *Rediscovery of the Ordinary* (Manchester, England: Manchester University Press, 1991), 67.

40. Nadine Gordimer, *A Sport of Nature* (London: Cape, 1987), 33.

"A Story for This Place and Time"

An Interview with Nadine Gordimer
about *Burger's Daughter*

SUSAN GARDNER

◆   ◆   ◆

IN JULY 1980 SUSAN GARDNER sought an interview in Johannesburg with Nadine Gordimer to discuss her 1979 novel, *Burger's
Daughter*. This was banned for import and distribution in South Africa one
month after its London publication on a range of grounds specified in the
Publications Act of 1974, including propagating Communist opinions; indecency and offensiveness to public morals and religious feelings or convictions of some inhabitants of South Africa; being prejudicial to the safety
of the state, the general welfare, peace, and good order; creating "a psychosis of revolution and rebellion"; and making "several unbridled attacks
against the authority entrusted with the maintenance of law and order and
the safety of the state."[1]

Susan Gardner (SG): Could you tell me how and when you decided that
Burger's Daughter was a story that had to be told about this particular place
and time?

Nadine Gordimer (NG): Well, I was fascinated by the *idea* of the story for
a long time. I can't tell you exactly when because these things always begin
very much in the subconscious. I can't say which came first, the general
idea or the story. Maybe first of all there was the idea: the role of white
hard-core Leftists. But that would be a kind of theoretical approach, a

historical or a sociopolitical approach, and I'm an imaginative writer, I don't write that kind of thing. One could have written a factual book about that: it has been done, I think, very thoroughly. But that is approaching it as a phenomenon—a sociological/political phenomenon. So perhaps it occurred to me originally in that form.

But then something—as an imaginative writer—really took hold of me, and that was the idea of what it would have been like—what it would be like—to be the son or daughter of one of those families. I became fascinated to see how, as time went by, in my own life, for instance, my own generation, we moved away from our parents' lives and our parents' political beliefs (or lack of them): we changed our whole attitude. But—the children of Communists, of white Communists, and of hard-core Leftists generally, but particularly of Communists, did *not*: they simply took up the torch. It was a relay race of generations, so to speak, and they did not seem to question the way of life that these political beliefs dictated. It wasn't just simply a matter of saying I think this or I think that, and voting, and going to a political meeting. It was putting your whole *life* on the line. Your political beliefs as a Communist completely dominated your whole way of life in a country like this, even before the Communist Party was banned. And you must remember, the Communist Party was formed in 1921, here. So the children of these Communists—and perhaps even their grandchildren—were Communists during a much more trying period: because in 1950 the Communist Party was banned.

Now, what happened to these young people? The amazing thing was that it was quite clear—since they got arrested, since they went to prison, since they took part in all sorts of activities *after* the party was banned—that they had *not* thrown off, or abandoned, their parents' beliefs or their parents' incredibly disciplined way of life. I became fascinated by this long ago, I should think—perhaps as long ago as 1949, the first big Treason Trial. . . . I had never been to a large political trial before; I don't think I had ever been to a political trial at all. This trial—the preliminary examination part of it—went on for nine months; then, indeed, that was the trial because everybody was dismissed. But it was the beginning of a series of political trials where, alas, this didn't happen. After that they came thick and fast, and I went to quite a lot of them. And looked at some of these very young people—children or teenagers—left with the responsibility of the whole household and younger children. It must have affected their lives tremendously; it must have been a great intrusion on the kind of secret treaties that you have when you're an adolescent, you know, the time that you spend with your buddies, and don't want to be involved in grown-up responsibilities. That's how I became fascinated with these young people, and I suppose the character Rosa gradually began to take shape. Since I'm a woman myself, it was in the form of one of the young women, or one of the girls, that I saw the story.

SG: Why was it Rosa rather than her brother Tony who was given the job, in the novel, of critically inheriting the political task?

NG: It may be that women were particularly prominent; and also because I knew a number of women in this position, either as children, or in the position of Rosa's mother. And their relationship fascinated me.

SG: But why is Rosa's relationship to her ideological inheritance patriarchically presented? It is after all her mother, Cathy, who is in prison when the book starts, and who is identified as "the real revolutionary" both by Ivy Terblanche (who admired her and worked with her) and by Katya Bagnelli, whom Cathy supplanted as Lionel Burger's wife and comrade.

NG: Yes, but you see again, the incredible layers of meaning in the lives of people like this. The question of who was the more important person in party work would very often be covered up, in the eyes of the world, with the facade of the marriage. So that one would conveniently make use— particularly in this country, particularly because the Burgers are an Afrikaner family—of the convention that Papa is the master; meantime, probably, it was the woman who was the more important member.

SG: Who, perhaps, by capitalizing on sexual double standards, could be getting away with some political maneuvers?

NG: Yes, yes, in the end this was no protection, but it had to be tested, perhaps, to see whether it was. And, of course, a woman could be treated more leniently in court, when it came to bail: if a woman and her husband were arrested, their application for bail might also be on compassionate grounds, that her children were young and were left at home without anybody to care for them. The court was much more likely to let the woman out on bail than the man; yet that woman might be the brains of the whole organization. This kind of layer after layer of meaning in people's lives was so different from the lives of the sort of people that I grew up with, whose lives were simpler, whose *loyalties* were so much simpler. . . .

SG: Might your presentation of Rosa as a dissident Afrikaner woman who is betraying her racial heritage account for some of the Publications Control Board's hostility?

NG: I don't think so. It might, perhaps, on a certain deep psychological level, have influenced one of the censors who read the book originally and banned it. Rosa certainly would not seem to be a nice *Boere meisie*, (but) the whole idea of the *Boere meisie*, this good, quiet, church-going girl, has clearly become outdated. It's a concept not equal to the realities of the present life here. And I think one can draw an interesting parallel with the Voortrekker period. Think of the kind of role that women played then. When necessary they picked up a gun, and they gave birth to their children in the middle of the *veld*, without any medical help, without the proverbial kettle of hot water boiling. So they stepped out of this idealistic role of the woman in the background, the submissive woman, and now you have your Rosas and, indeed—what was her name?—Marie, her cousin, who in a different way went out into the big world to advertise South African oranges in Paris and ended up sheltering an international terrorist.

SG: C. J. van der Merwe, the "expert on security matters" consulted by the Publications Appeal Board, concluded that the book's readership would be limited to "literary critics and . . . people with a specific interest in subversive movements in South Africa."[2] Did you have an implied or envisaged audience in mind while you were writing the book?

NG: I don't write that way. I never have anybody in mind; I think that's death to any writer. You can't get anywhere near the truth as you know it if you have any idea—if you're wondering what this one's going to think of it, what that one's going to think of it. I've said before, and for me it's a truth that must be repeated—I think the best way to write is as if you were already dead. This is sometimes misunderstood. I don't mean that you *ignore* the reality around us. Far from it. My idea is that, in order to come to grips properly with that reality, you must have no fears for yourself, for the embarrassment that it's going to cause your family, for the embarrassment that it's going to cause *you*. One can refuse to answer questions, but when one is sitting down and writing something, one must not refuse *any* truth that comes to mind, one must not censor oneself from following any line of thought. I'm analyzing this now, but it's to me absolutely natural. I simply *don't* think about it. When I first began to write, and was not politically aware (when, indeed, there was no political danger as there is now), again, I didn't think at all about whether I was going to offend when I wrote my first novel (*The Lying Days*, 1953), which obviously, like most first novels, has elements of my own childhood. My mother was alive. Afterward, when it was published, I thought, Oh my God, what's she going to think when she reads it? But had I begun to think about this while I was writing it, I should never have written it. That's the answer, I think. For me.

SG: *Burger's Daughter* is an appealing book for feminists because it explores that movement's basic contention that "the personal is political." And I'm intrigued by the attraction for Rosa of other women: Marisa Kgosana, the wife of an imprisoned black political leader, and Katya, her father's first wife. They seem to be very important, emotionally and as models, and although Rosa is said to be trying to understand and relate to her dead father, Lionel, she could also be regarded as searching for her mother. And I think the novel is relevant to feminists not least because the "women's liberation meeting" (if that is what one could call it), described as a "harmless liberal activity" and organized by the fellow traveler Flora Donaldson, may be too pessimistic and dismissively presented. Do you think there are any South African women's organizations that could be effective in the struggle against South Africa's racial capitalism?

NG: There are, and there have been. *But*—and it's a big but—as soon as they say, "We are completely apolitical," they might as well shut up shop. Because there's no issue in this country—I defy anybody to bring up an issue, except perhaps the very personal one of the love relationship between men and women. . . . But all the other issues—can you have a bank account in your name, the ownership of property, the rights over your children, what happens when you get divorced, all these things, not to mention of course the most important of all, equal pay for equal work, and other conditions, maternity benefits and so on—as soon as you touch any of the real feminist issues you are going right into the heart of the racial problem.

SG: But I think Flora represents a facile, and rather biological, notion of sisterhood, and she's too optimistic and sentimental about it; perhaps very generation-bound as well. She doesn't realize that any solidarity between black and white women would have to be constructed and fought for, and always changing.

NG: It's also curious because Flora is the kind of woman who has been—well, all right, she's been on the fringe of real political action, but then she's moved into the typically feminine position of being warned by her husband. And this happens so much here. After Sharpeville—but it was always there, it must have been quite a source of conflict within the bourgeois marriages here (white marriages I'm talking about, of course), that the husband said, right—I admire you for your courage, I admire you for your views, I share them of course, but I don't want you going to prison, what benefit is it going to bring to anybody? It was then that somebody like Flora, with the very genuine feelings that she had about liberation, would look around for another outlet. It's interesting, too, because it relates to a little theory I have about the basis of this society still being so colonial, especially in personal relationships, and how this affects one's effectiveness in the outside world. Women in our frontier society (the ordinary women, not politicized women) were the first really to begin to have uneasy feelings about blacks, and about the conditions under which blacks lived. And, for example, the problems that black women have with their children; there were few if any nursery schools for blacks, so this kind of thing began to interest public-spirited women. Again, of course, it was not "political"; no, it was not even reform; it was charity. So that kind of activity, along with fringe artistic activity . . . I can remember as a child in a mining town where I was born and brought up, the choirs, the amateur theatricals—right, there would be men in the casts of these amateur plays, but the audiences were likely to be predominantly female. When a musician came from abroad, or a ballet company, perhaps, came from Johannesburg to this mining town—again, the audience would be 90 percent female. So that culture and charity, with a slapdash kind of social reform, were a woman's domain. A social conscience was a leisure-time activity, because the man was busy earning a living; he was the breadwinner and protector. This was a real frontier society conceptualizing of the roles, the "ordained" roles. . . . And I think this lingers, and it has lingered to the extent that it has produced Floras. Highly intelligent, well-educated women who are still in that kind of relationship to the husband.

The Black Sash organization, which I admire very much, is a most interesting example of this. I've often said to people, "Why is there no Black Sash for men?" The Black Sash is now open to men, and I have one or two friends (I think Sydney Kentridge, the Biko lawyer, is one who belongs), but this is obviously just a nominal thing. The fact is—who are the husbands of these women? Why are the women so much more enlightened? Why are the women defiant of public opinion, defiant of the police, and certainly *not* apolitical? The Black Sash is a women's organization that is trying to bring about real social reform, that is opposing this government, that is opposing National Party policy, and is now going radically further than the Progressive-Reform Party policy and all the white political parties. And these *women* have the guts to do this. Now what happens when they go home, I wonder? What are the discussions at home? I know of two cases where the man has been politicized by the wife, to a very interesting extent. So far, insofar as it has affected the children (again influenced by the mother)—the children, having started off with some sort of liberal teaching from the mother, move on and become more and more radical. I know of one who is indeed in exile now, having had to flee on an exit permit. When this girl was detained—in prison without trial—her father, a conventional and conservative man until then, made a stand on principle, which is so rare. He had been politicized by his wife and by his children. Yet there is no men's Black Sash. Men do *not* go and stand in protest outside the university or in John Vorster Square. And there is no feminist lobby at all in the Parliament. But it would be by proxy, because there would be a couple of white women talking about the disabilities of black women. And as far as black women are concerned, their concern is the oppression under which all blacks live. The feminist battle must come afterward.

SG: I think it must come simultaneously, but it's very difficult for black women to admit that, especially if under pressure in their own communities.

NG: Yes, it's very difficult. My view is a different one. I feel that if the real battle for human rights is won, the kingdom of . . . feminine liberation follows. Because if we are all free individuals, that's all we need, we don't have to have any special feeling because we are women. But I know this view is not shared by feminists.

SG: About relations with blacks as they are experienced and recounted by white characters, Anthony Sampson in the *New York Times* said that no one had better described certain aspects of township, in this case Soweto, life. Yet one of the copublishers at Ravan Press, Mothobi Mutloase, as reported in the *Star* (Johannesburg), has stated (12 July 1980):

> I feel that whites writing about blacks is just nothing but an academic exercise. It is not authentic. It lacks that feeling of the people. Good writing should have emotions and a purpose. . . . Whites, be they writers or politicians, experience only the life of the privileged. All they can do is to just imagine the Black Experience. (p. 12)

What are the prices that whites must pay for acceptance by, and collaboration with, blacks? To what extent are these still possible?

NG: There are really two questions here, because the point you're getting from Mothobi's argument is a political one, it's about political action, and the other question is its reflection in literature. My comment about that statement is that it ignores completely the very large areas of contact between black and white, here, *all our lives*. This, indeed, is the failure and lie of apartheid; it has *not* succeeded.

SG: But Mothobi's statement seems to uphold or echo apartheid, in fact.

NG: In some ways apartheid has succeeded only too well. I've said this before; there are areas of black experience that no white writer can write about. But there are vast areas of actual experience—rubbing shoulders with blacks, having all kinds of relationships with blacks. . . . It's not as simple as it sounds . . . all kinds of conflicts, of a very special nature, arise between black and white. . . . And this leads whites to know quite a lot about blacks. And it leads blacks to know quite a lot about whites. The author of that statement cast no opinion on white characters in black books. Are we to say then that no black person can possibly create a white character? Of course, this is nonsense. I do believe that when we have got beyond the apartheid situation—there's a tremendous problem for whites, because unless you put down cultural roots, unless whites are allowed in by blacks, and unless we can make out a case for our being accepted and we can forge a common culture together, whites are going to be marginal, because we will be outside the central entities of life here. To a large extent we are now. But there's still that area of conflict which is from an artistic point of view fruitful. But when that is gone, if we are not integrated, we have not cut loose from the colonial culture. . . . And make no mistake about it, blacks are hampered by it, too. The very fact that the black writer, Mothobi Mutloase, who gave that interview, edits a magazine, or the fact that he is interviewed—these are all the tools of white culture that he has taken over, and why not? Why not use them? They are there. I object to the attempt to convince people that blacks do not want to use any of these tools at all. The fact is, you cannot have a literature without them. And you can't have a modern culture without them. And all blacks want a modern culture. Why on earth not? This is a heritage that belongs to all of us.

But there are areas where I know there are things I cannot write. For instance, if I were to want to write a novel about a black child growing up between 1976 and now—not so much in Soweto, because all my life I have had contacts with city blacks and all my life I've been in and out of townships, I may not have lived there, but I know something about it . . . — but a black child, say, living in a country area, who perhaps doesn't even speak a word of English—there are many like that—and perhaps a few broken words of Afrikaans—I think that the concept of reality, the relation to the entities in the life of that child would be something beyond my imaginative powers as a writer, even though writers are extraordinary people. They're monsters in a way, they can enter other people's lives. Imagination is a mysterious thing.

SG: Is there anything about the style of *Burger's Daughter*—or any of your other work, for that matter—that you regard for whatever social or genetic reasons as most likely to have been written by a woman?

NG: No. I don't think so. It's difficult to judge. And of course, I have written one book in the first person as a man, and I've written two or three from a male point of view. Perhaps some man will say, as some blacks may say, how can she possibly know? But I don't really feel we're all that different. I have this feeling that there's this overriding . . . humanity—not in a "humanitarian" sense, but just what it is to be a human being, to know hurt, pain, fear, discouragement, frustration, this is common to both sexes—

SG: And sexuality. Your "inside" descriptions of male sexuality astonish me.

NG: Yes, but I've often been astonished by the "inside" descriptions of female sexuality written by men. So perhaps we know each other on these levels. Below our consciousness. And when you come to write, that's what you tap.

SG: Would you regard the style of *Burger's Daughter* as different, or a development from, your previous work? How would you compare it vis-à-vis stories in *A Soldier's Embrace* (1980), for instance?

NG: For me it's very, very simple. For each idea, there's never been anything but one right way to say it. Perhaps that way is going to be in the first person, perhaps it's going to be in the past tense, perhaps it's going to be a monologue, perhaps it's going to be a free association, perhaps it's going to be . . . classical. If I don't find it, I can't write. In *A Soldier's Embrace*, there's a story called "Oral History," where the title is the key to the right style for the story. I wanted to tell it the way you tell something that has actually happened (an episode in the chronicle of a village, a people). Then it has to have these echoing *tones*, like a bell tolling, that you've heard many times before, but the sounds mean something, you can retell it a hundred times. That was for me the right way to tell that story; I had to find it. Then there is the story about the unborn child. Well, there's no way to "tell" that in a direct narrative fashion. Because it is a mystery. It's surrounded by strange waters in a womb; it's projecting yourself into a journey we've all taken, and God knows what it is like, it's like going into space. So the style has to be something that suggests an apprehension of the world much removed from normal senses.

But—with *Burger's Daughter*—here again there's this slippery fish, Rosa, who is herself a girl like any other girl; she has roles imposed upon her by her mother and father; underneath those roles there's her own. For instance, she's sent to visit the young man in prison: there is a role imposed upon her, but she's playing another role, and the young man is playing yet another. So there are three roles somehow to be conveyed by the same character. It came to me, when I was pondering about writing that book, since she was someone who had so much imposed upon her from the outside; since these were people who lived with layers of protective coloring in order to carry out what they thought was their purpose in life; since it had been my own experience, knowing people like that, that there are infinite gradations of intimacy. . . . I had somebody, a woman friend, whom I've known all my life, and terribly intimately, who lived in this house—but there are areas of her life I've known nothing about. I would, almost certainly, if she'd not been a devout Communist, but there were things she didn't tell me and there were probably other things she didn't tell other people. Life lived in compartments, well, how do you approach somebody like that? And so the idea came to me of Rosa questioning herself as others see her and whether what they see is what she really is. And that developed into another stylistic question—if you're going to tell a book in the first person, to whom are you talking? You asked me earlier when I write, what is my audience. And I told you I have none, and that is the truth. But if a character of mine is speaking in the first person there's an audience assumed, which is one person or the whole world. It's always there. And that is why Joseph Conrad uses the device of Marlow—because then Marlow is speaking to him. Conrad is somebody who's living the individual life that she's never tried, she's testing his word against hers all the time. This hippie son of a scrap dealer, brought up with a completely different idea about what's meaningful in life, in her life. And when she's talking to him, she's indeed appealing to him: this is how it was for me, how is it for you? Then—it's obvious, but the thing is, it only really came to me afterward—if she goes to Europe, to whom would she go? She must go to Katya, to her father's first wife.

SG: That wasn't originally planned?

NG: No. When I began to write the book, I knew she would go to Europe, and under very strange circumstances (guilty over having compromised herself for a passport). She doesn't know her father's first wife, and she has a certain curiosity about her; and Katya lives at a remove from the active political exiles whom Rosa has more or less undertaken to avoid. She goes to Katya, it seems, because there is nowhere else to go. And then, as so often in life, the unconscious motive appears: Rosa thought to learn from Katya: how to defect? Because Katya has "defected" from Lionel Burger.

To turn to the question of the different people whom Rosa addresses. Inevitably, in the end, she does talk to her father, but perhaps only after he's dead. So you can see how for me style really grew out of content. I couldn't have told that story the way I did *The Conservationist*, which was without any concessions explaining anything to anybody. If you didn't catch on—who was who and what was missing and what was assumed, then you were just left in doubt. But, in *Burger's Daughter*, you see there was too much—take for instance the whole question of what the Communist Party *was*, here. I couldn't *not* explain that, so I had to find a way to do it, and fortunately for me the device of the biographer of Lionel Burger enabled me to fill some of that in.

SG: You have called *Burger's Daughter* a political novel, and a novel of ideas. And you've also distinguished contemporary white South African writing by saying that it's predominantly critical, analytical, "protestant in mood," while black writings are "inspirational" "and that is why the government fears them." You've claimed that the inspirational presently predominates over satire in black writing, for instance, because satire requires "a license for self-criticism that loyalty to the black struggle for a spiritual identity does not grant at present."[3] But would you further claim that *Burger's Daughter* is *not* inspirational—in intention or in effect?

NG: *Burger's Daughter* is—much more, I think, than my other books. My method has so often been irony. I find irony very attractive in other writers, and I find life full of irony, my own life and everybody else's; somehow one of the secret locks of the personality lies in what is ironic in us. In *Burger's Daughter* irony is like a kind of corrective, a rein. It comes from Rosa, she has that in her confrontation with Clare (a contemporary of hers, also the daughter of Communist parents), but very often the inspirational took over. Because there are things—it comes from what is here, if you look at what happened in Soweto in 1976 and what has happened again now (school and meat workers' boycotts, municipal workers' strikes in Johannesburg), there's so much inspiration in it· a reaching out, a bursting forth . . . the very recklessness comes from that. The very courage to risk, with your stone in your hand, being shot down. You know, if you look at the history of Africa or any other country—let's confine it to here—the famous time when the Xhosas burnt their crops and said, "the white man is going to be pushed into the sea", "on a certain day the sun will come up twice, two blood-red suns will rise," and they feared nothing. There was the same thing in Madagascar. There were bloody riots against the French and they believed that bullets would turn to water (that same legend really comes from Africa; it has been inspirational here before, too). There was something of that in these school kids in 1976—something that suddenly took fear away.

SG: If, voluntarily like Joyce or forced like Solzhenitsyn you had to leave South Africa, what then would be your available source and substance?

NG: I've lived here for fifty-six years, all my life. I've still got a great deal inside me and don't know if now, at this stage of my life, I have it worked out. It would depend, too, on how I got involved in the society I went to live in. This theory that you lose your roots—I know that this is very true, and there are very few writers who have the strength, and the character, and the talent, to overcome it. If you look at what happens to black writers in exile, you don't know. It's very bad. But—if you look at Doris Lessing, if you look at Dan Jacobson, particularly with Lessing, it's possible for some writers to transplant and grow.

SG: Have any critics missed what you regard as especially important aspects of *Burger's Daughter*?

NG: I think some critics discovered things in it I didn't know about. Two reviewers pointed out that it is also the story of a daughter-father relationship and of a child-parent relationship. And I hadn't thought about it in that way, but of course it is. And then Conor Cruise O'Brien says that it's a profoundly religious book. Which, of course, is written by an atheist. But that could happen, most certainly.

SG: Well, Conor Cruise O'Brien once editorialized in the *Observer* that E.P. Thompson is not a Marxist, and neither is Christopher Hill—so he's twisting his own definitions.

NG: But I think he had a profound point in that in the book was the idea of redemption being entered into through suffering. Taking it on in one way or another, politically or religiously motivated, that is the only choice you have. You can't opt out of it. One thing I think lots of people have missed—the reason why Rosa goes back to South Africa and, ultimately, to prison. It's not just because she has that terrible midnight telephone call with her former black stepbrother, Baasie, and that really brings her nose to nose with reality. It started long before, it started in France, in that village, when she met that woman in the street in her dressing gown, who doesn't know where she is. And it really hits Rosa that you get old, lonely, dotty. That you suffer. That Katya, running from political suffering, has simply postponed what is coming. And Didier is also very important, because he shows Rosa what the alternatives are. The alternatives have some horrible sides to them, too. That young man is living for pay with a woman much older than he, a kind of prisoner who thinks he's free.

SG: I wonder if the terminology of redemption and suffering—which gives history a metaphysical cast—isn't too fatalistic and amorphous a formulation for what is really systematic, structural exploitation and oppression in South Africa—which can be transformed.

NG: Oh, quite, and that's why Rosa comes back. If you sit around on a

Greek island and . . . I don't know, take a purely feminine example, have a face lift and tint your hair, what's happening is staving off the suffering that will come to you. It's a fact of life, that kind of animal suffering. But there's *another* kind of suffering that you *can* fight and that human beings have been fighting generation after generation, for thousands of years. And I think Rosa's overcome by disgust; this passivity, this submission. And wants to become embattled with suffering.

SG: Do you think that the sensuous-redemptive appeal of blacks is romanticized in the book, especially through the character of Marisa?

NG: I think the sensuous-redemptive thing is dangerous. But I've seen it even among my—my Burger-type friends. It's very strong, you know. And it's powerful. It also sounds so sentimental, but it's true that when we whites go away we miss that certain warmth. Even now, I find when I'm in New York I just can't believe that the vibrations that come from the blacks I see are what they are. Because I'm used to a different relationship with blacks. It's just incredible that this endures, has endured. With all the awful resentments that there are between us, and all the troubles, there still is this strong bond.

Notes

1. Nadine Gordimer et al., *What Happened to* Burger's Daughter; *or, How South African Censorship Works* (Emmarentia, South Africa: Taurus, 1980), 6–14. The reasons are listed in a letter from the directorate of publications to Nadine Gordimer's lawyer, 16 July 1979. The eventual release of *Burger's Daughter*, and the Publications Control Board's attempts further to polarize black and white South African writers by selectively unbanning the work of some white writers while massively suppressing work by black writers, are discussed by Nadine Gordimer in "Censorship and the Word" (reprinted in *The Bloody Horse*, this is the text of her speech—during which a government official walked out—accepting the 1979 CNA literary award for the best South African book in English); "New Forms of Strategy—No Change of Heart," *Critical Arts* 1, no. 2 (June 1980): 27–41, repr. in *Index on Censorship* 10, no. 1 (Feb. 1981): 4–9, and (with others), *What Happened to* Burger's Daughter, *or, How South African Censorship Works*. Other discussions of South African censorship appear in Kelwyn Sole, "The Abortion of the Intellect: Literary Circles and 'Change' in South Africa Today," in *Dead in One's Own Lifetime* (Rondesbosch, Cape Town, South Africa: National Union of South African Students, 1979), 62–91; *English in Africa* 7, no. 2 (Sept. 1980); Gerald Gordon, "The Right to Write: A Critical Appraisal of the South African Publications Act of 1974," *Index on Censorship* 4, no. 2 (Summer 1975): 41–44; John D. Jackson, *Justice in South Africa* (London: Penguin, 1980); and Louise

Silver, comp., "Publications Appeal Board: Digest of Decisions" (Johannesburg, South Africa: Centre for Applied Legal Studies, University of the Witwatersrand, recurring).

2. C. J. van der Merwe, "Report on *Burger's Daughter* of Nadine Gordimer," in *What Happened to* Burger's Daughter, 57.

3. Gordimer, "New Forms of Strategy—No Change of Heart," 27–33.

Waiting for Revolution

CONOR CRUISE O'BRIEN

❖   ❖   ❖

NADINE GORDIMER, like many of the great Russian novelists of
the nineteenth century, lives in two worlds at the same time. She
lives, as the Russians did, in a police state, and she also lives, as they did, in
the wider culture of the West, receiving the reflections of the kinds of freedom that the West has enjoyed over two centuries or more. But it is more
than a question of living under a police state. A whole analogous social
structure is involved. Whites in South Africa, in relation to blacks, have
much in common with the nobility in tsarist Russia in relation to the serfs.
Turgenev and Tolstoy rejected serfdom but were nonetheless themselves
distinctive products of a leisured serf-owning society. South African whites
constitute an aristocracy of pigmentation, and even if they do not want to
belong to it, they still do belong. A great writer in South Africa—and I believe Nadine Gordimer is a great writer—is living and working in a culture
that is closer to nineteenth-century Russia than it is to the contemporary
West.

Of all the great Russians, it is Turgenev whom she most brings to mind.
Like him, she is alienated from the society which produced her and, as in
his case also, that society, at work within her, makes her something of a
stranger in the wider world. These conditions produce *detachment*, strange
angles of insight, and a kind of stereoscopic lucidity. There is also in their

works—by reason of the kind of world these writers willy-nilly share—an inherent aristocratic sense of leisure, of time to wait and to watch. In Nadine Gordimer's writings, the conditions of South African life have produced a glorious anachronism.

THE STYLE OF *Burger's Daughter* is elegant, fastidious: a high style belonging to a cultivated upper class. Superficially, there is an opposition between this style and the subject matter of the book. *Burger's Daughter* is the story of Rosa, the daughter of a revolutionary, the Communist doctor Lionel Burger, who dies in a South African jail. The style is appropriate, nonetheless, and not just because Lionel and Rosa belong to the white, educated middle class—important though their so belonging is, and is shown to be. It is appropriate because the revolutionary's daughter is an aristocrat of the revolution, feels herself to be such, and is used to being seen as such. Nadine Gordimer knows revolutionaries and knows them to feel themselves as being, not struggling underdogs, but patricians of a present underworld, and of a future society. Rosa is the daughter of a revolution only just beginning, yet her style has already something in common with a Daughter of the South African Revolution, in the American sense of such a daughterhood: "She didn't understand the shame of the need to please, as royalty never carries money." And again, as she talks to a friend from outside the charmed revolutionary circle.

> —You seem to think people go around talking revolution as if they were deciding where to go for their summer holidays. Or which new car to buy. You romanticize.— The cartilage of her nostrils stiffened. The patient manner patronized him, displayed the deceptive commonplace that people accustomed to police harassment use before the uninitiated.

Burger's Daughter is constructed with properly deceptive art. For much of its course—indeed considerably more than half—it seems to be one of those books in which "nothing happens"; or rather in which what happens is an accumulation of small events, individually ambiguous but making a significant pattern, established in a calm and leisurely manner. The events after Rosa's father's death are handled in this way. The house—a good, big one with a swimming pool—has to be sold, the plate with Dr. Burger's name removed:

> She returned before dark with an unhealthy-looking fair man with long hair and a straggling moustache, wearing the fashionable garb of shirt with Balkan embroidery, jeans, and veldskoen. He had a screwdriver but found

some difficulty in turning it in the grooves caked with layers of metal polish turned to stony verdigris. She did not get out of the driver's seat. The oblong where the plate had been showed whitish in the twilight. He put the plate in the boot of her car and they drove away.

As she talks with a friend outside the house she is aware of a small change within: "The telephone had stopped ringing in the house. Rosa knew by some faint lack of distraction in her ears. Somebody living there now had picked it up."

IN THIS PART OF THE BOOK Rosa's relations to her father, to the revolution, and to South Africa are established with loving precision. She is intensely proud of her father and his revolution, yet she desperately longs to cut loose from them both. She experiences a kind of envy for her conventional, acquiescent Afrikaner farmer cousins,

> secure in the sanctions of family, church, law — and all these contained in the ultimate sanction of color, that was maintained without question on the domain, dorp and farm, where she lay. Peace. Land, Bread. They had these for themselves.
>
> Even animals have the instinct to turn from suffering. The sense to run away. Perhaps it was an illness not to be able to live one's life the way they did with justice defined in terms of respect for property, innocence defended in their children's privileges, love in their procreations, and care only for each other. A sickness not to be able to ignore that condition of a healthy, ordinary life: other people's suffering.

That sickness is something she cannot escape, yet she can escape, physically, from South Africa, and she does, for a time. The incident that precipitates her departure is one of two great thunderstorms in the book, deliberate eruptions out of its marmoreal course, like interpolations by Dostoevsky into a story of Turgenev's. They light up the South African landscape in a way which is wonderfully complementary to the calm perceptions of most of the book. These magnificent passages are pivotal to the novel: the first of them determines Rosa's departure from South Africa, the second her return to it.

The first passage, which to do it justice I shall quote in full, concerns the beating of a donkey:

> I gained a cambered dirt road without signposts just as one of those donkey-carts that survive on the routes between these places that don't exist was approaching along a track from the opposite side. Driver's reflex made me

slow down in anticipation that the cart might turn in up ahead without calculating the speed of an oncoming car. But there was something strange about the outline of donkey, cart and driver; convulsed, yet the cart was not coming nearer. As I drew close I saw a woman and child bundled under sacks, their heads jerked rocking; a driver standing up on the cart in a wildly precarious spread of legs in torn pants. Suddenly his body arched back with one upflung arm against the sky and lurched over as if he had been shot and at that instant the donkey was bowed by a paroxysm that seemed to draw its four legs and head down towards the centre of its body in a noose, then fling head and extremities wide again; and again the man violently salaamed, and again the beast curved together and flew apart.

I didn't see the whip. I saw agony. Agony that came from some terrible centre seized within the group of donkey, cart, driver and people behind him. They made a single object that contracted against itself in the desperation of a hideous final energy. Not seeing the whip, I saw the infliction of pain broken away from the will that creates it; broken loose, a force existing of itself, ravishment without the ravisher, torture without the torturer, rampage, pure cruelty gone beyond control of the humans who have spent thousands of years devising it. The entire ingenuity from thumbscrew and rack to electric shock, the infinite variety and gradation of suffering, by lash, by fear, by hunger, by solitary confinement—the camps, concentration, labour, resettlement, the Siberias of snow or sun, the lives of Mandela, Sisulu, Mbeki, Kathrada, Kgosana, gull-picked on the Island, Lionel propped wasting to his skull between two warders, the deaths by questioning, bodies fallen from the height of John Vorster Square, deaths by dehydration, babies degutted by enteritis in "places" of banishment, the lights beating all night on the faces of those in cells—Conrad—I conjure you up, I drag you back from wherever you are to listen to me—you don't know what I saw, what there is to see, you *won't* see, you are becalmed on an empty ocean.

Only when I was level with the cart, across the veld from me, did I make out the whip. The donkey didn't cry out. Why didn't the donkey give that bestial snort and squeal of excruciation I've heard donkeys give not in pain but in rut? It didn't cry out.

It had been beaten and beaten. Pain was no shock, there is no way out of the shafts. That rag of a black man was old, from the stance of his legs, the scraggle of beard showing under an old hat in a shapeless cone over his face. I rolled to a stop beyond what I saw; the car simply fell away from the pressure of my foot and carried me no farther. I sat there with my head turned sharply and my shoulders hunched round my neck, huddled to my ears against the blows. And then I put my foot down and drove on wavering drunkenly about the road, pausing to gaze back while the beating still went on, the force there, cart, terrified woman and child, the donkey and man, bucked and bolted zigzag under the whip. I had only to turn the car in the empty road and drive up upon that mad frieze against the sunset putting out my eyes. When I looked over there all I could see was the writhing black shape through whose interstices poked searchlights of blinding bright dust. The thing was like an explosion. I had only to career down on that scene with my car and my white authority. I could have yelled before I even got out, yelled to stop!—and then there I would have been standing, inescapable, fury and right, might, before them, the frightened woman and child and the drunk, brutal man, with my knowledge of how to deliver them over to the police, to have him prosecuted as he deserved and should be, to take away from him the poor suffering possession he maltreated. I could formulate everything they were, as the act I had witnessed; they would have their lives summed up for them officially at last by me, the white woman—the final meaning of a day they had lived I had no knowledge of, a day of other appalling things, violence, disasters, urgencies, deprivations which suddenly would become, was nothing but what it had led up to: the man among them beating their donkey. I could have put a stop to it, the misery; at that point I witnessed. What more can one do? That sort of old man, those people, peasants existing the only way they know how, in the "place" that isn't on the map, they would have been afraid of me. I could have put a stop to it, with them, at no risk to myself. No one would have taken up a stone. I was safe from the whip. I could have stood between them and suffering—the suffering of the donkey.

As soon as I planted myself in front of them it would have become again just that—the pain of a donkey.[1]

ROSA NOW LEAVES SOUTH AFRICA herself conniving to do so with the connivance of a sophisticated *verligte* Nationalist politician (a distant relative)—a splendid hate portrait—and goes to live in the south of France where she has, for a time, a very good time, with pleasant, hedonistic people. Some of them give themselves political airs sometimes, but they are not political, as South Africa knows politics:

—You didn't betray anybody.—
"Oppress." "Revolt." "Betray." He used the big words as people do without knowing what they can stand for.

She listens to a political argument at a party:

—Yes, yes, exactly what they are saying—whether it's the Communist Party or some giant multinational company, people are turning against huge, confining structures—

—Our only hope lies in a dispassionate morality of technology, our creed must be, broadly speaking, ecological—always allowing the premise that man's place is central—

Bernard met Rosa in the thicket of the others' self-absorption.—For them it livens up a party.—

She shrugged and imitated his gesture of puffing out the lower lip: for all of us. She gave a quick smile to him.

Rose has grown more humble in exile: she feels she has betrayed others by leaving South Africa, she has come down to the level of ordinary mortals.

Then she attends another party, involving some real politics this time, since it is in honor of a Frelimo delegation. Here she meets Baasie again. Baasie is a black, of her own age, whom her father had taken into his house as a child. His father was a revolutionary organizer, generally on the run. The two children were brought up as brother and sister, sharing the same bed, in a household which regarded color as irrelevant. After the death of the two fathers in prison, the children become separated. Rosa is over-joyed to see her childhood friend, but he receives her coldly, refusing to let her call him Baasie. After the party is over, and Rosa is asleep in bed in her own flat, the telephone rings. There follows the second, and more terrible, of the book's two thunderstorms.

The voice from home said: Rosa.

—Yes.—

—Yeh, Rosa.—

—It's you, Baasie?—

—No.—A long, swaying pause.

—But it is.—

—I'm not "Baasie," I'm Zwelinzima Vulindlela.—

—I'm sorry—it just came out this evening . . . it was ridiculous.—

—You know what my name means, Rosa?—

—Vulindlela? Your father's name . . . oh, I don't know whether my surname means anything either—"citizen," solid citizen—Starting to humor the other one; at such an hour—two much to drink, perhaps.

—Zwel-in-zima. That's my name. "Suffering land." The name my father gave me. You know my father. Yes—

—Yes.—

—Is it? Is it? You knew him before they killed him.—

—Yes. Since we were kids. You know I did.—

—How did they kill him?—You see, you don't know, you don't know, you don't talk about that.—

—I don't . . . because why should I say what they said.—

—Tell it, say it.—

—What they always say—they found him hanged in his cell.—

—How, Rosa? Don't you know they take away belts, everything.—

—I know.—

—Hanged himself with his own prison pants.—

"Baasie"—she doesn't say it but it's there in the references of her voice, their infant intimacy—I asked if you'd come and see me—or I'd come to you, tomorrow, but you—

—No, I'm talking to you now.—

—D'y'know what time it is? I don't even know—I just got to the phone in the dark.—

—Put on the light, Rosa. I'm talking to you.—

She uses no name because she has no name for him. —I was fast asleep. We can talk tomorrow. We'd better talk tomorrow, mmh?—

—Put on the light.—

Try laughing. —We'd better both go back to bed.—

—I haven't been in bed.— There were gusts of noise, abruptly cut off, background to his voice; he was still somewhere among people, they kept opening and shutting a door, there.

—The party going strong?—

—I'm not talking about parties, Rosa.—

—Come tomorrow—today, I suppose it is, it's still so dark.—

—You didn't put the light on, then. I told you to.—

They began to wrangle. —Look, I'm really not much use when I'm woken up like this. And there's so much I want . . . How old were we? I remember your father—or someone—brought you back only once, how old were we then?—

—I told you to put it on.—

She was begging, laughing. —Oh but I'm so tired, man! Please, until tomorrow.

—Listen. I didn't like the things you said at that place tonight.—

—I said?—

—I didn't like the way you went around and how you spoke.—

The receiver took on shape and feel in her hand; blood flowing to her brain. She heard his breathing and her own, her breath breathing garlic over herself from the half-digested sausage.

—I don't know what to say. I don't understand why you should say this to me.—

—Look, I didn't like it at all.—

—I said? About what?—

—Lionel Burger, Lionel Burger, Burger—

—I didn't make any speeches.—

—Everyone in the world must be told what a great hero he was and how much he suffered for the blacks. Everyone must cry over him and show his life on television and write in the papers. Listen, there are dozens of our fathers sick and dying like dogs, kicked out of the locations when they can't work any more. Getting old and dying in prison. Killed in prison. It's nothing. I know plenty blacks like Burger. It's nothing, it's us, we must be used to it, it's not going to show on English television.—

—He would have been the first to say—what you're saying. He didn't think there was anything special about a white being a political prisoner.—

—Kissing and coming round you, her father died in prison, how terrible. I know a lot of fathers—black—

—He didn't think what happened to him more important.—

—Kissing and coming round you—

—You knew him! You know that! It's crazy for me to tell *you*.—

—Oh yes I knew him. You'll tell them to ask me for the television show. Tell them how your parents took the little black kid into their home, not the backyard like other whites, right into the house. Eating at the table and sleeping in the bedroom, the same bed, their little black boss. And then the little bastard was pushed off back to his mud huts and tin shanties. His father was too busy to look after him. Always on the run from the police. Too busy with the whites who were going to smash the government and let another lot of whites tell us how to run our country. One of Lionel Burger's best tame blacks sent scuttling like a bloody cockroach everywhere, you can always just put your foot on them.—

Pulling the phone with her—the cord was short, for a few moments she lost the voice—she felt up the smooth cold wall for the switch: under the light of lamps sprung on the voice was no longer inside her but relayed small, as from a faint harsh public address system in the presence of the whole room. . . .

—Why should I see you, Rosa? Because we even used to have a bath together?—the Burger family didn't mind black skin so we're different for ever from anyone? You're different so I must be different too. You aren't white and I'm not black.—

She was shouting. —How could you follow me around that room like a man from BOSS, listening to stupid small-talk? Why are we talking in the middle of the night? Why do you telephone? What for?—

—I'm not your Baasie, just don't go on thinking about that little kid who lived with you, don't think of that black "brother," that's all.—

Now she would not let him hang up; she wanted to keep the two of them nailed each to the other's voice and the hour of night when nothing fortuitous could release them—*good, good*, he had disposed of her whining to go back to bed and bury them both.

—There's just one thing I'm going to tell you. We won't meet, you're right. Vulindlela. About him and me. So long as you know I've told you. I was the one who was sent to take a fake pass to him so he could get back in from Botswana that last time. I delivered it somewhere. Then they caught him, that was when they caught him.—

—What is that? So what is that for me? Blacks must suffer now. We can't be caught although we are caught, we can't be killed although we die in jail, we are used to it, it's nothing to do with you. Whites are locking up blacks every day. You want to make the big confession?—why do you think you should be different from all the other whites who've been shitting on us ever since they came? He was able to go back home and get caught because you took the pass there. You want me to know in case I blame you for nothing. You think because you're telling me it makes it all right—for you. It wasn't your fault—you want me to tell you, then it's all right. For you. Because I'm the only one who can say so. But he's dead, and what about all the others—who cares whose "fault"—they die because it's the whites killing them, black blood is the stuff to get rid of white shit.—

—This kind of talk sounds better from people who are in the country than people like us.— Impulses of cruelty came exhilarating along her blood-vessels without warming the cold of feet and hands; while he talked she was jigging, hunched over, rocking her body, wild to shout, pounce him down the moment he hesitated.

—I don't know who you are. You hear me, Rosa? You didn't even know my name. I don't have to tell you what I'm doing.—

—What is it you want?— the insult thrilled her as she delivered herself of it. —You want something. If it's money, I'm telling you there isn't any. Go and ask one of your white English liberals who'll pay but won't fight.

Nobody phones in the middle of the night to make a fuss about what they were called as a little child. You've had too much to drink, Zwelin-zima.— But she put the stress on the wrong syllable and he laughed.

As if poking with a stick at some creature writhing between them—You were keen to see me, eh, Rosa. What do you want?—

—You could have said it right away, you know. Why didn't you just stare me out when I came up to you? Make it clear I'd picked the wrong person. Make a bloody fool of me.—

—What could I say? I wasn't the one who looked for you.—

—Just shake your head. That would've been enough. When I said the name I used. I would have believed you.—

—Ah, come on.—

—I would have believed you. I haven't seen you since you were nine years old, you might have been dead for all I know. The way you look in my mind is the way my brother does—never gets any older.—

—I'm sorry about your kid brother.—

—Might have been killed in the bush with the Freedom Fighters. Maybe I thought that.—

—Yeh, you think that. I don't have to live in your head.—

—Goodbye, then.—

—Yeh, Rosa, all right, you think that.—

Neither spoke and neither put down the receiver for a few moments. Then she let go the fingers that had stiffened to their own clutch and the thing was back in place. The burning lights witnessed her.

She stood in the middle of the room.

Knocking a fist at the doorway as she passed, she ran to the bathroom and fell to her knees at the lavatory bowl, vomiting. The wine, the bits of sausage—she laid her head, gasping between spasms, on the porcelain rim, slime dripping from her mouth with the tears of effort running from her nose.

Recoiling in horror from her own insults to Baasie, Rosa decides to return to South Africa, to the revolution, and so to prison—all without expectation of success. She isn't really a revolutionary.

> I don't know the ideology:
> It's about suffering.
> How to end suffering.
> And it ends in suffering.

She knows—and not only from Baasie—that in a revolutionary movement now dominated by Black Consciousness her kind could have no in-

fluence either over the course of the revolution, or over the society resulting from it. She does not share the revolutionary confidence in the future,
the simple confidence that makes one of her Communist contemporaries
say that her generation is necessarily luckier than that of their parents:
"lucky to be born later."

Essentially, her return stems from something she had noted much
earlier in the book, about the house in which she grew up: "The political
activities and attitudes of that house came from the inside outwards, and
blacks in that house where there was no God felt this embrace before the
Cross." The trouble was that Baasie hadn't felt that embrace, or, if he had,
would not now admit the fact. But even if Baasie were no longer there, the
cross itself was there. That much could be relied on.

Burger's Daughter is not a revolutionary book but a religious one, and seems
specifically a Christian one. The Christian theme is only twice overtly introduced, but its introduction in each case is crucial—in the double sense
of that word. The first introduction prepares a way for a terrible reverber-
ating contrast in the second. The first is the "embrace before the Cross"
passage, which occurs early in the book. In this passage Rosa is imagining a
common acceptance of sacrifice and suffering, in her father's house: blacks
and whites embracing before the cross. The weakness in this, of course, is
that the whites could choose or reject suffering: the blacks had it inflicted
on them, whether they chose it or not.

The second overt Christian reference occurs when Rosa receives the
telephone call that disabuses her of that vision of black and white embracing. When, then, Rosa feels the need to hurt and humiliate the black who
had hurt and humiliated her, the cross is there again: "She wanted to keep
the two of them nailed each to the other's voice." Black and white are no
longer, now, embracing before the cross: they are on the cross, nailed there
by one another. Rosa's return from the joys and pleasures of Europe
to South Africa—the "land of suffering" after which her "Baasie" was
named—is the acceptance of the cross.

I do not know whether Nadine Gordimer thinks of herself as Christian,
but I do recognize *Burger's Daughter* as the work of an imagination profoundly permeated by Christianity. Although *Burger's Daughter* is written
without the least hint of self-pity, it nonetheless reflects the pain, loneliness, and hopelessness of being a white South African who is *really* opposed
to the regime. The "really" needs emphasis, because it is not at all painful
or lonely to be notionally opposed to the regime, and vote against it at
election times: most affluent, English-speaking South Africans are in op-

position to that extent, and accommodate themselves very well to that which they oppose.

It is quite different to be a white who rejects the system totally, and who is an artist capable of entering into the minds of blacks who also reject it, but whose rejection takes the form of rejecting all whites. Baasie's telephone call tells that story; and Baasie there speaks, in essentials, for almost all politically conscious young blacks in South Africa today. A white who really understands what Baasie is saying, and why he must say it, is cut off, in virtue of that understanding, from ease in either black or white society.

Cut off, also, from hope. An artist who takes politics seriously—as distinct from taking up political causes for the sake of relaxation, exercise, and display—is condemned to be lucid about politics, and lucidity about South African politics is a form of despair. For whites, that is, and some others. The Baasies have considerable, rational grounds for hope. After the fall of Angola and Mozambique, and as white Rhodesia falls, they can reasonably expect that power will be in black hands in South Africa during their lifetimes. That expectation alone is enough to light up their days with hope. Those who have to endure the systematic humiliation and privation of the apartheid system are not going to worry, in public at any rate, over such questions as: Whose black hands? Or, how will those hands use that power?

In private, the first question is certainly present in a number of active and ambitious minds; factions in revolutions—or, as at present, in a prerevolutionary situation—reflect not just differences about ideology or tactics but the struggle for future power. That is what Lenin was about, and that is what the South African Lenin—whoever he may be—has to be about now.

One thing can be said with certainty about the South African Lenin: he will not be of the same pigmentation as his precursor. Lionel Burger is dead and buried, and his hopes for a nonracial revolution in South Africa are dead and buried along with him. His daughter may enjoy a feeling of solidarity with blacks in prison, but outside she will be excluded from all their councils. The future, as she knows, is not for her. For her and her kind the future can hold nothing good except for a liberation from the guilt of being, in virtue of their color, partners in a particular system of oppression, now doomed.

On that liberation there is a daunting price tag. Before any system acceptable to the Afrikaner *Volk* can be succeeded by any system acceptable to Black Consciousness, it is likely that blood will flow in great quantities, over many years. And at the end of that time? The lucid and (perforce) detached observer has to see that what ensues is very unlikely to take any democratic or liberal form. There is nothing in South Africa's past to prepare for democracy or liberalism, nor is it likely that the coming period of transition will include such preparation. The future, then, at the end of a bloody struggle, is likely to bring not the talked of "majority rule" but the rule of a determined minority, hardened in the struggle against the whites—and also probably against other tough and determined black minorities disputing the final seat of power.

AFRIKANERS AT PRESENT like to say that the end of white power will be followed by *Mfecane*—the word for the fearful intertribal crushing of peoples which accompanied the great Zulu migrations of the nineteenth century. It is, of course, in the interests of defenders of the present system to make such dire predictions, but these may nonetheless be uncomfortably close to the truth. Certainly in Rhodesia, as white power approaches its end, intertribal differences, whose significance was submerged under the whites, are becoming salient again—as they were before the white man came.

Black minorities—or even helpless majorities—are likely to suffer, but "nonblack" minorities—whites, Asians, coloreds—seem virtually certain to do so. The Asians may be the most endangered of all. When I was in South Africa recently, a white journalist told of a joke told him by a black colleague. The joke took the form of advising the white man to be in Durban on the day of the revolution. Durban has the largest Indian community of any South African city. "So we'll be so busy cutting the throats of the Indians first, there'll be just time for you whites to leave town." I take this blood-curdling pleasantry to be intended as a caricature of white fears of what black power would mean. All the same, if I were a South African Indian, I should not find the joke very funny.

Such grim intimations about the post-apartheid future do nothing to justify apartheid. On the contrary it is part of the case against apartheid that this is the kind of future that it has been preparing, and is still preparing, for the people who live under it and the people who devised it. There is a South African novel about a future in which blacks rule and Afrikaners survive as abjectly poor peasants, whose bare physical survival is tolerated, but who are occasionally swooped on and savaged by the police of their new masters. In these conditions an Afrikaner is showing a stranger, by candlelight, over his ramshackle old farmhouse. He shows him a set of portraits of the great Nationalist leaders of the past—Malan, Verwoerd, Vorster. He explains his pride in these men: "They made us what we are today."

Burger's Daughter reflects a doomed society,[2] about to be overthrown by a probably doomed revolution—probably doomed, that is, so far as the hopes are concerned of those who now see in it the impending dawn of human liberty. No wonder that Nadine Gordimer's work evokes comparison with those great Russians who painted *their* doomed society, in the years leading up to a revolution about which we no longer have to make predictions.

Notes

1. Excerpts reprinted with permission of Viking Press.

2. *Burger's Daughter* is banned in South Africa (or "prohibited"; there, "banning" is something they do to human beings). It might have been prohibited for nearly anything—for "obscenity" or for giving a favorable picture of a Communist. I like to think myself that it was banned because in the person of the eminent *verligte* Nationalist who gets Rosa her passport some people are likely to see an odious portrayal of the sophisticated and charming *verligte* who is currently the president of the *Broederbond.*

The Subject of Revolution

STEPHEN R. CLINGMAN

❖ ❖ ❖

Wait for it: waiting for it.
> —Nadine Gordimer,
> "A Lion on the Freeway"

I N *The Conservationist* there are no white characters whose task it is to respond positively to the prospect of revolution; it is part of the novel's prophetic release that this is not deemed to be necessary. However, in the two novels that followed, *Burger's Daughter* and *July's People*, Gordimer returned to the question that *The Conservationist* leaves out: whether whites can participate in the future it predicts. Yet she did so in very different circumstances. As independence came to Mozambique, Angola, and, later, Zimbabwe, the prophecy of *The Conservationist* seemed to be fulfilled on a regional level; but in South Africa its price was made clear. The explosion of the Soweto Revolt of 1976 indicated just how tortuous the path of change was gong to be, at the same time thrusting the position of dissident whites into radical ambiguity; the easy mood of celebration of just a few years earlier was dramatically displaced.

In *Burger's Daughter* and *July's People* Gordimer therefore comes down from the symbolic plane of *The Conservationist,* and what she attempts to do is assess whether there can be a role for whites in the context of Soweto and after, and what the practical implications of such a role might be. The two novels are in some ways very different; Rosa Burger, in *Burger's Daughter,* comes from an official and conspicuous political tradition; Maureen Smales, in *July's People,* is among the most ordinary of Gordimer's characters, politically considered. But the underlying themes of the two novels unite them, at the same time suggesting new developments in Nadine Gordimer's consciousness of history. Both are deeply concerned with the climactic historical moment that Gordimer's fiction increasingly seems to be "waiting for": the moment of revolution in South Africa. And both of them deal with the subject of revolution by scrutinizing its effect on the subject: Rosa Burger in *Burger's Daughter* and Maureen Smales in *July's People*. Dealing with social transformation as it affects the individual is the primary way in which Gordimer's novels develop a consciousness of history. And it may be that the future that is written here, especially in *July's People*, is the ultimate subject of Gordimer's historical consciousness.

IT IS, HOWEVER, HISTORY as a sense of the past, that for the first time, enters Gordimer's work in her seventh novel, *Burger's Daughter*, published in 1979.[1] Also for the first time she concerns herself with an obviously recognizable public figure. This dual interest appears in the novel in its investigation of Lionel Burger, Rosa Burger's father. For, both positively and negatively, Rosa's career is measured out in the novel in relation to that of her father; and her father was a man with a significant, though fictional, personal history. Born an Afrikaner of staunch Nationalist stock, Lionel Burger had "betrayed" his people by becoming a member of the Communist Party of South Africa (CPSA; later SACP) in the late 1920s. Involved in the ideological swings of the party at that time and in the decade following, and in the campaigns of the 1940s and 1950s, Burger had remained a member of its Central Committee when the party dissolved itself in the face of the Suppression of Communism Act, and went underground. Captured in the mid-1960s and sentenced to imprisonment for life, he died in jail in the early 1970s. His fictional career has therefore coincided with most of the major developments in the revolutionary opposition in South Africa in the twentieth century.

In most of these respects the character of Lionel Burger bears a strong resemblance to the real-life figure of Abram "Bram" Fischer, one of the most prominent leaders within the SACP, upon whose personal history Burger's career has evidently been based.[2] We have seen that in the mid-1960s Gordimer was very much interested in Fischer; at the time of his arrest and trial she wrote two articles in which her admiration for his integrity and heroism are evident.[3] This interest comes to the fore again here. Certain details have been changed; Fischer joined the Party somewhat later than Lionel does in the novel, and Lionel Burger is cast as a doctor, whereas Bram Fischer was a lawyer. Other particulars, especially insofar as they concern the Fischer Family, have been changed in the life of the Burgers, though sometimes only by rearrangement; for example, at one stage the Fischers took into their household a young black child, the niece of a servant; in the novel this is changed into the figure of Baasie/Zwelinzima, the son of a political colleague, whom the Burgers take in.[4]

But in the end it is not the details that matter. Primarily Gordimer has been concerned to capture the *spirit* a man like Fischer represented. In this way the Burger home, with its symbolic centerpiece, the swimming pool, represents in the novel the social warmth and historical optimism for which the Fischer household (along with its own swimming pool and "open house" policy) was renowned. And in drawing in Lionel a charismatic figure—doctrinaire, but first and foremost full of what Rosa at the end of the novel considers to be his "sublimity"—the figure of Fischer most of all appears.

In being concerned to capture the spirit rather than the details of Fischer's life, Gordimer has been after a specific typification: notwithstanding whatever faults the Burgers may exhibit, it is the very best heritage there has been in the white revolutionary tradition. Nevertheless, insofar as Burger *is* based on Fischer, Gordimer has extended her usual practice of close observation in the present into historical research of the past. Not only has she made direct use of basic political and historical texts (as we shall see) but she also undertook interviews with people connected with Fischer and his times.[5] So the figure of Burger acts as a bridge in the novel between fact and fiction, and past and present, as the methods of the novelist and a more orthodox historian coincide.

This does not mean that Gordimer's view of the past is somehow "neutral." We have seen the role that ideology has played in her fiction so far, and in *Burger's Daughter* it enters again, though ultimately by no means in anything like simple fashion. It first becomes apparent in the novel's view of the Communist Party, to which its response is to some extent mixed. Subtly, for example, a distinction is drawn between Communist doctrine and Communist performance. In contrast to the usual basis upon which such a distinction is made, however, the Communist performance in South Africa is, if anything, seen to be superior to its doctrine. Where Rosa rehearses the "litany" (her word) of Party dogma, the mood is frequently—though not stridently—ironical; on the other hand, it is demonstrated in the novel that the historical record of the SACP is a proud one.

In her own commentary on the novel Gordimer has suggested why a figure such as Lionel Burger should have joined the Communist Party. In the late 1920s when he did so, she has pointed out that there was no other political party in South Africa that incorporated blacks into its membership and leadership as equals, and envisioned them as such in the running of the country.[6] This is a fundamental good faith, the novel suggests, which the Communist Party kept up throughout its history. If this is so, then the basis of the novel's (and perhaps Gordimer's own) approval is clear. It is primarily a human and democratic approval; the Party's human record is affirmed, and its politics only at the "nonideological" level of performance. This is most definite in the figure of Burger; for where he, as the representative of the revolutionary tradition, is shown in his most favorable light, it is because of his magnificent qualities as a human being: his warmth, generosity, and dedication. In this regard the novel's respect for him is entirely unambiguous and so in an important way—though it is by no means exaggerated—theory is separated from practice; the novel's reading of the past is selective. It is thus not entirely surprising that one of the only unfavorable reviews *Burger's Daughter* received appeared in the *African Communist*, official organ of the SACP.[7]

Although the character of Lionel Burger bears a significant resemblance to the real-life figure of Bram Fischer, Gordimer's novel is not about Lionel Burger himself, but about Burger's daughter, Rosa. In this respect there would be little point in attempting to trace any real-life parallels between the book and Fischer's family, though parallels exist. To assume that these are what are finally important for the figure of Rosa, however, is to miss the central thrust of the novel's concerns. For in Rosa, more so than in the case of Lionel, Gordimer has given an even clearer example—perhaps the clearest in all of her novels—of her practice of typification at work; a particular social "space" has been carefully constructed for the imaginative exploration of the historical possibilities and necessities applying to a certain kind of figure in a given situation. At this level Gordimer is primarily concerned with the predicament facing the inheritor of a revolutionary tradition in the context of South Africa in the mid-1970s. Precisely because Lionel Burger is a recognizable type of historical figure, this is what he enables Gordimer to explore most imaginatively through Rosa. But for the same reason Rosa herself does not depend on any correspondence with living persons; there is a sliding scale of typification in the novel—from Burger, who establishes the historical situation, to Rosa, through whom its implications are examined. It is, finally, because Gordimer is concerned with the deepest internalities of Rosa's existence on the one hand, and the broadest of social and historical themes on the other, that the figure of Rosa far transcends whatever documentary-like parallels exist, which ultimately function only to set the basic context of her struggle.

By an apparent paradox, considering its overall framework, one of the major themes of *Burger's Daughter* concerns a challenge to the whole idea of political or historical commitment. On one level this is conducted through the novel's categories of analysis. Thus along with Marx, who stands behind the text of *Burger's Daughter* as a kind of symbolic analytical figurehead, are two others: Freud and, less so, Christ.

On occasion Lionel Burger is compared to Christ, and it becomes apparent that, if there is any meaning at all to a Christ figure in South Africa, it is likely to be found in a character such as Lionel Burger. Also, the phrase that Rosa most frequently (and ironically) uses to describe the Party members is that of "the faithful," as if they belonged to a religion. This kind of interest does not proceed much beyond the realm of analogy in the novel, however, and is only of minor concern.

More important to *Burger's Daughter* is the figure of Freud. A Freudian discourse is first represented in the vicarious, and degraded, form of Conrad, the self-absorbed hippie with whom Rosa takes up, and for whom the entire experience of the world can be reduced to two words, *sex* and *death*. But at a deeper level, an intriguing attempt is made in the novel to psychoanalyze political commitment itself. In meeting Marisa Kgosana, the activist wife of an imprisoned African leader, Rosa recognizes just how much the strictly political dedication of her family was mediated by the sensuality and warmth that Marisa both embodies and represents, acting as an unconscious physical and emotional attraction for whites. Marisa is physically the promise of "return," of reintegration, which is at once a subjective and objective issue in South Africa. As Rosa says, addressing Conrad in her mind, the Burger household was "closer to reaching its kind of reality through your kind of reality than I understood" (p. 135).

But the novel's psychoanalytic politics go deeper than this. The basic organizing motif of the text is that of the family; we see Rosa not only in relation to her father, but also in relation to her surrogate mother, Katya, in France; and the relationship between Rosa and Conrad is presented in what are finally incestuous terms, as if they were brother and sister. The Communist Party itself is presented as if it were a "family" (this was in fact the code name for the SACP when it was underground) but it is one in which Rosa is always regarded as a "daughter." *Burger's Daughter* might then be regarded as a *Bildungsroman* with a difference, in which Rosa is eventually expelled from the womblike infantilization she is subjected to from so many sources into the mature acceptance of her own life history (which of necessity leads her into another kind of womb, the prison cell).

Judie Newman has shown that the most important "family relationship" of the novel politically is also a psychological one—it is that between Rosa and Baasie, the black boy who had been her virtual brother. Brought into the Burger household as a child because of his own father's political involvement, he and Rosa had taken baths together, discovered the world together, slept together in the same bed. Yet this is a sibling relationship in which primary issues had remained unresolved. For it too had been an "infantile" relationship, held forever in amber in Rosa's mind, as it were, due to the fact that Baasie had been removed from the Burger "safe" environment when his father took him away. There are unresolved questions of sexual displacement, and there is a basic problem of projection; Baasie has remained a construct in Rosa's mind, and a childish construct at that, something of an eternal playmate or plaything. Drawing on psychological and cultural theories of colonialism, in particular Mannoni's *Prospero and Caliban*,[8] which Gordimer had been reading at the time, Newman then argues that this forms the basis of Rosa's political development. Whereas blacks had never been truly Other for her, by the end of the novel Rosa has reached the point where they are objects neither of mental projection nor of displacement, but exist fully in their own right. This allows her own authentic political reengagement.[9]

If this is so—and the argument is in many respects a fascinating and persuasive one—then much of the force of this exploration in the novel must derive from its own historical context in the second half of the 1970s. We shall see that the primary phenomenon to which *Burger's Daughter* responded in this period was the movement of Black Consciousness and its culmination, the Soweto Revolt. The primary question that Black Consciousness posed for whites who were politically involved was that of their authenticity. Despite their outward protestations, Black Consciousness proponents argued, at certain levels—most likely including subconscious levels—whites, no matter what their political persuasion, still participated in deep-rooted patterns of white supremacy.

In the late 1970s Gordimer showed herself much exercised by the question of "white consciousness" as a response to Black Consciousness. This by no means had anything to do with a white racist response; on the contrary, as a term that was in currency at the time, especially among white students, in its very phrasing it accepted the point the Black Consciousness movement was making. It primarily denoted an attempt by whites to transcend the horizon of even an unwilling complicity in the patterns of supremacy by recognizing the real possibility of its existence, and thereby being able to construct an authentic alternative.[10] *Burger's Daughter* can be seen as a fictional way of working out the same problem. Thus, the only way in which the novel, and Rosa as a character, can avoid the accusation of even a subconscious participation in the supremacist syndrome is to internalize this accusation by first displaying it, then analyzing and eradicating it. Moreover, *Burger's Daughter* does so in explicitly psychoanalytical terms, which in one respect indicates just how seriously it takes the problem with which it is dealing. The novel's explorations in this area have a certain autonomy and are of great interest in their own right. At the same time, seeing them in this wider context is to analyze the novel's own psychoanalysis, within a historical framework. In this view, the pressure applied by the challenge of Black Consciousness added force to the novel's researches into the unconscious of a white political response, making Rosa's development to some degree hinge on the eradication of deeply embedded subconscious patterns.

The idea of political commitment comes under even more direct challenge in *Burger's Daughter* in the figure of Rosa herself. For much of the course of the novel Rosa is in straightforward revolt against both her historical heritage and the demands of her current situation. After her father's death, rejecting what she regards as the oversimplifications of Communist Party ideology—and, more immediately, rejecting her father himself, who had made her deny her own individuality in favor of political needs—Rosa opts for what she has never had: the experience of a private life. Considering her only past experience of love, she remembers how she subjected herself to her father's wishes by undertaking a pretended betrothal to a political prisoner in order to carry messages more easily back and forth from prison. Rosa is not scandalized by her past performance; as she says, in her family "prostitutes" were regarded as victims of necessity while certain social orders lasted (p. 68). But what lay behind her pretense was an even deeper one, for in fact Rosa *really* loved this prisoner— something that out of exigency and sensitivity she never allowed anyone else to know, neither her parents nor her "betrothed" himself.[11] There is no great sentimentalization of such issues in the novel, and part of their force is their indication that in the South African political context sentimentality is an inadmissible luxury. Nevertheless, for Rosa herself it means that she has never explored a private existence. The need now to do this determines her to go to Europe, to leave the site of all these problems, the site of revolutionary struggle itself. In this her motivation is plain enough; the key word Rosa uses to describe her reason for going is "defection."

Quite simply Rosa Burger goes to Europe to learn how to "defect" from her father and the historical legacy he has handed to her.

Adding to her feelings in this matter is the sense that Lionel's ideology is ultimately inadequate to cope with the complexities of existence as such and, particularly for Rosa, the complexities of existence in South Africa. This becomes evident in two separate scenes in the novel where Rosa confronts the human condition in its barest and simultaneously almost abstract forms. The first occurs at lunch time in one of Johannesburg's city parks, where a hobo, sitting on one of the benches near Rosa, suddenly dies where he is, without ceremony, as it were, in public; this to Rosa seems to signify the blunt and blank realities of life—and death—which are beyond the scope of a purely political framework to comprehend.

The second scene occurs when Rosa is returning to Johannesburg from Soweto and she comes across what seems to her to be the very incarnation of cruelty and despair. She sees a black man, violent in drunken anger and tiredness, repeatedly whipping a donkey that can no longer pull the cart in which a woman and child sit starkly terrified.[12] Social and political conditions have conspired to produce this scene, but to Rosa what she is witnessing appears to be an existential essence and total or, as she puts it, the "sum of suffering" (p. 210). She identifies it with all the suffering there has ever been, including that of her own country:

> the camps, concentration, labour, resettlement, the Siberias of snow or sun, the lives of Mandela, Sisulu, Mbeki, Kathrada, Kgosana, gull-picked on the Island, Lionel propped wasting to his skull between two warders, the deaths by questioning, bodies fallen from the height of John Vorster Square, deaths by dehydration, babies degutted by enteritis in "places" of banishment, the lights beating all night on the faces of those in cells. (p. 208)

Precisely because the scene has such a vast significance, however, Rosa feels powerless to act to end it. Also, it appears that the only way she could intervene to stop the immediate cruelty at hand would be to exploit her position of white authority; in this case she will be yet one more white who evidently cares for animals more than she does for people. This need not necessarily be true; it is easy to think of action Rosa might take that would show her concern for the people involved as much as for the animal, and there is no reason why she should not use the power she has to help. But Rosa simply feels that things have gotten beyond her. Confounded by the implications of her situation she just does not know what role to play. Absorbing the fact of her own impotence, she recognizes that she no longer knows "how to live in Lionel's country" (p. 210). This is another way of say-

ing that she is defecting from politics in search of other ways of understanding and living out her life. The scene acts as a final spur to send her on
her way to Europe.

The idea of social engagement is thus brought under severe test in the
novel. Freud is posed strongly against Marx, existence is posed against history, and Rosa is moved to "defect." Looking back on Gordimer's other
novels it is clear that this procedure of contestation is very much an intrin-
sic component of her work—ever since Helen, in *The Lying Days*, took her
own decision to "defect" from South Africa to Europe. (In this respect the
donkey-whipping scene in *Burger's Daughter* functions in much the same way
as the killing of the man in the May Day riots; both episodes indicate the
central character's historical exclusion.) This theme of defection is present
in the other novels as well. From a moral point of view Toby Hood in *A
World of Strangers* is a defector from social responsibility for much of that
novel; Jessie Stilwell opts for "existence" at the price of politics in *Occasion
for Loving*; for most of *The Late Bourgeois World* Elizabeth believes that social engagement is no longer possible; and Bray in *A Guest of Honour* is faced with a
further option of "defection" upon his return to his African country. For
Gordimer, then, a sense of history is itself a site of struggle; it is by no
means easily given, but comes under challenge again and again.

In *Burger's Daughter*, as in the other novels, this contestation is itself only a
part of the overall movement of the work. In Europe Rosa is on the point
of finding the personal fulfillment she has never had. She falls in love, and
is making plans to defect on a permanent basis. But precisely at this moment (for good historical reasons, as we shall see) she comes to understand
that it is after all imperative for her to return to South Africa and take up
the social engagement she had tried to avoid.

And so the overall pattern of *Burger's Daughter* takes on a dialectical form.
In the first movement we have Rosa, together with her revolutionary inheritance; in the second she rejects this inheritance in favor of her personal
life; in the third she reunites with that inheritance, simultaneously finding
her personal identity in becoming socially and historically committed.
From one point of view this procedure of contestation can be seen as a
method of self-probationary verification; only through having challenged
the category of historical engagement to its utmost can there be any certainty as to its necessity when at last it is confirmed. It is the historical
equivalent of a philosophical procedure of "methodical doubt," which is in
the end all that can verify what is doubted in the first place. Furthermore,
this pattern of self-probation is recognizably present in all of Gordimer's
novels; after the challenge against a social and historical destiny (even

Mehring opts for a private seclusion on his farm) comes the confirmation of its final necessity. This pattern of challenge and probation must therefore be considered a major component of the way a consciousness of history is tried and tested in Gordimer's work.

This phenomenon is also revealing from another point of view. It has been suggested before in this study that if Gordimer had not been a writer in South Africa she might have been a different kind of writer. From this standpoint what appears in her work as a procedure of verification looks more like one of renunciation. There are whole dimensions of existence and its understanding that Gordimer recognizes must be surrendered in favor of historical priorities. This can be seen as a direct consequence of living in South Africa, in which history must be seen, for better or for worse, as the category of comprehension that includes all others, and as the dimension of engagement that must take precedence.

In pursuing these themes so far we have dealt very little with the novel's treatment of the present—the area that, overall, appears to be of greatest concern for Nadine Gordimer's consciousness of history in general. The "present" to which *Burger's Daughter* responded was one of momentous importance. On 16 June 1976 some fifteen thousand schoolchildren gathered at Orlando West Junior Secondary School in Soweto to protest against the enforced use of Afrikaans as a medium of instruction in certain subjects in black schools. The meeting began with peaceful intentions, but by the time it ended two children had been shot by the police.[13] They were the first of many to follow, for what came after was one of the most climactic periods of modern South African history, as an unexpected phase of resistance burst with extraordinary intensity. It is impossible here to give a full and detailed account of what came to be known as the Soweto Revolt, since its ramifications were vast as well as geographically dispersed; nevertheless some of its central patterns can be delineated.[14] It was for one thing a sustained episode of cultural as much as political resistance; not only was there the issue of the use of Afrikaans (widely regarded by blacks as the language of their oppression) in schools, but feeding into the revolt as well as burgeoning from it was the Black Consciousness ethos, with its emphases on cultural revival and the assertion of black dignity and identity. It was also, preeminently, a revolt of children. For the schoolchildren consciously saw their assertion as being not only against the white state, but also against their parents whom they felt had been passive for too long. This was a revolt that started in schools, spread through schools, and sometimes reached the universities, but in which the youth led, and their elders, if anything, followed.

For any (including the government) who thought that a children's eruption could be easily contained, the course of the revolt proved the opposite. Where children confronted the police they often seemed fearless, marching into police bullets. The path of the revolt also spread like wildfire, darting from place to place throughout the country, being quelled here, but then flaring up there, and then back again where it had begun. Scarcely an area of the country was not in some way touched by the Soweto Revolt. In some respects the youthful leadership of the insurrection was not equipped to deal with wider issues of political organization;[15] but also it showed great ingenuity. Thus the Soweto Students Representative Council (SSRC), which led the revolt in Soweto, had a rotating leadership. Partly this was due to necessity, as successive leaders were forced to flee or were taken into detention, but it was due to astuteness as well, since a revolving leadership was that much more difficult to pin down.[16] Nor was the revolt without its successes; it brought down the Urban Bantu Council in Soweto and some local schoolboards; there was a mass resignation of teachers; stay-aways of workers were organized (though there were other failures in relation to migrant workers); both in Cape Town and Johannesburg student marchers penetrated into the city centers.

The impact of the countrywide revolt as a whole is best measured in the fact that it took the full force of the police, with all the resources and laws at its disposal, a good deal more than a year to bring it to an end; indeed they were kept at full stretch for much of that time. When the revolt finally subsided toward the end of 1977 there had been a significant migration of black youth across the borders to join the ANC. On the other hand the toll paid during the uprising was a heavy one. Among those who died violently during its course was the Black Consciousness leader Steve Biko, kept naked and manacled in police custody.[17] And the numbers of dead were tragically far greater than this; official (and probably underestimated) counts put the figure at 575—most of them schoolchildren shot by the police—with some 2,389 wounded.[18] Yet by the time it ended Soweto had become a historical landmark. The quiescence of the previous decade had ended, the tone for the decade to come had been set. The Soweto Revolt had earned a central place in the calendar of resistance in South Africa.

This was the context from which *Burger's Daughter* grew. How was it, how could it all be, transformed into a consciousness of history in Gordimer's fiction? Some of it was translated directly. One striking motif is that of the revolt of children against parents; this occurred in Soweto and this is what Rosa Burger goes through in relation to her father. An added dimension is the feeling in the novel that new forms of struggle are required for new circumstances, that the heritage of the fathers must be evaluated, modified, and reformulated; again, this was the immediate import of Soweto. However, if this was the positive impact of the revolt on the novel, there was nevertheless another side. *Burger's Daughter* is inspired by its circumstances, but there is also a sense in which it was sidelined by them. We saw in relation to *The Conservationist* that in as much as the Black Consciousness movement constituted a threat to official white supremacy, it was equally a challenge to white liberalism; for it classed the paternalism it found there with white supremacy itself. But if Black Consciousness was the challenge in theory, then the Soweto Revolt was that challenge in practice. Moreover, it was a challenge not just to liberalism but also to white radicalism. Black children were being shot while white liberals and radicals could at most only look on in horror. Now mountains of words spoken in the past could only seem sickeningly shameful in view of the blood of children running in the streets. If anything seemed to demonstrate the irrelevance of white dissidents on the periphery of the democratic struggle, that event was the Soweto Revolt.

Ever since the early 1960s Nadine Gordimer had occupied a narrowing margin within the domain of white society. Now that margin itself was qualitatively different; for the whites who occupied it were being rejected in theory and bypassed in fact by their only historical source of relevance, the oppressed black world itself.

Gordimer was deeply affected by these events in the second half of the 1970s. In a speech published in 1977 she said that though rationally she understood Black Consciousness, and even considered it necessary, as an experience she found it "as wounding as anyone else" (this marked a change from her calmer acceptance of it earlier in the decade).[19] As to those whites who maintained a commitment to an eventual and authentic meeting ground of liberation, all they could do, she suggested, was make a "Pascalian wager" on their commitment.[20] Elsewhere, her response to the events of 1976 was filled with a mood of outrage, horror, and impotence. In the aftermath of Soweto she wrote:

> We whites do not know how to deal with the fact of this death when children, in full knowledge of what can happen to them, continue to go out to meet it at the hands of the law, for which we are solely responsible, whether we support white supremacy, or, opposing, having failed to unseat it.[21]

Burger's Daughter is an attempt to deal with the practical and moral implications of this massive psychohistorical problem. Generated from this mood, it is a grave examination of what can remain of white "action" when it has been so fundamentally called into question, and in what terms such action can be revived.

Black Consciousness is central to this. Its challenge is implicit in the novel's major themes, but it is represented explicitly as well. It first enters directly at Fats Mxange's party where some of the younger blacks reject the class analysis of South Africa offered by the Communist fellow traveler Orde Greer. Their spokesman, Duma Dhladhla, angrily dismisses him:

> *This* and *this* should happen and can't happen because of *that* and *that.* These theories don't fit us. We are not interested. You've been talking this shit before I was born. (p. 162)

In the novel it is Rosa who is made to confront Black Consciousness in a most direct way. In London, at a party given in honor of some Frelimo representatives, she comes across Baasie, the little boy who had once been like a brother to her. She thinks she recognizes him at the party, but he refuses to acknowledge her. Later that night, however, he does so, and with a vengeance. After Rosa has gone to sleep he telephones her; what follows is one of the most powerful and extraordinary scenes in Gordimer's fiction (pp. 318–23). He tells Rosa he is no longer her "Baasie"—his real name, and the one Rosa never knew, is Zwelinzima Vulindlela (*Zwelinzima* means "suffering land"). And Rosa should set no sentimental store by his past in the Burger household, for this too was not without its ambiguities. For his part he now bitterly rejects the false brotherhood he had with Rosa and the (almost literal) paternalism of Lionel, which both set him aside from the rest of his people in privilege and, at the same time, he feels, belittled him; the name he was given ("Baasie"—"Little Boss") says it all. Most of all he rejects the heritage of Lionel Burger himself; there are hundreds of black men, including his own father, who have also died in jail, often more violently than Lionel (his own father died of an improbable prison "suicide"). But the black names have been forgotten, their heroism remains untold; instead it is white men, such as Lionel Burger, who get all the accolades and glory. "Whatever you whites touch," he tells Rosa, "it's a takeover"; the Burgers, and Rosa in particular, are no different from any other whites. As Zwelinzima urges her to turn on the lights (she has been speaking to him in the dark) and she confronts the full import of what is happening, Rosa is literally sickened, finally vomiting up the remains of what she has consumed at the party in anguish, shame, and anger.

The symbolic significance of this scene is a powerful one in the context of South Africa in the mid-1970s. Here the accusations of Black Consciousness are clearly hitting home. Actions taken with the best of intentions and out of genuine care are rejected as compromised and hypocritical. If a previous generation of whites devoted their best energies and talents to the liberation struggle, they should not expect any gratitude. The allegorical setting of the multiracial "family" gives a perfect and exact sense of earlier assumptions of interracial harmony and solidarity that were not being ripped apart, as well as the intimate violence aroused by the passions surrounding Black Consciousness.

As far as Rosa and Zwelinzima are concerned, there are also wider resonances. These two inheritors of a previous politics, who in principle are in favor of the same political objectives, are in a sense divided by the history uniting them. They are divided particularly by some of the undeniable insights of Black Consciousness, which Rosa seems merely to have proved in her "defection" from the struggle. The result is a love-hate relationship between these two "siblings" of the younger generation, which can be neither consummated nor set aside. In a far advanced form of the irony that contained Jessie and Gideon in *Occasion for Loving*, Rosa and Zwelinzima face one another on opposite sides of a chasm that, at some level, both are desperate to cross. But in contrast to *Occasion for Loving* (and possibly because of the very effects Gordimer is describing) what emerges from the scene is as a result not entirely negative. For one thing, if Rosa sees Zwelinzima as Other by the end of the novel, it is because he, with all his vindictiveness, *forces* her to do exactly that here. Moreover, she, confronting this fact, is then propelled toward her own separateness and assertion. Black Consciousness forces a white reassessment, but also provokes a new dedication; absorbing the impact of all that her encounter with Zwelinzima signifies, the revolt of Rosa's body presages the revolution of her identity once again. The direct challenge that Zwelinzima has leveled determines Rosa to return to South Africa to renew the social commitment her father left off. Taking up physiotherapy work at Baragwanath Hospital in Soweto, she is overtaken by the events of 1976. In this context she once again becomes involved in some form of undisclosed work in the underground, is detained under Section 6 of the Terrorism Act, and finds herself in solitary confinement, much like her father before her.

In the decade after 1976 the movement of Black Consciousness subsided in both intensity and significance, especially in its political forms. At the same time, however, whatever emerged in the aftermath of Soweto could never be free of some or other aspect of the Black Consciousness experience. And if one is looking for the classic condensation of what Black Consciousness *meant* at the apogee of its ideological authority, especially to sympathetic whites, then there is possibly no better place to find it than in the scene between Rosa and Zwelinzima. Yet the novel does not simply submit to the Black Consciousness onslaught in its own terms. It is significant that Rosa does again become "Burger's daughter" at the end of the novel, accepting her family identity and linking up with her father's tradition. If the events of the novel's present have governed its "remembrance of things past," then its research of that past has by no means been gratuitous. Rather it has scanned a previous history for a definite guideline in the present. Rosa does not become politically reengaged at the end of the novel in exactly the same terms as her father—for her the fact of suffering is paramount rather than any question of ideology:

> I don't know the ideology.
> It's about suffering.
> How to end suffering. (p. 332)

But she is acting in the spirit of her father's tradition and reconnecting with his heritage. The novel has looked to the past in order to find the only source of inspiration that could be adequate to its present. There are many places it might have looked, but that it found it in Lionel Burger's heritage confirms that *Burger's Daughter* is, despite its ideological qualifications, truly, as Gordimer has said, her most radical novel yet.[22] Fusing the needs of the present with the traditions of the past there is a strong revolutionary alignment in the novel.

One of the ways this alignment enters is in aspects of the novel's form. This should be no surprise; form has consistently been a bearer of historical consciousness in Gordimer's other novels, and in *The Conservationist* was the key to its historical consciousness. In its own way *Burger's Daughter* embodies two kinds of formal operation less easily discernible in Gordimer's other writing, but both have wider resonances. The first is perhaps unexpected, and concerns form as a matter of *quotation. Burger's Daughter* is full of quotations.[23] The most obvious example of this is the pamphlet attributed to the SSRC, which appears in the novel on pages 346–47. Considered solely within the text there is no way of telling whether the pamphlet is a reproduction of an actual one, or has merely been simulated by Gordimer, but in fact this pamphlet did appear on the streets of Soweto during the revolt, and has simply been inserted in full into the text.[24] This, in an explicit way, is quotation, and other instances of it abound in the novel. Thus, when Duma Dhladhla says black liberation cannot be divorced from Black Consciousness "because we cannot be conscious of ourselves and at the same time remain slaves" (p. 164), he is quoting Steve Biko, who expressed the same sentiments in almost exactly the same words.[25] More distantly, as

Orde Greer suggests (and as Biko himself acknowledged), Dhladhla is quoting Hegel. Similarly, when Lionel Burger, in his speech from the dock, talks of national liberation as being the primary objective of political struggle in South Africa, and the rest being a matter for the future to settle (p. 26), his words echo those actually spoken by Bram Fischer in his own trial before sentence was passed.[26]

Gordimer's chief written source for *Burger's Daughter*, however, seems to have been Joe Slovo's essay "South Africa—No Middle Road" first published, appropriately enough, in 1976.[27] This source is particularly interesting in that Joe Slovo has been a long-standing member of the SACP, and his essay is a historical review of South Africa from the point of view of tactics required in the revolutionary struggle; as such it has provided many of the most memorable encapsulations within the text of *Burger's Daughter*.[28] When Rosa Burger talks of the small group of white revolutionaries who are supposed to have solved the "contradiction between black consciousness and class consciousness" (p. 126), the phrase comes directly from Slovo, although the context has been changed.[29] Similarly, when she talks of the sixth underground conference of the SACP in 1962, at which Party ideology was finally evolved in the form of the thesis that "it is just as impossible to conceive of workers' power separated from national liberation as it is to conceive of true national liberation separated from the destruction of capitalism" (p. 126), this account comes verbatim from Slovo.[30]

In the novel's numerous quotations—of which these are only the most obvious, there is sometimes—as in the examples just cited—an oblique suggestion that there may be quotation involved. Elsewhere quotations are clearly marked, even though their source is seldom given; on yet other occasions quotations are not indicated in any way at all.[31] In one elaboration of the novel's quotational gymnastics, a statement by Marx, given in a footnote by Slovo, appears in unattributed quotation marks as a central sentiment in Lionel Burger's speech from the dock.[32] Elsewhere, Marx, Lenin, and others are quoted regularly.

In this way a textual collage is built up in *Burger's Daughter*, cutting across temporal, geographical, political, and ideological space. Once again in Gordimer's work, however, there is a distinct logic to her fictional procedures that goes beyond any pure formalism. Regarding the SSRC pamphlet, Gordimer has explained why it entered the novel as quotation. The document was a necessary part of the book as a whole, she maintained; she presented it as it was because her "stylistic integrity as a writer" demanded it:

I reproduced the document exactly as it was . . . because I felt it expressed, more eloquently and honestly than any pamphlet I could have invented, the spirit of the young people who wrote it.[33]

There is a particular functionalism at work here. If the original document is good enough, there is no reason, for the sake of convention, to invent another one that looks exactly like it; and the same may be said, one supposes, of the phrases reproduced from Slovo's essay. This functionalism is also a method particularly suited to the revolutionary subject matter dealt with by the novel; spare and economic, it not only introduces the actual mood of the time (in the case of the SSRC pamphlet) but from the point of view of authorship it overrides the conventions of bourgeois property relations—in this sense "ownership" of the documents or phrases used. The novel opts for use-value in preference to exchange-value; what is important is that the words are reproduced, and not the exchange of ownership rights denoted by the "purchase" of textual attribution. Also, to put words into the mouths of the SSRC leaders would be to fall guilty of the sin of patronization; instead the novel lets them speak for themselves.

This is the most important function fulfilled by the quotations that Gordimer uses. They give voice to a certain social or historical presence, and this in its own authentic form. Thus, the Soweto students are represented in *Burger's Daughter* in their own voices, as is the historical analysis of Slovo. This is not to say that the novel, or Gordimer herself, necessarily approves of or confirms the import of the sentiments quoted. Sometimes they are put in an ironical context (although this is invariably muted); sometimes, as in the case of the pamphlet, presented with complete dispassion. But this always means that the reader is given a chance to make up his own mind. Whatever irony there may be, Gordimer has given SACP doctrine a chance to claim what respect it deserves by the force of its own arguments. By this method, furthermore, she has allowed her novel to act as a vehicle for presenting sentiments, documents, and opinions that would otherwise be unavailable in South Africa—a function traditionally fulfilled by fiction in oppressive societies—and this is the final legitimacy for abstracting the quotations from her various sources. In this light Gordimer's novel has played an important role, especially in a country such as South Africa, where access to certain ideas and even to certain forms of thinking is so overwhelmingly constrained. In political terms, too, quotation in this form is not to be underestimated; there are few other ways that Joe Slovo, as an official in the SACP, could have "got into" South Africa.[34]

Although quotation is used in an emphatic form in *Burger's Daughter*, it enables us to recognize an aspect of Gordimer's fiction less marked in her other novels: all of them, either explicitly or implicitly, employ a method of quotation. In *A Guest of Honour* it is perhaps most obvious of all; Fanon is quoted directly, Shinza alludes to Cabral and Mweta to Senghor, Nkrumah is an underlying presence. At this level Gordimer's work reminds us of what she has always insisted, that her novels are also novels of ideas (all of them, as we remember, are prefaced by epigraphs from Yeats, Thomas Mann, Turgenev, Gramsci, and so on).[35] Even in the text of *A World of Strangers* there is, in a different way, a form of quotation. When Steven Sitole says he is "sick of feeling half a man," it is not necessarily as if Gordimer is reproducing someone's actual words. Rather, these words are representative of the sentiments that could well have been expressed (and sometimes possibly were) in the kind of situation Steven inhabits. In this sense quotation in Gordimer's work is typification at the level of verbal representation, and its essential function is to represent a social or historical voice in its most intense and resonant form. Conversely, as was suggested in that novel, typification may be thought of as a social "quotation"; in this case the character, though concretized and individualized in his own voice, is also a generalized reference drawn from, and alluding to, broader social patterns.

A second formal aspect of *Burger's Daughter* invites examination; this can be approached obliquely by first considering the novel's reception in South Africa. When *Burger's Daughter* was first published there it was immediately embargoed, and then soon after banned. Some time after that it had what was at that stage the unique experience of being unbanned due to an appeal by the director of publications against the decision of his own committee. All this is dealt with—and some of the reasons for this strange turnabout analyzed—in a booklet that Gordimer later produced, with the collaboration of some others, entitled *What Happened to "Burger's Daughter."*[36] Many reasons were given for the original banning, but all of them seemed to center upon the chief one, which was, in the committee's own words, that "the authoress uses Rosa's story as a pad from which to launch a blistering and full scale attack on the Republic of South Africa."[37] In its banal way the committee was perhaps trying to be poetic in its suppression of Gordimer's novel.

This decision has been examined by Robert Green, who has demonstrated its essential absurdity (not difficult to do on the grounds of common sense, but Green has been more sophisticated).[38] His primary objections are set up on formal grounds; the Censorship Board, he maintains, made the fundamental critical error of identifying the politics of the author with the politics of her text. Over and above this, he argues, there is in fact no necessary politics of the text *at all* in *Burger's Daughter*; this can be shown by exploring its narrative structure. Thus, in contrast to *A Guest of Honour*, in which there is a single narrative voice, in *Burger's Daughter* Green shows there are five. In his ordering these are: (1) Rosa's internal narrative, which is by definition identical with her view of the world; (2) a sympathetic third-person narrative that focuses on Rosa; (3) a third-person narrative in which Rosa is presented neutrally and dispassionately; (4) a narrative hostile to Rosa (usually that of a Security Police dossier); and (5) a narrative in which Rosa disappears altogether, as in the SSRC pamphlet. In the light of this compound structure Green argues it is impossible to claim that any one view of Rosa triumphs, or has priority in the text. Consequently, there can be no single point of view in the novel, and Green believes he has shown

> the ineffectuality of any reading of *Burger's Daughter* that approaches it as a "univocal" text, as a novel that simply expounds the author's own views. The plurality of narratives ensures instead that no single straightforward judgment on Rosa Burger is tenable. Only a novel of such stature can persuade the reader that Rosa's dilemma was at once massive and historically marginal; that her father's political devotion was both saintly and sterile.[39]

Effective as Green's argument is in showing the central narrative features of *Burger's Daughter*, however, it may reveal some mistakes in interpreting them. First, Green has possibly underestimated the number of narrative voices involved in the novel, or at least the degree to which they modulate through, or are interfused with, one another; sometimes this occurs within the course of a single sentence.[40] A second and more important point is that Green is, in a sense, hoist by his own formal petard; for there is no reason in principle why a multivocal text should be more "objective" than a simple third-person narrative. Both are simply conventions, and (given certain technical skills) one form may be as potentially manipulable as the other, or similarly employed in self-effacing exploration by the writer. Both, after all, are generally written by only one author; in this regard it seems likely that the differences in Gordimer's methods of narration are ones of degree rather than of kind. *A Guest of Honour*, despite its univocal narration, is clearly intended to be as objective as possible; nor can it, any more than *Burger's Daughter*, be regarded as a novel that "simply expounds its author's own views." As to the supposed social complicity of the realist text à la Barthes, that is another question, but even then there are not likely to be any straightforward answers.

As far as *Burger's Daughter* is concerned, from another point of view Green's argument can and must be turned on its head (though once again he has provided the basis for further investigation). For what Green sees as the construction of an indeterminacy in *Burger's Daughter* by means of a narrative plurality can, from a different angle; be seen as the construction of an *overdeterminacy* instead. The epigraph to *Burger's Daughter* comes from Lévi-Strauss: "I am the place in which something has occurred." As a statement, what that epigraph connotes is inevitability, necessity, and, primarily, the objective construction of identity. In this sense we have seen that Rosa Burger's identity has been objectively constructed. For most of her life, except in her revolt against her father, Rosa's private existence has been "empty," responding only to objective political needs, and shaped by her family around her; in her return to South Africa she once again places her identity at the disposal of such needs. In this respect, however, the empty individual, like Walter Benjamin's *Unmensch*, is not the most indeterminate, but on the contrary the most determinate, subject, constructed only by the objective forces of her historical situation.[41]

Moreover, of this objective construction the convention of the novel's narrative plurality stands as the formal sign. It is not that Rosa Burger has been seen from so many points of view as to become dispersed and indistinct in her commitment. Rather, seeing her from every point of view has merely led to an apparently necessary outcome: that this is the destiny Rosa was born to, that this is the commitment she must undertake. Certainly, her commitment has been seen to have many sides, but then all those sides accumulate toward that commitment. Like a sculpture around which there is circumambience, the novel, in "walking around" Rosa in its narrative plurality, has increased rather than decreased her final concreteness. Its procedures have set up the narrative space in which Rosa has occurred, defined (if not filled) from both inside and outside, and proceeding toward her historically necessary destiny.

As Green points out, this does not by itself mean that any specific political ideology has been necessarily affirmed in *Burger's Daughter* (in this regard there is an interesting tension in the novel between its post-humanist construction of Rosa, its humanist appropriation of Lionel Burger's tradition, and its basic revolutionary alignment). But what has primarily been affirmed is Rosa's sense of historical engagement; in the context of the Soweto Revolt this engagement alone has had final meaning for her. This has been explored not only thematically but, as we have seen, also formally. From every point of view, it seems, this is the step Rosa must take. It is a sense of necessary engagement that has been underwritten by the novel itself.

Here *Burger's Daughter* once again allows us to discern a basic pattern within Gordimer's novels as a whole. For all of Gordimer's novels are geared toward constructing an overdeterminancy in this sense. All of them are designed to find out what is absolutely necessary for their time and situation, to test it from every possible point of view and by thematic challenge. And all of them confirm that necessity all the more forcefully when it is discovered. This, fundamentally, is the historic form underlying Gordimer's novels, and the basic disposition underlying the historical consciousness of her work.

Rosa Burger finds her own necessity when she decides to return to South Africa, and then becomes involved in the underground struggle. The final vision of the novel, as in Gordimer's others, has a good deal to do with its sense of history; its resolution contains a perfect embodiment not only of Rosa's position, but also of that of the novel itself. Literally Rosa ends up in solitary confinement, but she is solitary in a different way as well. We have seen that "Burger's daughter" reconnects with the tradition of her father. On the other hand, in the aftermath of Black Consciousness and the Soweto Revolt there can be no special glory attached to her situation. In contrast to Lionel, whose role as a white leader had been preeminent, after the events of 1976 Rosa's can at best be secondary, supportive, peripheral. And so there is a far greater solitude than ever her father knew. In emphasis of this the narrative as a whole begins to withdraw from Rosa toward the end of the novel. Whereas up until now we have had fairly consistent access to her thoughts and feelings (despite the novel's narrative plurality) this domain is now sealed off; even what Rosa has done in the underground remains undisclosed.

It may be suggested that this withdrawal embodies a recognition relating to Gordimer's own position; if the novel cannot speak what Rosa has done, this is because fiction cannot do what Rosa might speak. By this separation, however, Rosa's dignity and heroism are only increased. Both she and the narrative withdraw to their respective solitudes, and perhaps from our point of view "solitude" is an exact image of the position of the white radical in South Africa in the years immediately following Soweto. There is in addition a slight but distinct note of elegy in the novel's final view of Rosa; here mood is possibly as sure an index of historical consciousness as anything else. Nonetheless, for Rosa Burger in her way, and for Gordimer's novel in its own, there is the affirmation of a historical synthesis, of the inheritance of Lionel Burger in its post-Soweto form. The revolutionary "subject" of *Burger's Daughter* has been constructed.

Notes

1. *Burger's Daughter* (London: Cape, 1979); all page references given hereafter in the text; cited where necessary in further footnotes as *BD*.

2. Something that Gordimer herself has not concealed. See "I Know I Have Not Been Brave Enough," interview with Diana Loercher, *Christian Science Monitor*, 21 Jan. 1980, p. 21.

3. See chapter 4, pp. 95–96, of Stephen Clingman, *The Novels of Nadine Gordimer: History from the Inside* (Amherst: University of Massachusetts Press, 1992).

4. I am indebted for this information to Ruth Eastwood. A pair of more tragic details has also been reversed in the novel; Bram's wife, Molly Fischer, was drowned in a car accident, and their son, Paul, died of cystic fibrosis of the pancreas. In *BD* Rosa's brother drowns in the Burger swimming pool, and her mother, Cathy, dies of multiple sclerosis.

5. Gordimer, interview.

6. Nadine Gordimer et al., *What Happened to "Burger's Daughter"; or, How South African Censorship Works* (Johannesburg, South Africa: Taurus, 1980), 18; hereafter referred to as *WHBD*.

7. Z. N., "The Politics of Commitment," *African Communist*, 1st quarter 1980, pp. 100–101. There was perhaps another reason (though unspoken) for the review's objection to *BD*—that Gordimer had dared to "annex" SACP history in the first place. For details of the review and Gordimer's response, see n. 28 below.

8. O. Mannoni, *Prospero and Caliban: The Psychology of Colonization*, trans. Pamela Powesland (London: Methuen, 1956).

9. "Prospero's Complex: Race and Sex in *Burger's Daughter*," *Journal of Commonwealth Literature* 20, no. 1 (Sept. 1985): 81–99. The only mistake that Newman makes, apart from her assumption that South Africa is simply a "racist" society, is to imply that Rosa is entirely contained within its framework—which she evidently is not.

10. See Nadine Gordimer, "What Being a South African Means to Me," *South African Outlook* (June 1977): 87–89, 92.

11. Although there is an alarming suggestion that the Security Police knew; see n. 40.

12. The scene recalls the horse-beating incident in Dostoevsky's *Crime and Punishment*, but is in fact based on an incident that actually occurred while Gordimer was writing the novel, "I Know I Have Not Been Brave Enough," p. 21.

13. Tom Lodge, *Black Politics in South Africa since 1945* (London: Longman, 1983), 328.

14. Ibid., chap. 13, gives a summary of the events of the revolt as well as a discussion of previous analytical approaches to it. For a full account and analysis, see Baruch Hirson, *Year of Fire, Year of Ash—The Soweto Revolt: Roots of a Revolution?* (London: Zed, 1979); also John Kane-Berman, *South Africa: The Method in the Madness* (London: Pluto, 1979). For a day-to-day account of the revolt, see M. Horrell, T. Hodgson, S. Blignaut, and S. Moroney, comps., *A Survey of Race Relations in South Africa 1976* (Johannesburg: South African Institute of Race Relations, 1976), 51–87, and L. Gordon, S. Blignaut, S. Moroney, and C. Cooper, comps., *A Survey of Race Relations in South Africa 1977* (Johannesburg: South African Institute of Race Relations, 1977), 55–82.

15. Hirson, *Year of Fire*, is especially critical of the failure of the Black Consciousness organizations to generalize the revolt more widely in society, especially by linking up with workers. This he sees as following directly from the weaknesses of Black Consciousness as an ideology. Lodge, *Black Politics*, 325, suggests that the "sheer emotional power" of Black Consciousness should not be underestimated as an organizing and political force of its own kind.

16. After twenty members had been detained, in August 1977 the SSRC announced that in future it would be led by a secret executive committee of six members (probably for this exact purpose). *A Survey 1977*, 35.

17. For a full description of Biko's detention and death, as well as the eventual decision at the inquest that no one could be held "criminally responsible" for it (a decision that seemed incredible to most from the evidence), see *A Survey 1977*, 159–64.

18. Lodge, *Black Politics*, 330.

19. "What Being a South African Means to Me," 89.

20. Ibid., 92.

21. Nadine Gordimer, "Letter from South Africa," *New York Review of Books*, 9 Dec. 1976, p. 3.

22. "I Know I Have Not Been Brave Enough," 21.

23. A suggestion by Stephen Watson set off this line of inquiry.

24. This was one of the reason for *BD* being banned, since the pamphlet had been declared "undesirable" and the SSRC had itself been declared an unlawful organization on 19 Oct. 1977. See *WHBD*, 11.

25. "Liberation . . . is of paramount importance in the concept of Black Consciousness, for we cannot be conscious of ourselves and yet remain in bondage." Steve Biko, "The Definition of Black Consciousness," in his *I Write What I Like*, ed. A. Stubbs (London: Heinemann, 1979), 49. This paper, first given by Biko in 1971, has evidently been an important source for Gordimer. On the other hand, it should not be thought that Gordimer was simply plagiarizing; Biko's sentiments were part and parcel of the common discourse of Black Consciousness, which he helped fashion.

26. Reproduced in Mary Benson, ed. *The Sun Will Rise*, rev. ed. (London: International Defence and Aid, 1981), 41.

27. Basil Davidson, Joe Slovo, and Anthony R. Wilkinson, *Southern Africa: The New Politics of Revolution* (London: Penguin, 1976).

28. Gordimer has revealed her sources for *BD* in a most interesting way. The review of the novel that appeared in the *African Communist* (n. 7 above) claimed that its politics "derived almost entirely from Roux's *Time Longer than Rope* and the gossip that floats about in left-wing circles, is a travesty." (Edward Roux was a lapsed member of the SACP.) Gordimer wrote a letter of reply (*African Communist,* 3d quarter 1980, p. 109) in which she pointed out that her political sources were, on the contrary, "principally the impeccable ones" of Jack Simons and Ray Simons, *Class and Colour in South Africa 1850–1950* (London: Penguin, 1969), Slovo's "No Middle Road," and the Black Community Programme publications edited by Mafika Pascal Gwala, B. A. Khoapa, and Thoko Mbanjwa (for the Black Consciousness politics). In relation to the SACP her sources could not have been more "impeccable," since the Simonses, like Slovo, have been long-standing officials and ideologists within the party.

29. See Slovo, "No Middle Road," 119.

30. Ibid., 161.

31. For example, when Orde Greer asks Duma Dhladhla, without any apparent reference or quotation, whether "a capitalist society which throws overboard the race factor entirely [could] still evolve here?" (*BD*, 157), the question and its phrasing come almost directly from Slovo, "No Middle Road," 142. Similarly when Dhladhla "quotes" Biko, no references are given.

32. "World history would indeed be very easy to make if the struggle were taken up only on condition of infallibly favourable chances." Slovo, "No Middle Road," 185; *BD*, 27, leaves out only the "indeed."

33. *WHBD*, 30.

34. When the Censorship Committee initially banned *BD*, citing some of the quotations that have just been given as reasons for doing so, this was usually on the grounds of the sentiments expressed, and not on account of the source, which in virtually every case was already banned material, and hence reason enough for banning the novel. That is, when the committee cited Slovo, it did not know it was Slovo it was citing. This adds a suitably ironic element to the fact that *BD* was later unbanned. I would have been more reticent about revealing Gordimer's sources had she not done so herself.

35. Gordimer, interview, in *WHBD*, 19. Gordimer says that *BD* is "a novel of ideas."

36. *WHBD*, passim.

37. Ibid., 6.

38. "Nadine Gordimer's *Burger's Daughter*," paper presented at Conference on Literature and Society in Southern Africa, University of York, Sept. 1981.

39. Ibid., 21.

40. For example, on p. 177, the Security Police narrative seems to end up partially inside Rosa's own mind: "But activity within the country suggested by the fact that she should attempt to pass out and in again was what was of concern; there was no hope at all for her that she would get what she had never had, what had been refused her once and for all when she tried to run away from her mother and father after the boy she wanted."

41. See Terry Eagleton, *Walter Benjamin; or, Towards a Revolutionary Criticism* (London: Verso, 1981), 150: "Benjamin's *Unmensch* is a purged space, a deconstructed function of historical forces." This would apply perfectly to Rosa.

Leaving the Mother's House

JOHN COOKE

✦   ✦   ✦

I N   T H E   1 9 7 2   R E V I E W   "A Private Apprenticeship," Gordimer focused on Carson McCullers's obsessive concern with adolescence in her
journals and novels. Gordimer's own "private apprenticeship" shows a
preoccupation as great as her subject's; Gordimer can accurately be
termed, to vary a phrase she applied to McCullers, "the high priestess of
childhood." As Gordimer told Lionel Abrahams in the late 1950s, "the ways
of seeing we acquire in our youth remain with us always."[1] In her fiction
those ways of seeing are determined, above all else, by unusually possessive
mothers. Gordimer's "strange childhood" provides a clear motivation for
this focus, yet her novels by themselves reveal her obsessive concern with
domineering mothers and the resulting resentment and sense of power-
lessness of their children. Gordimer deals with such relationships most
concertedly in *The Lying Days, Occasion for Loving*, and *Burger's Daughter*, which
form an extended *Bildungsroman* centering on the attempts of daughters to
break free of their mothers' power and establish lives of their own.[2] But
with the exception of *A World of Strangers*, whose protagonist can scarcely be
said to have a private life, all of Gordimer's novels show her returning,
again and again, to such strange childhoods as her own.

Mothers in Gordimer's novels respond with remarkable persistence in
one of two ways to their children: by attempting to prolong the child's de-

pendence or, conversely, if they acknowledge this desire in themselves, by renouncing the care of the child. The mother most conscious of this dynamic is Liz Van Den Sandt in *The Late Bourgeois World*. She decides to bring her son Bobo a treat when visiting his school at the novel's outset, for she knows:

> It is my way of trying to make up for sending him to that place—the school. And yet I had to do it; I have to cover up my reasons by letting it be taken for granted that I want him out of the way. For the truth is that I would hold on to Bobo, if I let myself. I could keep him clamped to my belly like one of those female baboons who carry their young clinging beneath their bodies. And I would never let go.[3]

This is not just a chance metaphor, provoked by the strain of her ex-husband's suicide the previous day, for later in the novel Liz busies herself with an icon of her powerful possessive urge—"the head of the baboon mascot I brought back for Bobo from Livingston" (p. 92). Liz does resist the desire to clamp on to her son, but only through exiling him to a school she describes as being "like a prison."

Both the urge to possess and its sublimated reflection to reject completely are manifested again and again by mothers in Gordimer's novels. In *The Lying Days* Mrs. Shaw's success in maintaining control over her daughter Helen is reflected in the action which gives the narrative its shape, Helen's compulsion to return repeatedly to her mother's house. In *Occasion for Loving*, Jessie Stilwell struggles to keep from acting like "her mother [who] had sucked from her the delicious nectar she had never known she had" by using the pretext of a heart condition to prolong Jessie's dependence (p. 45). Mrs. Burger usurps Rosa's early years by using her relentlessly in the service of her political goals; Rosa is even persuaded to feign engagement to a political prisoner in order to smuggle messages into prison. The reverse process, denial of the child, figures recurrently as well. Like Liz Van Den Sandt, Jessie Stilwell attempts to escape her son Morgan through shunting him off to a boarding school, and during his vacations she eagerly awaits the day of his return there. Rebecca Edwards, James Bray's lover in *A Guest of Honour*, has left her children in the care of her husband; and when Maureen Smales in *July's People* is confined in the same hut with her children, it is striking how little they figure in her thoughts.

Over the course of Gordimer's career, the mothers do reveal—as Liz's very awareness of the problem indicates—an increasing desire to overcome this possessiveness. Jessie Stilwell will finally show the impulse to accept Morgan's nascent manhood; Liz wants to free Bobo from her suburban world, which she knows is destructive. When Rebecca Edwards journeys alone to London after Bray's death, she fleetingly conceives of a new life for herself through taking her children back. But these are impulses which find no expression in action. It is finally outside the family that a kind of restitution is actually made for the wounds inflicted by mothers on children. Rosa Burger, the only Gordimer heroine except for the young Helen Shaw who chooses not to become a mother, exhibits the most selfless motherly instinct of all of Gordimer's characters by working in a hospital for children. Her treating children, "whom it was her work to put together again if that were possible," is a telling contrast with Liz's putting together of the image of her desire for Bobo's continued dependence (p. 345).

In the world of Gordimer's later novels it is possible, as Rosa hopes, to put children back together. Indeed, only children, whose "ways of seeing" are still being formed, are capable of regeneration. By *Burger's Daughter*, this hope lies in identification with an African world in which children are granted a life of their own through the African family, in which, as Gordimer wrote in *The Black Interpreters*, "there is never any suggestion that mother love can become warping." The regeneration of the white children with whom Gordimer is concerned occurs through a double process over the course of her career. One of its parts is the gradual loss of importance, and finally the eradication, of the white house in which the mother's power was supreme. Where the white house serves as the focal point in *The Lying Days* and *Occasion for Loving*, by *The Late Bourgeois World* is has diminished to an apartment. In the following novels it is absent: Rebecca Edwards has a house in Kenya, but it is never seen in the novel; the Burger house has been sold before *Burger's Daughter* begins; the Smales house has been abandoned in a wartorn Johannesburg before the start of *July's People*. Only in the later novels, however, is there any replacement for this white house. It is prefigured in small ways such as the maternal feeling of the African nurse Edna Tlume in *A Guest of Honour*, who expresses a purer grief for the departure of the Edwards children than does their own mother, and in the greater rapport of the conservationist's son Terry with the African farm laborers than with his own father. It is claimed by Rosa Burger through her identification with the 1976 black children's revolt, which leads to her "sense of sorority" in a multiracial prison. It is manifested, unmistakably, in the integration of the Smales children into July's house.

Gordimer's later novels finally reveal a complete unification of her private theme of children gaining freedom from possessive mothers and her public theme of Africans taking control of the South African house.

In her earlier novels she had conceived of these processes as separate, as she expressed it to John Barkham in 1963: "First, you know, you leave your mother's house, and later you leave the house of the white race."[4] In the later novels these developments merge. For Rosa Burger and the Smales children, these two leave-takings are one.

GORDIMER HAS SAID that *Burger's Daughter* was inspired by the children of South African Communists, whose parents were recurrently on trial or in prison. She was struck by these "children or teenagers, left with the responsibility of the whole household and younger children. It must have affected their lives tremendously; it must have been a great intrusion on the kind of secret treaties that you have when you're an adolescent."[5] At the outset of *Burger's Daughter*, one of those waiting outside a prison with the fourteen-year-old Rosa Burger to deliver goods to the detainees says that "the child was dry-eyed and composed, in fact she was an example to us all of the way a detainee's family ought to behave. Already she had taken on her mother's role in the household" (p. 12). The novel is about the discovery of "secret treaties" by this child whose parents have taught her so well how she "ought to behave."

The household the child takes over is better described as a political institution than a family. Lionel Burger was born in 1905, the year of the revolt against the czars; he married Cathy Burger during the 1946 African mineworkers strike; and their daughter Rosa was born in May 1948, the very month the Nationalist party assumed power. Rosa is indeed apartheid's child; the stages in her life are marked not by graduations or proms but by the 1956 treason trial and the 1960 Sharpeville massacre. Even her fondest childhood memory, taking refuge in her father's hairy chest as she swims in the family pool with Baasie, the child of an African nationalist reared by the Burgers, is put in a political context: "In 1956 when the Soviet tanks came into Budapest I was his little girl, dog-paddling to him with my black brother Baasie, the two of us reaching for him as a place where no fear, hurt or pain existed" (p. 115). Rosa will need to assess the Burger Communist vision, called into question by the Russian tanks, but she will have much more difficulty ceasing to be Burger's "little girl." Like Helen and Jessie before her, Rosa will remain bound to her parents' house, as her continuing perception of her father as a haven from the world's pain indicates. Rosa will find it especially difficult to confront, much less express, her own feelings, for she has been disciplined to remain "dry-eyed" in the face of such painful experiences as two called up by the pool scene. The black brother had been cast out of the Burger house at the age of eight, shortly after this remembered scene, when no schools could be found for him nearby, and her brother Tony had drowned in the pool some years later. The confrontation of such private issues awaits Rosa, the exemplary radical child.

Unlike the earlier novels, *Burger's Daughter* is given shape by the presence of a strong man. Lionel Burger is a public man who is the peer of Nelson Mandela and Bram Fischer, a private man who could expand the boundaries of his house to truly take in an African child.[6] It is the unrelenting attention to Rosa as this martyred man's daughter that most stifles her attempts to become Rosa Burger. She must assist her father's biographer; a Swede enters into a love affair with her in order to further work on a Lionel Burger documentary; "it is understood" among her friends that she will dedicate her life to the struggle as Lionel Burger did his. But like Helen Shaw and Jessie Stilwell, Rosa attributes her loss of freedom as a child and young woman largely to her mother. The novel's opening scene reveals Rosa's desire to express her personal self to her mother even as she fulfills the political responsibilities given her. As she waits outside the prison, she holds a hot-water bottle with a concealed message indicating that her father has not yet been detained. But Rosa seeks to convey a private message as well; experiencing menstrual cramps for the first time, she has chosen the womblike hot-water bottle to carry the message. Standing "in that public place on that public occasion," Rosa makes a small gesture to express her private self (p. 16).

Rosa's mother does not apprehend such gestures, large or small. Her preoccupation with the Communist struggle leaves her oblivious to her daughter's private needs. She requires Rosa, in the most bitter incident of her young life, to pose as the fiancée of a detained comrade, Noel de Witt, so that Rosa will be allowed visitor's privileges and can once again carry messages in her parents' cause. Rosa will later reflect bitterly, "Those were my love letters. Those visits were my great wild times" (p. 69). She comes to see herself not as her mother's daughter but simply one of those who can be used in the Burger cause, "one of my mother's collection of the dispossessed, like Baasie or the old man who lived with us" (p. 84). Rosa is particularly struck by her mother's use of another member of this collection—an old-maid schoolteacher, who is detained and, lacking the Burgers' strength of purpose, turns state's evidence against Lionel Burger. Rosa accedes to her mother's demands as thoroughly as this woman and finds them as difficult to fulfill. Where this woman turns state's evidence, Rosa will pathetically fall in love with Noel de Witt and attempt to join him abroad to develop a private life. Rosa will later actually defect from the Burger cause, for a time, to southern France. Like this woman who couldn't meet her father's gaze in court, Rosa will not be able to address him—the novel is constructed around her addressing others in the attempt to define herself—until her return to South Africa at the novel's close.

Initially, Rosa simply seeks escape in a private world by living with Conrad, a wanderer with no political interests, indeed no strong commitments of any kind. His garden cottage, soon to be destroyed to make way for a freeway, appeals to her because it is "nowhere," a private place for a private occasion. Through Conrad, Rosa is able to distance herself from her parents' house and begin to feel some of the anger which, as "an example to us all," she has repressed. This process is at its most intense in her recollection of "the engagement" to Noel de Witt:

> Mine is the face and body when Noel de Witt sees a woman once a month. If anybody in our house—that house, as you made it appear to me—understood this, nobody took it into account. My mother was alive then. If she saw, realized—and at least she might have considered the possibility—she didn't choose to see. Alone in the tin cottage with you, when I had nothing more to tell you, when I had shut up, when I didn't interrupt you, when you couldn't get anything out of me, when I wasn't listening, I accused her. I slashed branches in the suburban garden turned rubbish dump where I was marooned with you. (p. 66)

Conrad has helped Rosa to distance herself from her home, making it "that house," and to rail at her mother. But Rosa's persistent use of negatives—she knows what wasn't done for her, and she defines her behavior to Conrad by what she doesn't do—reveals her lack of alternatives to "that house." Indeed, Rosa projects its atmosphere onto the world of the tin cottage; Conrad becomes someone, like her mother, who is interested in getting things "out of her." She will finally conceive her relationship with Conrad in terms of her upbringing. Because of their closeness she views them as siblings, "treating each other's dirt, as little Baasie and I had long ago," and she stops making love to Conrad, "aware that it had become incest" (p. 70). Even before she leaves him, she begins again to refer to "that house—our house," reversing the formulation she used when expressing anger toward her mother. Clearly, she still carries "our house" with her.

Rosa's behavior is not simply a compulsion, like Helen's, to relive an unhealthy past; for the world of her parents, unlike the Shaws or Fuechts, has much to offer. Rosa recurrently thinks of the sense of community in "our house," most often of the close and broad circle of friends who gathered there on Sundays. Even more, she misses the sense of what she calls "being connected," in contrast to being "marooned" at Conrad's, that her parents' struggle provided. This "connection," what Helen and Jessie termed "continuity," derived from the Burgers' sense of a life's purpose, the Communist vision of a just society growing from the past and extending to the future. But Rosa's selfhood has been so thoroughly denied in the service of this vision that she cannot claim it until she has developed a sense of personal worth. She needs, in short, first to become Rosa Burger before she can again be the Burger's daughter.

Rosa finds establishing a life of her own particularly difficult because, having been used so much in the service of her parents' cause, she has no friends of her own. After her parents' deaths when Rosa is in her teens, her only associates, except Conrad, are their long-time comrades who have the same expectations of her as her parents. Of Ivy Terblanche, the most important of them, Rosa tells Conrad, "In the enveloping acceptance of Ivy's motherly arms—she feels as if I were her own child—there is expectance, even authority. To her warm breast one can come home again and do as you said I would, go to prison" (p. 114). Behind the unwillingness to be enveloped by a surrogate mother lies Rosa's awareness that commitment to her parents' cause means prison, where her father died an early death and she had already wasted the sweet times of her youth.

The first book of the novel shows Rosa looking for "connection," the sense of a future growing from her past. The only other past Rosa has been exposed to is the Afrikaner past of the Nels, her father's relatives, whom she had visited at the age of eight when her parents were imprisoned during the 1956 treason trial. Not only her father's but her aunt's tradition is reflected in Rosa's name. She assumes she has been named after Rosa Luxemburg, "But my double name contained also the claim of Marie Burger and her descendants to that order of life, secure in the sanctions of family, church, law" (p. 72). At the Nels' Rosa feels the seduction of a life governed by an order so clearly lacking in her private life:

> All this ordered life surrounded, coated, swaddled Rosa; the order of Saturday, the order of family hierarchy, the order of black people out in the street and white people in the shade of the hotel stoep. Its flow contained her, drumming her bare heels on Daniel's box, its voices over her head protected her. (p. 61)

She fleetingly enjoys this new feeling of being protected and "swaddled"; like Jessie, she desires the "flow" of a peaceful life. Yet she is not free to explore this claim, for choosing the Nels' order would be a betrayal—a word often summoned up in the novel—of everything the Burgers have fought for. But betrayal, public and private, is at issue in a society so polarized by two orders, the Nels' and the Burgers', each demanding unquestioned adherence. The picture of young Rosa surrounded by this order is followed by reference to it as "the heritage of his people that Lionel Burger betrayed" (p. 61). Rosa will, in turn, temporarily betray his heritage by seeking a private life in France which offers a serene order such as this. Indeed, the school teacher, with whom Rosa identifies, cannot "look at him whom she had betrayed" in court (p. 87). And the Burgers have betrayed Baasie, as he will remind Rosa later, by casting him out just before her visit to the Nels. Rosa's exploration of her place is hindered by the severity with which any deviation from the group will be judged; her world seems to offer only choices for betrayal.

Rosa is forced to confront betrayal only later, for at first her two heritages offer no images of herself worth claiming. Their restrictiveness is revealed through the use of the rose, the flower associated with her name. She recalls sitting across from de Witt in prison, "a flower standing for what lies in her lap. We didn't despise prostitutes in that house—our house—we saw them as victims of necessity while certain social orders lasted" (p. 69). Set against this prostitution masquerading as engagement is an image of even greater inauthenticity at the Nel farm, where the grave of Rosa's grandmother is decorated with a glass dome "under which plastic roses had faded" (p. 77). Rosa feels her identity to be, like the roses, artificial and faded, removed from the world under glass. Neither the Burger nor the Nel past offers a sense of what she desires to be, a beautiful girl whose symbol is a living rose.

An incident during a party in the Orlando location links Rosa's search for meaning in her name to her future as well as her past. As so often, Rosa is treated as Burger's daughter and has to "describe again, as Lionel told a political anecdote, a family chronicle, what was really his love affair with my mother" (p. 168). During her recounting, an African grandmother gives a baby a cap with a rosette on it to present to Rosa. The hat—a sign of acceptance and, in the grandmother and baby, of the continuity of past and future—pleases Rosa. But it is given to the daughter of the Burger love affair, not to a woman valued for herself, as Rosa realizes; she puts it away in a drawer on returning home.

The possible futures, much discussed in the novel, seem to exclude her as well. The most important is, once again, her parents': the future, often italicized or capitalized, of Communist victory. "*That house*," Rosa thinks, "made provision for no less than the Future. My father left that house with the name-plate of his honourable profession polished on the gate, and went to spend the rest of his life in prison, secure in that future" (p. 111). Aunt Nel offers "the future—it's the same as now. It will be occupied by her children, that's all" (p. 131). For Africans, "through blackness is revealed the way to the future. The descendants of Chaka, Dingane, Hintsa, Sandile, Moshesh, Cetawayo, Msilekzai and Sekukuni are the only ones who can get us there" (p. 135). The first future, with its prospect of prison, Rosa fears; the second she denies; and the third, as the disdain with which all whites are held by the young Africans at the Orlando party indicates, seems to be denied her.

Her attempts to find a private life in the present are unsuccessful as well. "Now you are free," she thinks again and again after her parents' deaths, but she is disconnected, as the setting of her new job indicates: "Up on the twenty-sixth floor the smoked glass windows made the climate of each day the same cool mean, neither summer nor winter, and the time something neither night nor day" (p. 77). In this world divorced from environment and time she remains a rose behind glass. When she descends for lunch in a park one day, she experiences the first of the two events, both marked by disconnection and stasis, which are to precipitate her "betrayal" of the Burger cause. In the park Rosa and the other lunchers find one among them suddenly and inexplicably dead. The entire scene is marked by immobility and frustrated action: the dead man sits "solid as the statue of the landrost"; a pantechnicon is unable to turn at the traffic light; an errant child is caught by its mother; two young lovers display a "fondling half-mating." Rosa can find no context for this event, a death without ostensible cause or meaning. Rosa, formed entirely by her parents' code of opposition to institutional injustice, is arrested by this action in the present, this simple death. The second event, the beating of a donkey, has no spatial context; it occurs as Rosa drives through the fringes of an African location, a place "not on any plan of the city environs" (p. 207). Again, the incident is marked by arrested motion. She sees a donkey cart, and driver "convulsed, yet the cart was not coming any nearer" (pp. 207–8). As she becomes aware of the senseless beating of the exhausted beast, which she calls a "mad frieze," she too becomes immobilized: "the car simply fell away from the pressure of my foot and carried me no farther" (p. 209).

Rosa senses that her life in "our house" is the cause of her paralysis in the face of death and pain. Shortly after leaving the dead man in the park, she recalls "the paralysis that blotted out my mother limb by limb," and she makes a more specific connection, that her mother despised "those whites who cared more for animals than people," to explain her failure to stop the man from beating the donkey. Rosa has sought in part one of the novel to break free from her parents by searching for a past from which her future can grow. Failing to find this connection, she remains the little girl, Burger's daughter, who sought her father in the pool as "a place where no fear, hurt or pain existed."

Rosa's condition at the time of the donkey beating recalls Helen Shaw's at the close of *The Lying Days.* Both women are disconnected and, consequently, paralyzed; both remain in their parents' thrall; both run. But where Helen failed to acknowledge her parents' influence and simply sought to "go away," Rosa realizes, "I don't know how to live in Lionel's country" (p. 210). Rosa's formulation, implying that it is his country, not her own, which she seeks to inhabit, shows her incipient awareness of her problem's cause. And where Helen made cheery claims about accepting disillusion as a beginning rather than an end and exited claiming she would return, Rosa leaves disillusioned, knowing that her running will be seen as betrayal.

Rosa's vehicle for escape from Lionel's country is Brandt Vermeulen, a cosmopolitan Afrikaner with influential government connections. Like the Burgers and Nels, he offers Rosa another version of a continuous history, "dialogue, beginning with Plato, the dialogue with self, culminating in 'the Vorster initiative,' the dialogue of peoples and nations" (p. 194). A more intellectual version of her employer on the twenty-sixth floor, Vermeulen has shut himself off from the South African environment by accepting the ingenious notions of the *verlighte* Afrikaners. Where the Burders have fought for "Peace, Land, Bread," Vermeulen uses what Rosa calls "the long words"— separate freedoms, multilateral development, and the like—in a vain attempt to reconcile the viewpoints of the Burgers and Nels.

Set against Vermeulen's constructs is the real South African environment, which Rosa observes on her first trip to his house. She perceives in the landscape the history which had informed her parents' lives and which, in the end, will inform hers—the history of a land in which the only legitimate home is prison. Her drive takes her toward Pretoria, where she sees "Ndebele houses like a mud fort" and "the monumental shrine of the volk," signs of the African battle against domination and the molding of the victorious Afrikaner nation, and then

> in past the official's house in the fine old garden, the trunk of the huge palm-tree holding up its nave of shade, the warders' houses in sunny domestic order, the ox-blood brick prison with the blind façade on the

street—the narrow apertures darkened with bars and heavy diamond-mesh wire, impossible to decide, ever, which corresponded with which category of room for which purpose, and along which corridor in there, to left or right, there was waiting a particular setting of table and two chairs; the police car and van parked outside, a warder come off duty flirting with a girl with yolk-colored hair and a fox terrier in her arms; the door; the huge worn door with its missing studs and grooves exactly placed for ever. (p. 178)

The historical allusions continue in this depiction of the prison, "the ox-blood brick" recalling the Afrikaner teams trekking north from the Cape and "the diamond mesh" recalling the discovery which led the whites to settle the veld. The huge door is what confronts those, like Rosa, waiting to deliver parcels to the detained at the novel's outset, those waiting to deliver them to Rosa at the close. That door is there "for ever" for Lionel Burger after his life sentence. That it will be for Rosa as well is further indicated by the "narrow apertures," which provide a small patch of light for those inside, a detail with which the novel closes. The description of the prison is bracketed by allusions to gardens, the private life Rosa has sought in order to escape it. The "sunny domestic order," a contrast with the darkness behind the apertures, recalls the order of the Nels' life which had entranced Rosa, and the flirtation of the man and girl, the pleasures of a young woman she was denied and still craves. The landscape thus calls up at once the harsh realities of South African history, the private life Rosa has been denied in the past, and the future in prison she is trying to escape.

For Rosa to seek a passport through one such as Vermeulen is betrayal of the Burger cause with a vengeance. By putting her defection in such stark terms, Gordimer makes her strongest statement of the need, whatever the consequences, of a child to claim a life of her own. Rosa seeks that life with Madame Bagnelli (nicknamed Katya), the first wife of Lionel Burger, who had bridled under the discipline of the Communist Party and betrayed its cause by establishing a personal life in southern France. For most of the novel's second part, Katya is the vehicle for Rosa's search for a private life; Rosa now addresses her, as she had Conrad in part one. The initial appeal of Katya's world is the liberty it allows Rosa to experience the childhood she was denied in a house dominated by stories of the Sharpeville massacre and prison visits. As Rosa thinks, "I giggle with *their Katya* like the adolescent girls at school, who were in that phase while Sipho Mokema was showing Tony and me the bullet hole in his trouser-leg and I was running back and forth to visit prison, the first prison, where my mother was" (p. 326). Katya also offers Rosa a world, unlike South Africa's in which a historical continuity can be assumed. "If you live in Europe . . . things change," Katya says, "but continuity never seems to break. You don't have to throw the past away. If I'd stayed . . . at home, how will they fit in, white people?" (p. 249). The breaks in her speech—a parenthetical glance, the ellipses—are an early sign of the problems with continuity in Katya's life that Rosa will see later. But at the outset of her visit, Katya presents, and Rosa eagerly accepts, a society in which continuity never "seems" to break. This sense of continuity has allowed Katya to live for the present, and as the room she has prepared for Rosa indicates, Katya knows the need of present, sensuous experience for a young girl:

> It was a room made ready for someone imagined. A girl, a creature whose sense of existence would be in her nose buried in flowers, peach juice running down her chin, face tended at mirrors, mind dreamily diverted, body seeking pleasure. Rosa Burger entered, going forward into possession by that image. Madame Bagnelli, smiling, coaxing, saw that her guest was a little drunk, like herself. (pp. 229–30)

Rosa doesn't need much coaxing; she has wanted to take possession of a room catering to her senses, a room in which her face, not Lionel Burger's, is attended to.

Already on her first day in France, Rosa, the model of restraint, is intoxicated. The development of the latent desire for pleasure in the sensual world of the present comes through a love affair with a married French professor, Bernard Chabalier. The sense of Rosa's luxuriating in the present is evident as she observes the furnishings of the bar which is their rendezvous: "All these were strongly the objects of Rosa's present. She inhabited it completely as everything in place around her, there and then. In the bar where she had sat seeing others living in the mirror, there was no threshold between her reflection and herself" (p. 272). "Everything in place around her," Rosa is beginning to see herself as the focal point of her world; and for the first time in her life she finds no disparity—no threshold—between what she is and what her appearance shows her to be, as she so painfully had when posing as de Witt's fiancée.

Chabalier offers Rosa love simply for herself unalloyed with feelings about her august father, but when he proposes a life together for them, it is simply a continuation of the present they share. The prospect of Rosa's living in Paris as his mistress—what more private life could there be, she thinks—is introduced as they view two Bonnard canvases, one from 1894, the other from 1945. The women in them, Chabalier holds, were the same to Bonnard, as if Fascism, two wars, the Occupation had never occurred, because they have no "existence any more than the leaves have, outside this lovely forest where they are. No past, no future" (p. 287). Rosa's response, "if I did come to Paris," shows her assumption that it holds a life with "no past, no future." She tries out the idea soon after, watching people from a hill "as if completing a figure that was leading to a tapestry on a museum wall" (p. 288). But the prospect of this life doesn't hold her. As she and Chabalier lie together, she gives a glance down "in a private motivation of inner vision as alert and dissimulating as the gaze her mother had been equally unaware of" (p. 290). This is the look Rosa noticed when her mother suddenly realized she would make use of someone, like the pathetic schoolteacher, in her cause. Instead of being used as she had been throughout her early life, Rosa acts as her mother had; she uses Chabalier in her cause, the affirmation of her desirability as a woman. She will not join him in Paris.

Katya has given Rosa a sense of herself as well—as Rosa, so proper and withdrawn when Burger's daughter, thinks, "I've never talked with anyone as I do with you, incontinently, femininely" (p. 262). Rosa has realized that "something is owed us. Young women, girls still"; what she felt owed—what she has now claimed—is the right to be girlish, incontinent if she pleases (p. 300). But the dangers of being only this are conveyed to her in a chance meeting in the street with an old woman, who "didn't know, couldn't remember what was wrong" (p. 300). Her problem is the same, if more extreme, as Mrs. Fuecht's, whose life changed "suddenly" for no apparent reason. Both of them have lived without looking for a pattern in their lives; having no sense—no remembrance—of the past, they live a series of isolated presents. After calming the woman in her room, Rosa takes her leave:

> I wanted to go and she wanted to keep me with her in case the woman I had met in the street took possession of her again. I came flying up the hill to look for you singing while you upholster an old chair or paint a brave coat of red on your toenails. I wanted to ask who she was and tell you what happened. But when I saw you, Katya, I said nothing. It might happen to you. When I am gone. Someday. When I am in Paris, or in Cameroun picking up things that take my fancy, the mementoes I shall acquire. (p. 301)

Unstated is Rosa's realization that the life of the present in Paris means it might happen to her. In short, there is a fine line between entering into possession of rooms made for the moment's pleasure as Rosa did on arrival and being taken possession of by a discontinuous series of them. At best, what might appear as taking possession can, without a purpose to one's life, become merely "taking a fancy." Rosa has needed the life of the present that Katya has given her, but she sees that its prospect may be worse than the prison she has fled. She doesn't tell Katya about this incident; indeed, Rosa will address her no longer in her thoughts.

Before returning to South Africa, Rosa encounters Baasie at a gathering in London. He phones her later that night, drunk and denouncing the past they had shared. The confrontation is, in short, the same as Gideon and Jessie's at the close of *Occasion for Loving.* But the effect is not elegiac as it had been for Jessie, who waits, helpless, for Gideon to remember their time together, when he certainly will not. For Rosa, by contrast, the confrontation is cathartic. She cries for only the second time in her life—the first was on leaving Chabalier—over the loss of her black brother Baasie and of her drowned brother Tony, whose death her vomiting sausage and "gasping between spasms" recalls. She realizes that in the house pool where she and her brothers swam, Lionel Burger had only seemed to provide "a place where no fear, hurt or pain existed." By accepting that her father did not have the power to nullify the pain of Tony's death and Baasie's rejection, Rosa ceases to see him as the "place" defining her life. In the words of the novel's epigraph, she now feels that "I am a place in which something has occurred."

Only through her private time in France, Gordimer stresses at the close of part two, could Rosa sever the hold of her father and feel herself as the place at the center of her world: "Love doesn't cast out fear but makes it possible to weep, howl, at least. Because Rosa Burger had once cried for joy she came out of the bathroom and stalked about the flat . . . sobbing and clenching her jaw, ugly, soiled, stuffing her fist in her mouth" (p. 324). Her private occasion of loving and being loved as Rosa Burger allows her to mourn the end of the Burger house, to leave behind the composed, dry-eyed girl—Burger's daughter—who waited, motionless and silent, before the prison door.

Having become Rosa Burger, she is free to return to South Africa to fashion her own life. Rosa cannot say why she returned, but she is clearly changed by her confrontation of her past through Baasie's phone call, the experiencing of a private life of the present she can claim as her own, and the understanding that without a sense of continuity one may become the woman she met in the street. Rosa's own sense of this continuity is shown in the peace she finds at the Nels' farm after her return: "I went to bed in the rondavel and slept the way I had when I was a child, thick pink Waverly blankets kicked away, lumpy pillow punched under my neck. Anyone may have come in the door and looked down on me, I wouldn't have stirred" (p. 352). Her blankets kicked away, she is no longer "swaddled" as she had been by the Nels' order of Afrikaner life. This change derives, in part, from the deflation of her aunt's vision of the future. She had been certain it was to be the present, only "occupied by her children," but her daughter Marie has been implicated in terrorist activities. For Rosa Marie Burger, the two heritages in her name have become one, both heralding the same future. Certain of her heritage and future, it no longer matters to the girl who was so concerned with what people saw in her—the girl whose first words in the novel are "*When they saw me outside the prison, what did they see?*"—should they happen to look at her sleeping (p. 13). She knows; she sleeps secure in an African hut, in place.

Having found in France a life of her own, Rosa is now undaunted by those who controlled her past. She can finally address her father as an equal, telling him that his vision of the way to "the future" was wrong. Rosa sees the future in the revolt of the Soweto children in 1976. The spontaneity of their action, unguided by the discipline urged by the older opposition leaders, carries a condemnation of not only her parents' political methods but the discipline imposed on the young Burger daughter. Rosa says to her father: "The sins of the fathers; at last the children avenge on the fathers the sins of the fathers. Their children and children's children; that was the Future, father, in hands not foreseen" (p. 348). This is at once a statement about historical change and an assertion by Rosa Burger, his child, that the future lies in her hands.

Her sense of self secure, Rosa can now carry on, in her own way, the struggle to which Lionel Burger dedicated his life. She chooses his profession, working with crippled children: "I am teaching them to walk again, at Baragwanath Hospital. They put one foot before the other" (p. 332). In this calling she has found a means of alleviating the paralysis she had felt as a child under her parents' demands. She can act when faced with the inexplicable suffering of crippled and wounded children. One can be sure she would not run from a dead man in a park or a tormented donkey.

During the October 1977 school boycott, Rosa is one of the many detained. In a women's prison at the novel's close, she has assumed the position of her mother at the outset. Having learned how to act on her own volition, Rosa has claimed her maturity. Other women are no longer the massively powerful figures that they had been for Helen Shaw. Rosa is their equal; as she says, "My sense of sorority was clear." Rosa gets permission to draw pictures, which visitors recognized as the women inside "and understood that these women were in touch with each other, if cut off from the outside world" (p. 356). Rosa is once again "connected" but she is not carrying messages from and about others—her father not yet being detained, her parents' news to de Witt. She now sends her own.

The importance of her private time with Katya remains clear as well. Rosa draws, again and again, childlike sketches of a hill by a sea filled with bright, tiny boats, renditions of Katya's village. The most striking aspect of the drawings is the light "which appeared to come from everywhere; all objects were sunny" (p. 355). In her dark cell, Rosa is sustained by the bright private time she spent in southern France. But she does not mourn its loss, realizing that it belongs to a world with different codes, different possibilities than the one into which she was born and has now claimed as her own. In a letter to Katya which closes the novel, the prison censor deletes Rosa's reference to the "watermark of light" which is reflected into her cell every evening. Katya is simply perplexed by his deletion, where Lionel Burger had taken delight in trying to decipher the censored material. He, and now Rosa after him, have accepted and managed to find small pleasures in their chosen world; he had described the watermark as "delicate pearly light" (p. 64). Rosa had realized while at Katya's that "there is a certain range of possibilities that can occur within the orbit of a particular order of life" (p. 238). Rosa's story ends with her acceptance of the possibilities allowed by her order: the few sensual pleasures like that watermark of light, her sorority, and a belief in her future. The view may not be as good as from the hill in southern France—or even the twenty-sixth floor of the office building—but Rosa's company is better and her sense of place, and time, secure.

Notes

1. Lionel Abrahams, "Nadine Gordimer: The Transparent Ego," *English Studies in Africa* 3, no. 2 (1960): 150.

2. *The Lying Days* (1953; repr. London, 1978); *Occasion for Loving* (1963; repr. London, 1978); *Burger's Daughter* (New York: Viking, 1979). Subsequent references in the text are to the editions from the 1970s.

3. *The Late Bourgeois World* (New York: Viking, 1966), 11. Subsequent references in the text are to this edition.

4. John Barkham, "South Africa: Perplexities, Brutalities, Absurdities," *Saturday Review*, 12 Jan. 1963, p. 63.

5. Susan Gardner, "'A Story for This Place and Time': An Interview with Nadine Gordimer about Burger's Daughter," *Kunapipi* 3, no. 2 (1981): 100.

6. Fischer's life served as a model for Lionel Burger's, from his family background and trial to his death in prison, and the original for the woman who turned state's evidence against Burger is the woman who did so against Fischer. See Nadine Gordimer, "The Fischer Case," *London Magazine* 5 (Mar. 1966): 21–30, and "Why Did Bram Fischer Choose Jail?" *New York Times Magazine*, 14 Aug. 1966, pp. 30ff.

Prospero's Complex

Race and Sex in *Burger's Daughter*

JUDIE NEWMAN

✦　✦　✦

NADINE GORDIMER has remarked that all South African novels, whatever their political intentions, involve the question of racism: "There is no country in the Western world where the creative imagination, whatever it seizes upon, finds the focus of even the most private event set in the social determination of racial laws."[1] There are those who have argued that the white South African novelist is automatically corrupted by a privileged position, that Gordimer's audience can only be other privileged whites, and that the products of her creative imagination are therefore intrinsically a part of a racist society.[2] In *The Conservationist* Gordimer focused upon the disjunction between the internal, subjective reality of her white protagonist and the external reality of political consensus, employing as her principal strategy the translation of political problems into other languages, particularly into sexual terms. In the novel sexual fantasy functions as a surrogate for colonial lusts. The sexual body of woman and the body of a murdered black combine to form one massive image of colonial guilt. As her use of the language of Zulu culture, and Zulu dreams, indicates here, Gordimer is clearly aware of the dangers of solipsistic art, an art which may articulate only the dominating power of the white imagination.[3]

Rosa Burger begins her tale with the recognition that: "one is never talking to oneself, always one is addressed to someone . . . even dreams are performed before an audience."[4] In *Burger's Daughter* Gordimer focuses upon the fantasies of the white subconscious, in order to undermine their power. Once again, a body lies below the level of conscious articulation, here the body of a white woman. In the opening scene of the novel Rosa is presented as she appears to other observers, as seen by casual passers-by, as reported on by her headmistress, and as transformed by the rhetoric of the Left, which converts her into "Little Rosa Burger," "an example to us all" (p. 12). The later Rosa reflects on her invisibility as a person: "When they saw me outside the prison what did they see? I shall never know. . . . I saw-see-that profile in a hand-held mirror directed towards another mirror" (pp. 13–14). As the daughter of a Communist hero, it is assumed by others that Rosa's views reflect her father's. Rosa is thus trapped in a hall of mirrors, an object in the eyes of others whose internal reality remains unknown. A figure in an ideological landscape, she is placed by observers only in relation to their own political position: an image of the struggle in the "bland heroics of badly written memoirs by the faithful" (p. 14), a suspicious object under state surveillance. This public rhetoric of South Africa contrasts with a bleeding body, invisible to all shades of South African opinion. For Rosa these external views are eclipsed by her awareness of the pains of puberty: "real awareness is all focussed in the lower part of my pelvis . . . outside the prison the internal landscape of my mysterious body turns me inside out" (p. 15). In the novel Rosa's sexuality forms the point of entry to an exploration of the topography of the racist psyche. The disjunction between external and internal realities is rendered in the form of the novel, in the alternation of first- and third-person narratives, narratives which interact in order to explore the roots of racism.

Burger's Daughter poses the question of racism as a primary or secondary phenomenon. Is racism the product of a political system (capitalism) as Lionel Burger would argue? Or is racism a screen for more primary sexual insecurities? The central images of the novel are drawn from an informed awareness of the principal arguments involved here. Racism has been generally understood by various commentators as a product of sexual repression. In his early, classic study of prejudice, Gordon Allport noted that to the white the "Negro" appears dark, mysterious, and distant, yet at the same time warm, human, and potentially accessible.[5] These elements of mystery and forbiddenness are present in sex appeal in a puritanical society. Sex is forbidden, blacks are forbidden; the ideas begin to fuse. White racism expresses itself in response to ambivalence toward the body, conceived of as both attractive and repugnant. In *White Racism: A Psychohistory*,

Joel Kovel developed the argument, describing aversive racism as the product of anal repressions.[6] In his view the "Negro" is not the actual basis of racism but a surrogate or substitute. In white culture bodily products are seen as dirt. The subject therefore splits the universe into good (clean, white, spiritual) and bad (dirty, black, material). Things associated with the sensual body are dirty; those things which may be seen as nonsensuous are clean. Racism therefore depends upon the displacement of dirty activities onto an alter ego. Fantasies of dirt underlie racism, which is a product of sexual repressions.

Octave Mannoni offers a rather similar analysis, though with greater emphasis on sexual fantasy.[7] Nadine Gordimer entitled her Neil Gunn Fellowship Lecture "Apprentices of Freedom," quoting Mannoni.[8] In *Prospero and Caliban* Mannoni argues that colonial racism simply brings to the surface traits buried in the European psyche, repressed in Europe but manifest in the colonial experience. Colonial countries are the nearest approach possible to the archetype of the desert island. Colonial life is a substitute life available to those who are obscurely drawn to a world of fantasy projection, a childish world without real people. For Mannoni, European man is always in inner conflict between the need for attachments which offer emotional security, and the need for complete individualization. Revolt against parents is an important factor here. When a child suffers because he feels that the ties between him and his parents are threatened, the child also feels guilt, because he would also like to break those ties. He therefore dreams of a world without bonds, a world which is entirely his, and into which he can project the untrammeled images of his unconscious. This desire to break every attachment is impossible, of course, in fact. But it is realized by the colonist when he goes into a "primitive" society, a society which seems less "real" than his own. In the modern world this urge may be realized by the substitution of depersonalized links for original attachments. Mannoni cites the film star and pin-up girl as examples. These people are still persons, but only just enough for the subject to form unreal relations with them. The more remote people are, the easier they appear to attract our projections. Prospero's relations with Caliban and Ariel, Crusoe's with Friday, are cases in point. In Gordimer's *July's People* a similar relationship obtains between white woman and black servant.[9] Maureen Smales comes to realize in the course of the action that the traits she admired in July were not his real character but only assumed characteristics, assumed in order to conform to Maureen's mental image of him. In the literature of colonialism the native woman is more commonly a focus for this type of projection. The white colonist marries the native girl because her personality is so little externalized that it acts as a mirror to his projections. He may then live happily among these projections without granting that the Other has autonomous existence. In Mannoni's words: "It is himself a man is looking for when he goes far away; near at hand he is liable to come up against others. Far-away princesses are psychologically important in this respect" (Mannoni, p. 111). As will become evident, Rosa Burger almost becomes identified with the image of the far-away princess, inhabiting a world of erotic fantasy, though in her case Europe becomes the magic island, and her guilty revolt against her father is only temporary.

In this connection Mannoni's analysis of the roots of racism in a patriarchal system is particularly important. For Mannoni the antagonism between Caliban and Prospero in *The Tempest* hinges upon Miranda's presence as the only woman on the island. Having first treated the black (Caliban) as his son, Prospero later accuses him of having attempted to rape Miranda, and then enslaves him. In short, Prospero justifies his hatred of Caliban on grounds of sexual guilt. Analyzing the "Prospero complex" Mannoni draws a picture of the paternalistic colonist whose racism is a pseudorational construct to rationalize guilty sexual feelings. In his view the sexual basis of racism is revealed in the old cliché of the racist: But would you let your daughter marry one? Uneasy incestuous feelings in the father are disturbed by this argument. For Mannoni it is easy to see why it is always a daughter, sister, or neighbor's wife, never his own, whom a man imagines in this situation. When a white man imagines a white woman as violated by a black man he is seeking to rid himself of guilt by projecting his thoughts onto another (Caliban), putting the blame for his "dirty" sexuality upon someone else. In *The Tempest* Prospero's departure from the colonial island is accompanied by his renunciation of his art, in this case magical arts which enable him to dominate a world created in his own image. Caliban remains behind, however, as disowned son and slave. There are clearly extremely interesting connections here with the character of Baasie (adopted as a son by Lionel Burger but later abandoned), with Rosa's relationship with her father, in whose shadow she lives, and with the nature of Gordimer's art.

Mannoni's is, of course, a highly ambivalent analysis of the colonial enterprise. His central thesis, that the dependence and inferiority complexes are present in rudimentary form in everyone, too easily elides into the untenable hypothesis that people are colonized because they want to be colonized, at least subconsciously. Communists, in particular, have denounced the search for psychological solutions, as too easily providing an alibi for those who refuse to confront political problems. In *Black Skin, White Masks,*

Fanon contested Mannoni in detail.[10] While Fanon allows that the "civilized" white may retain an irrational longing for areas of unrepressed sexuality which he then projects onto the Negro he argued that this image of the sexual-sensual-genital Negro can be corrected: "The eye is not merely a mirror, but a correcting mirror. The eye should make it possible for us to correct cultural errors" (Fanon, p. 202). For Fanon, sexuality need not remain at the level of frustration, inauthenticity, or projection. True authentic love is "wishing for others what one postulates for oneself" (Fanon, p. 41). Confrontation of one's psychic drives is only a necessary part of a process of cultural evolution: "The tragedy of the man is that he was once a child. It is through the effort to recapture the self and to scrutinize the self, it is through the lasting tension of their freedom that man will be able to create the ideal conditions for a human world. . . . Was my freedom not given to me in order to build the world of the *You*?" (Fanon, pp. 231–32).

Burger's Daughter charts just such a process of self-scrutiny. Rosa remembers and observes her past self, in an extensive attempt to recapture and reconstitute it and to engage with the world of the "you." Rosa's first-person narrative is directed toward three people, each addressed as "you": Conrad, a surrogate brother with whom she enjoys childish erotic freedom; Katya, a sexually permissive replacement mother; and finally Lionel Burger, the father to whom she eventually returns. "You" is obviously also the reader, who is initiated into these three identities. The reader participates in the fantasy while also measuring the distance between these surrogate people and herself. At key points Gordimer adopts Fanon's phraseology. For Conrad, the significant dynamic is "the tension between creation and destruction in yourself" (p. 47). Rosa describes Lionel, however, in antithetical terms. "the tension that makes it possible to live lay, for him, between self and others" (p. 86). In the novel Gordimer's narrative technique draws the reader into a tension of freedom, progressing from Conrad's inner psychological existence to a fresh orientation toward the world of the autonomous Other. The alternation between first- and third-person narrative creates a tension between external image and internal voice, between "she" and "I." As "you" the reader continually mediates the two, correcting the errors of the eye, emerging from the spell of the internal voice. The reader is therefore offered a choice. He may place the voice addressing him as initiating him into a secret intimacy. Or he may refuse to identify with a surrogate "you" and thus register the possibility of a world in which communication is not limited to depersonalized stereotypes.

In the first movement of the novel, Rosa Burger disowns her original attachments in order to enter a world in which surrogate brothers and mothers replace the originals in a fantasy landscape. She does so largely as a result of ambivalence toward the body, as one example will indicate. When Rosa meets Marisa Kgosana (gorgeously regal while buying face cream) their embrace is described as a step through the looking glass: "To enter for a moment the invisible magnetic field of the body of a beautiful creature and receive on oneself its imprint—breath misting and quickly fading on a glass pane—this was to immerse in another mode of perception" (p. 134). To the salesgirl Marisa appears in the image of the sensuous black woman, distant and unreal. She asks, "Where's she from? One of those French islands?" (p. 139). Marisa, however, has returned, not from the exotic Seychelles or Mauritius, but from Robben Island, the island to which white racist attitudes have banished her husband. From Marisa, Rosa's mind moves at once to Baasie, who is remembered quite differently as a creature of darkness and dirt. Rosa remembers Baasie wetting the bed which they shared as children: "In the morning the sheets were cold and smelly. I told tales to my mother —Look what Baasie's done in his bed!— but in the night I didn't know whether this warmth . . . came from him or me" (pp. 138–40). Quite obviously the two images suggest the twin racist strategies delineated by Kovel and Mannoni—the attempt to use blackness as a way to sensual liberation (Marisa), the attempt to blame dirty actions on the black (Baasie). Rosa exists in tension between these two forms of racism, but it is a tension Gordimer's complex art transforms into a political challenge. Key terms and images—island paradise, incestuous desires, projection onto mirrors, far-away princesses—recur in the novel, taken from Mannoni's thesis, as do images of dirt, guilt, bodily products, and repugnance, taken from Kovel. The language of racism is exploited, however, in order to confront the reader with a series of questions. Which vision of Rosa do we accept?—that of a white woman who is part of a racist society and who can address a "you" who exists only in her own projections? Or that of a woman confronting and correcting a stereotyped image and painfully learning to address herself to a world of other autonomous beings? It is my contention that the complex narrative art of *Burger's Daughter* refuses to maintain the text at the level of private fantasy or dream, and also avoids the danger of the depersonalized image. Gordimer employs the terms of the white racist subconscious in an attempt to free her art from Prospero's complex and to direct it toward a world where "you" is not a fantasy projection, but real.

Gordimer's daring strategy, here, is to select as the focus of the novel a white woman attempting to achieve autonomy by emerging from her father's dominance. As the daughter of a white Afrikaner Communist, Rosa is an extremely complex figure. She may be defined in terms of sex, race, and position in the class struggle, and thus encapsulates the warring explanations of South African racism. In order to assert her autonomy Rosa can rebel only against another rebel. Her father is fighting political repression, so to fight his psychological influence is to join with the forces of political repression. This paradoxical situation is made evident from the beginning. In the eyes of the faithful, Rosa is desexualized and infantilized, maintained in the image of the faithful daughter. In the opening scene Rosa is described as having already "taken on her mother's role in the household" (p. 12), "giving loving support" (p. 12) to her father. That father cheerfully permits Rosa to have boyfriends while laughing at them for "not knowing she was not for them" (p. 17). In the Burger household the children have few exclusive rights with their parents (p. 84) for whom intimate personal relationships are subordinate to the struggle. As a young woman Rosa gains her parents' approval by posing as the fiancée of Noel de Witt, a device to enable him to receive visits in prison. Decked out, scented, "a flower standing for what lies in her lap" (p. 68), Rosa presents herself as a sexual object in prison, conveying a political subtext beneath innocuous lovey-dovey phrases. She returns to her mother's welcoming expression, the expression reserved for her "as a little girl" (p. 67) returning from school, and to her father's "caress" (p. 67). Rosa's parents are blind to the fact that she is actually in love with Noel. They are happy to cast her in a surrogate sexual role, a role which denies the reality of her emotions, confining her sexuality within prison walls. In the overall action of the novel, Rosa moves from prison to prison. Infantilized as Little Rosa Burger at the start, she becomes in the final pages, once more a child. Flora describes her at the end: "She looked like a little girl. . . . About fourteen" (p. 360). In the eyes of the faithful Rosa has not changed at all. She is still her father's daughter and is living out the historical destiny prepared for her by him. Imagistically, the prison is connected to the dichotomy of inside and outside in the novel. The reader, with access to Rosa's internal voice, knows that Rosa defected from her father in a belated revolt against the ideology of the parental generation. Does Rosa return from France to continue the political struggle, making a free choice on the basis of internal understanding? Or has Rosa simply fled from the erotic life of Europe in order to return to a desexualized security, a prison of women where she is once more her father's daughter? Rosa is finally imprisoned on suspicion of abetting the schoolchildren's revolt—a revolt informed by consciousness of black brotherhood and directed against paternalism, whether white or black. Rosa's return follows her encounter with Baasie, who denies her "brotherhood." In external political terms the white is rejected by blacks and retreats into paternalism. In internal psychological terms, however, the position is more complex.

That Rosa's rejection of her father is connected to sexual assertion is made clear in the scene with Clare Terblanche, daughter of Dick and Ivy, who have been surrogate parents to Rosa. Rosa is tempted by the parental warmth of their welcome and recognizes their attraction: "In the enveloping acceptance of Ivy's motherly arms—she feels as if I were her own child—there is expectance, even authority. To her warm breast one could come home again and do as you said I would, go to prison" (p. 114). Clare Terblanche lives with her parents and her life is devoted to their cause. As a result she is desexualized, in contrast to Rosa who is beginning to emerge. Clare appears at Rosa's door as a shadow which "had no identity" (p. 118) glimpsed through a glass panel. In Rosa's eyes, Clare is still her childish playmate, sturdy as a teddy bear, suffering from eczema and knock-knees which went uncorrected by parents for whom the body is unimportant. Where Rosa's is a body with "assurance of embraces" (p. 121), Clare, faithful to her father's ideals, has "a body that had no signals" (p. 122) and is "a woman without sexual pride" (p. 123). Clare has two purposes here—to recruit Rosa as a political intermediary, and to rent a flat for her lover. The first is clearly the dominant motive. Rosa refuses on the grounds that she will not conform to her parents' image of her: "Other people break away. They live completely different lives. Parents and children don't understand each other. . . . Not us. We live as they lived" (p. 127). One event specifically links Clare to the earlier Rosa. When Rosa shows Clare the vacant apartment, Clare discovers a used sanitary towel in a cupboard. As they leave she removes this unmentionable object to the waste bin "and buried her burden . . . as if she had successfully disposed of a body" (p. 129). Disposing of her body is, of course, what Clare has done. Supposedly involved with the people's struggle, her background isolates her from the realities of the body.[11] Irony cuts both ways here, however. In the background a radio announcer is "reciting with the promiscuous intimacy of his medium a list of birthday, anniversary and lover's greetings for military trainees on border duty" (p. 119). Rosa's refusal to help Clare aligns her with this promiscuous intimacy. In South Africa there appears to be no possible mediation between the desexualized image and an erotic intimacy which is the voice of the repressive state.

This erotic intimacy is developed in the person of Brandt Vermeulen. Breaking her attachments to the original family, Rosa sets out to obtain a passport, aligning herself with an alternative family. In order to defect, she makes a series of visits to Afrikaners "whose history, blood and language made [Lionel] their brother" (p. 173). Of them all, she selects as her ally Brandt Vermeulen, a member of the Broederbond, the Afrikaner political "brotherhood" which runs South Africa from within Parliament. Brandt's house expresses the psychological reality of colonialism. The façade is that of a Boer farmhouse of seventy or eighty years ago. Within, however, all the internal walls have been demolished to create one large space of comfortable intimacy, with glass walls giving access to a secret garden. Behind the façade of historical legitimacy there exists a vast personal space, inhabited by the erotic male. Brandt runs an art publishing house, and is about to publish a book of erotic poems and woodcuts. By participating in a racist political system Brandt has found sexual liberation. Rosa's attempt to escape from her father has brought her to a "brother" whose façade of reverence for the traditions of his fathers conceals a sophistic eroticism. Rosa is placed here against a highly representative background of objets d'art. Brandt's walls are hung with Pierneef landscapes, modernist abstractions, a print of the royal Zulu line, and images of tortured bodies. The room is dominated, however, by a sculpture, a perspex torso of a woman's body, set upon a colonial chest. Described as suggesting both the ice of frigidity and the hardness of tumescence (p. 182), the sculpture presents an image of erotic woman as a reified object of display, possessed by the male and existing only in his internal space. It is on this erotic object that Brandt's more "sophisticated" art depends, as Prospero's art draws upon a complex of sexual motives. In the garden a small black boy plays, amid chairs spattered with messy bird droppings, indicating his place in Brandt's internal landscape. To escape desexualization by her father, Rosa has entered a landscape organized by a surrogate brother to reflect his own fantasy.

Conrad is another such "brother." (The watchman for whom he places bets describes him to Rosa at one point as "your brother" [p. 149].) Rosa's relation with Conrad is foreshadowed in the visit she pays to the Nels' farm when first separated from her jailed parents. At the farm, "more and more, she based herself in the two rooms marked Strictly Private—Streng Privaat" (p. 55). On the door hangs a wooden clock face on which visitors mark the time of their call. To Rosa it is "immediately recognizable to any child as something from childhood's own system of signification. Beyond any talisman is a private world unrelated to and therefore untouched by what is lost or gained" (p. 55). The dummy clock marks the entrance to the timeless world of the child's psyche, a place to which Rosa returns when separated from her parents. The visit to the Nels also marks the disappear-

ance from Rosa's life of Baasie. Rosa recalls that she and Baasie had both
been given watches, but that Baasie ruined his in the bath. To Rosa, Baasie
has become timeless, existing only in her memory. When Rosa is perma-
nently separated from her parents, she sets up house with Conrad in a
world which is also outside time and place. Their cottage, soon to be demolished in favor of a new freeway, is let without official tenure at "an address that no longer existed" (p. 21). Set in a jungle of palms, beneath a
bauhinia tree, the house is "safe and cosy as a child's playhouse and sexually arousing as a lovers' hideout. It was nowhere" (p. 21). In the dark of
their secret cottage, Conrad and Rosa act out their dreams of a private
erotic world in which parents are no longer controlling. For Conrad, a
man with no political affiliations, only psychological events matter:
Sharpeville passes unnoticed, obscured by the realization that his mother
had a lover. Freed from his Oedipal conflicts by the awareness that his
mother was no longer the sole possession of his father, Conrad becomes
obsessed with her: "I was mad about her; now I could be with someone
other than my father there already" (p. 44). Rosa admits a kinship with
Conrad: "We had in common such terrible secrets in the tin house: you
can fuck your mother and wish your father dead" (p. 63). Conrad's reaction to Lionel's death is "Now you are free" (p. 40). Freedom from the father liberates Rosa sexually, but is attended by guilt. She wished for this
freedom. She obtained it on her father's death. She concludes, "I know I
must have wished him to die" (p. 63). In the psyche there is no distinction
between what she has actually done and what she has imagined. This
criminality of the white imagination is seen as liberating by Conrad. For
him Rosa can only begin to live once she blasphemes her father's ideology.
He quotes Jung in his support: "One day when he was a kid Jung imagined
God sitting up in the clouds and shitting on the world below. His father
was a pastor. . . . You commit the great blasphemy against all doctrine
and you begin to live" (p. 47).

As Conrad's choice of example suggests, he and Rosa are still inhabiting
a world structured around the opposed terms of racist language. When
Rosa ends her relationship with Conrad she does so in terms which suggest
important connections with Lionel and Baasie:

> I left the children's tree-house we were living in, in an intimacy of self-
> engrossment without the reserve of adult accountability, accepting each
> other's encroachments as the law of the litter, treating each other's dirt as
> our own, as little Baasie and I had long ago performed the child's black
> mass, tasting on a finger the gall of our own shit and the saline of our own

pee. . . . And you know we had stopped making love together months before I left, aware that it had become incest. (p. 70)

Rosa recoils from Conrad's erotic activities—activities which depend upon the replacement of the father—because these activities are perceived as dirty and incestuous. The closer Conrad becomes to Rosa, the more he blasphemes against her family's beliefs, the more he approaches Baasie, the black "brother" with whom her first dirty acts were performed. For Rosa sexual freedom is forever connected to images of the black, and to imperfectly suppressed incestuous desires. Significantly Conrad later sails off on a yacht to islands in the Indian Ocean. Rosa departs for Paris—an unreal place, "Paris —a place far away in England" (p. 56), as she describes it to the Nels' maids—and thence to the south of France, to the arms of a surrogate mother, Lionel's first wife, who placed erotic freedom before the needs of the Party.

Rosa's arrival in the south of France is described in terms which establish it as the enchanted land of fantasy. "The silk tent of morning sea" (p. 214) tilts below her, glimpsed through the distorting glass of the window. Below, tables outside a bar become "tiny islands" (p. 217) in "a day without landmarks" (p. 217). On the verge "roadside tapestry flowers grow" (p. 217) and in the background "a child's pop-up picture book castle" (p. 217) stands against a landscape of sea and flowers, where "people were dreamily letting the car pass across their eyes an image like that in the convex mirror set up at the blind intersection" (p. 217). Rosa's perceptions are dazed here, as if entering a dream world, a world drowning in sensuality. Katya's dining room appears as "swimming colours, fronds blobbing out of focus and a sea horizon undulating in uneven panes of glass" (p. 220). Katya's reminiscences of the Party—vodka, parties, sexual affairs— accompany Rosa's meal while she is "dissolving" (p. 222) in the pleasures of wine and French sights, sounds, and tastes. A room has been prepared for Rosa at the top of the house, full of feminine bric-a-brac, flowers, mirrors, and peaches, "a room made ready for someone imagined. A girl, a creature whose sense of existence would be in her nose buried in flowers, peach juice running down her chin, face tended at mirrors, mind dreamily averted, body seeking pleasure. Rosa Burger entered, going forward into possession by that image" (pp. 229–30). Rosa is thus presented with an image of herself as sensual woman, created by Katya, an image which she delightedly assumes, enjoying the sensual pleasures of an unreal country, where her projections are reflected back to her, where she ceases to be her father's daughter and becomes instead the mistress of

Bernard Chabalier. The particular features of the landscape—islands, tapestry, flowers, mirrors, silk tent—are focused in the tapestry series *La Dame à la Licorne*, which is presented to the reader after Rosa's return to Africa.

Rosa's lover plans to show her these tapestries. He also takes her to see an exhibition of paintings by Bonnard. As he says, "In Africa, one goes to see the people. In Europe, it's paintings" (p. 286). The white in Africa sees people as objects to be contemplated, objects which mirror their own projections. In Europe art offers a timeless substitute reality. To Rosa the paintings of Bonnard are just as real as the French people she lives among. These people are "coexistent with the life fixed by the painter's vision" (p. 286). Bernard points out that Bonnard's style and subjects never changed. The woman painted in 1894 and the mimosa painted in 1945 during the war are treated in the same way. In the fifty years between the paintings there was the growth of Fascism, two wars, the Occupation, but for Bonnard it is as if nothing happened. The two paintings could have been executed on the same day. In Bernard's analysis, the woman's flesh and the leaves around her are equal manifestations: "Because she hasn't any existence any more than the leaves have, outside this lovely forest where they are. . . . Your forest girl and the vase of mimosa—C'est un paradis inventé" (p. 287). With Bernard, Rosa lives in a similar invented paradise, a world of sensual pleasure, divorced from the world of historical events, cut off from both future and past, a world in which she is only a timeless image. Rosa meets Bernard for the first time in the bar owned by Josette Arnys, a Creole singer. The bar is mirrored and suggests the solipsism of France for Rosa: "In the bar where she had sat seeing others living in the mirror, there was no threshold between her reflection and herself" (p. 272). In the background runs a recording of Arnys' unchanging voice, singing about "the island where she and Napoleon's Josephine were born" (p. 269). Arnys is quite unaware of the naive political content of the song. For her, art is timeless in its eroticism. She argues at one point that "the whole feminist thing" (p. 270) will mean the death of art, as women will no longer be able to sing of love. In her view, "the birds sing only when they call for a mate" (p. 270). Katya is associated with the same vision, when she takes Rosa to hear the nightingales singing. Rosa's final rejection of this world is liked to a different voice—that of Baasie—and to the image presented in the tapestry series.

The tapestries of the Musée de Cluny have been variously interpreted both by artists and scholars. Discovered by George Sand, who featured them in her novel *Jeanne*,[12] they were also the inspiration for a ballet created by Jean Cocteau in Munich in 1953.[13] Rilke was also attracted to them, and celebrates them in one of his sonnets to Orpheus, which begins "O dieses ist das Tier, das es nicht gibt" (This is the creature that has never been).[14] Rilke also described the tapestries in detail in *The Notebooks of Malte Laurids Brigge.* The hero, Malte, has found that growing up is a process of reducing and distorting experience to make it fit conventional categories, thus acquiring a false identity or mask. To his horror that mask becomes more real than his inner self; the self he sees in the mirror is more real than the person it reflects. When he observes the tapestries, however, Malte feels a restored sense of totality. From the tapestries he gains a sense of total or simultaneous time, with no sense of an absent future: "Expectation plays no part in it. Everything is here. Everything forever."[15] Forced as she grows up into a similar assumption of a fixed role, Rosa is also attracted at first to the tapestries, as part and parcel of her assumption of the role of Bernard's mistress. "Bernard Chabalier's mistress isn't Lionel Burger's daughter; she's certainly not accountable to the Future; she can go off and do good works in Cameroun or contemplate the unicorn in the tapestry forest. 'This is the creature that has never been'—he told me a line of poetry about that unicorn, translated from German. A mythical creature. Un paradis inventé" (p. 304).

Scholars have suggested various interpretations for the tapestries, seeing them as representing a Turkish prince and his lady, as celebrating a marriage between two noble houses, as an act of homage to the Virgin Mary, and most important, as a celebration of the five senses, to name only a few of the available explications.[16] A particular focus of difficulty is the sixth tapestry, in which the lady, on a blue island, against a rose background strewn with tapestry flowers, stands in front of a silk tent over which hangs the banner motto "A mon seul désir." The lady appears to be taking a necklace from a box and the tapestry has thus been understood as celebrating a gift of love. Nadine Gordimer draws upon both Rilke's vision of the tapestries and the most recent scholarly explanations. In the text, she describes the first tapestry, in which the lady holds a mirror in which the unicorn is reflected, and then simply lists the four following tapestries as "the representation of the other four senses" (p. 340), hearing, smell, taste, and touch. The text then moves to the sixth tapestry which is described in more detail. In 1978, Alain Erlande-Brandenburg agreed that the tapestries represent the five senses, but suggested that the meaning of the sixth tapestry lay not in the acceptance of a gift, but rather in its renunciation: the lady is not receiving the necklace but replacing it in the box.[17] The sixth tapestry may therefore be understood as signifying the need not to submit to the power of the senses, but to exercise free will in their control. The necklace is therefore a symbol of the renunciation of the passions, which may interfere with our ability to act morally. "A mon seul désir" translates as "by my own free will" and is linked to the *Liberum arbitrium* of Socrates and Plato. Where formerly the tapestries were seen as celebrating the senses, as embodied in a beautiful woman, the understanding of the sixth panel has now corrected the eye of the observer.

On the simplest level, therefore, the tapestries indicate that Rosa's decision to abandon the luxuriant sensual joys of life with her lover is an act of free will and a renunciation of the fantasy eroticism of projection, mirror images, and magic islands. Life with Bernard would remove her from her historical destiny to a "place" outside time; Gordimer's description of the tapestries is entirely in the present tense, a timeless participial present which creates an impression of enchanted stillness. "The Lion and the Unicorn listening to music. . . . The Lady weaving. . . . The Lady taking sweets from a dish" (p. 340). In France Rosa has been possessed by an image of herself as sensual, floating like the lady on "an azure island of a thousand flowers" (p. 340), hearing nightingales sing, delighting in the taste of French foods and the sights of France, enjoying the touch of a lover. For all their beauty, however, the tapestries were executed in "the age of the thumbscrew and dungeon" (p. 341). Bernard would take Rosa away from a similar world of pain and imprisonment in order to sequester her in a private world of sexual joy and art, a world in which he could show her the tapestry he loves—"to love you by letting you come to discover what I love" (p. 341). What Bernard loves is an image of Rosa to which she does not entirely correspond. In the extremely complex presentation of the tapestries, Gordimer describes a woman gazing at them, a woman who has all the time in the world to do so:

> There she sits gazing, gazing. And if it is time for the museum to close, she can come back tomorrow and another day, any day, days.
> Sits gazing, this creature that has never been. (p. 341)

In the "Sight" tapestry the lady is also gazing, into a hand-held mirror, but she sees only the reflection of the unicorn, the mythical creature which has never existed outside the human mind. In the tapestry the oval face of the lady with her hair twisted on top is echoed in the oval frame of the mirror and the unicorn's twisted horn. Rosa Burger may become, like the lady, a gazer into a hand-held mirror which reflects back to her only an unreal and mythical creature, a woman who has only existed in the projections of others. In returning to South Africa, however, Rosa chooses not to be such an image, an object to be displayed and desired, a figure in an erotic or political iconography. In South Africa, Rosa, like Rilke's Malte, acquired a false identity imposed upon her by others. Pursuing a personal erotic course, however, simply creates an alternative mask. Rosa's progress toward autonomy involves coming to terms with the mythic masks which men have fastened over the female face—whether desexualized or erotically reified—and correcting the errors of her own internal eye.

Where the tapestry series articulates the necessity of correcting the errors of the eye, Baasie's voice establishes the autonomous existence of "you." Rosa wakes in the night to "the telephone ringing buried in the flesh" (p. 318) and in the darkness at first assumes it is her lover, Bernard. When she realizes it is Baasie she tries to put him off. When Baasie keeps telling Rosa to put on the light, Rosa refuses on the grounds that it is late; she will see him "tomorrow—today, I suppose it is, it's still so dark" (p. 319). Rosa would very much like to keep this conversation in a timeless darkness. To her, Baasie is not a person with an autonomous existence, but a creature of her own mind: "The way you look in my mind is the way my brother does—never gets any older" (p. 323). She addresses him as Baasie. The childish nickname, insulting in the world of *baasskap*, infantilizes and desexualizes the adult male, converting him into a "boy." For Rosa his real name—Zwelinzima Vulindlela—is unknown and unpronounceable. Infantilized and desexualized by Rosa's impersonal greeting at the party, Baasie angrily insists that he is not her "black brother" (p. 321) and doesn't have "to live in your head" (p. 323). He will not enter into a relationship with her in which he functions as a psychological surrogate. His insults force Rosa to put on the light, transforming his voice: "the voice was no longer inside her but relayed small, as from a faint harsh public address system" (p. 320). Baasie's insults externalize his voice, no longer a part of Rosa, but a person in his own right, challenging her. By taunting her, "he had disposed of her whining to go back to bed and bury them both" (p. 322).

Buying the body is a part of Rosa's strategy, as much as it is Clare Terblanche's. She, too, would like to live in a world which corresponds to childish projections, a world in which the childish magical landscape is more real than a "suffering land" (Zwelinzima). In the conversation, Baasie can only be "you," a voice without pronounceable identity. Up to this point in the novel Rosa may be said to have addressed a "you" of fantasy. Now, however, "you" answers back. At the end of the conversation, vomiting in front of the bathroom mirror, Rosa sees herself as "ugly, soiled" (p. 324), "filthy" (p. 329), and "debauched" (p. 329). She comments, "how I disfigured myself" (p. 329). Disfiguration is an essential step in Rosa's progress toward autonomy, an autonomy which depends upon confrontation with her real body, repugnant as well as beautiful, a body which cannot be split into good, clean, white or bad, dirty, black.

The realization is also a product of the subject of Rosa's conversation with Baasie—their respective fathers. In the conversation Rosa tries to assume responsibility for Baasie's father. She says that she was responsible for getting a pass to him, a pass with which he was caught, and as a result died. Baasie, however, refuses to allow whites to assume responsibility for blacks: "it's nothing to do with you . . . who cares whose 'fault' " (p. 322). Baasie rejects Lionel as a spokesman for the black cause, as he rejects white paternalism. Rosa's desire to assume responsibility for her "brother's" father's death is finally checked here, as she emerges from the world of the psyche into the light of conscious action. What Baasie says to her ends her fantasy guilt over a white father, but does not absolve her from political responsibilities. She leaves behind an incestuous psychological world, in the recognition that blacks are autonomous beings, who are not bound to her by imagined ties of dependence.

Rosa returns to South Africa to take up her father's work again, in two senses: first, in terms of a renewed political commitment, and second, in the tending of black bodies. As a physiotherapist, Rosa (like her doctor father) restores feelings to the nerves of injured black people. Rosa's return is to a world of repugnant bodies—horribly mutilated in the Soweto riots—but she is now able to face these bodies and act in their world. When Rosa is charged with "aiding and abetting of the students' and schoolchildren's revolt" (p. 356), the reader knows of no external evidence for the truth of the accusation. Internally, however, Rosa has participated in a schoolgirl's revolt against paternalism, a revolt which has brought her to political consciousness. The novel ends with a revolt against parents, which is not the product of white fantasy, but a political and historical reality. The schoolchildren's revolt in Soweto is directed at the white paternalist state, but also at the political compromises of black fathers. Fats Mxenge is such a father, a man who appears at the end of the novel like "someone brought aboard out of a tempest" (p. 343).

The extent to which she has left Prospero's complex behind is indicated in the art of Gordimer's novel. Two points are important here. In the final pages of the novel the third-person view is emphasized and Rosa appears flatter and more distant than before. Gordimer also introduces into these final pages a statement from the Soweto Students Representative Council, ungrammatical, misprinted, and rhetorically crude. Rosa comments:

"They can't spell and they can't formulate their elation and anguish. But they know why they're dying" (p. 349). In prison, Rosa obtains drawing materials and produces paintings which are also crude in their expression. Failures in aesthetic terms, they are however politically valuable. One drawing is a Christmas card. Ostensibly an innocuous group of carol singers, the card represents the clumsily drawn figures of Marisa, Rosa, and Clare, signaling to its recipients that the women are in touch with each other. In the prison Marisa sings—not of love—but in order to announce her presence to the other prisoners. Rosa has also found her political voice and as a result her inner voice has become silent. The other picture is a "naive imaginary landscape that could raise no suspicions that she might be incorporating plans of the lay-out of the prison" (p. 355). In this crude drawing tiny boats appear "through some failure of perspective" (p. 355) to be sailing straight for a tower. Rosa's drawing is an analogy to the art of Gordimer's novel, which takes the landscape of the racist psyche and inverts it to political ends. At the end of the novel Rosa is distanced as a result of a creative change in the reader's perspective. The "you" of fantasy has disappeared, replaced by the political voice of autonomous blacks (the SSRC statement). The internal voice has been silenced in favor of communications directed toward the world of the Other. *Burger's Daughter* opens with the epigraph "I am the place in which something has occurred." Gordimer's aesthetics are directed against the constructs of a racist imagination, constructs which depend upon psychological displacement, in order to relocate the individual in a real political perspective.

Notes

1. Nadine Gordimer, "Literature and Politics in South Africa, "*Southern Review* 7, no. 3 (1974): 205–6.

2. See, for example, Ronnie Mutch, "Growing Up with Gordimer," *Literary Review* (Jan. 1982): 44–45.

3. As I have previously argued. See Judie Newman, "Gordimer's *The Conservationist*: 'That Book of Unknown Signs,'" *Critique: Studies in Modern Fiction* 22, no. 3 (1981): 33–44.

4. Nadine Gordimer, *Burger's Daughter* (London: Cape, 1979), 16. All subsequent references follow quotations in parentheses.

5. Gordon W. Allport, *The Nature of Prejudice* (Cambridge, Mass.: Addison-Wesley, 1954), 376–82.

6. Joel Kovel, *White Racism: A Psychohistory* (London: Penguin, 1970).

7. Octave Mannoni, *Prospero and Caliban: The Psychology of Colonization,* trans. Pamela

Powesland (New York: Praeger, 1956). First published as *Psychologie de la colonisation* (Paris: Seuil, 1950).

8. Nadine Gordimer gave the Neil Gunn Fellowship Lecture in Edinburgh on 29 May 1981, published as "Apprentices of Freedom," *New Society*, 24–31 Dec. 1981, ii–v. Mannoni uses the phrase "an apprentice to freedom" on p. 65 of *Prospero and Caliban*.

9. Nadine Gordimer, *July's People* (London: Cape, 1981).

10. Frantz Fanon, *Black Skin, White Masks*, trans. Charles L. Markmann (London: MacGibbon and Kee, 1968). First published as *Peau Noire, Masques Blancs* (Paris: Seuil, 1952).

11. A point instantly seized by one reviewer. See Z. N., "The Politics of Commitment," *African Communist* 80 (1980): 100–101.

12. George Sand, *Jeanne*, edited by Simone Vierne (Grenoble: Presses Universitaires de Grenoble, 1978), 132–33. Sand also described the tapestries in detail in "Un Coin du Berry et de la Marche," *L'Illustration*, 3 July 1847, 275–76.

13. René Gilson, *Jean Cocteau* (Paris: Segher, 1964), 39. Cocteau rejected courtly and allegorical explanations in order to place the tapestries in the tradition of "Beauty and the Beast."

14. Rainer Maria Rilke, *Sonnets to Orpheus*, trans. J. B. Leishman (London: Hogarth, 1946), 94–95.

15. Rainer Maria Rilke, *The Notebooks of Malte Laurids Brigge*, trans. John Linton (London: Hogarth, 1930), 122. I am indebted to E. F. N. Jephcott, *Proust and Rilke: The Literature of Expanded Consciousness* (London: Chatto and Windus, 1972).

16. For details of the various interpretations, see Pierre Verlat and M. Francis Salet, *La Dame à la Licorne* (Paris: Braun, 1960), and Charles Dédéyan, *Rilke et la France* (Paris: Sedes, 1964).

17. Alain Erlande-Brandenburg, *La Dame à la Licorne* (Paris: Réunion des Musées Nationaux, 1978). I am grateful to John Frankis of the University of Newcastle upon Tyne for assistance in obtaining this documentation.

Nadine Gordimer

The Degeneration of the Great South African Lie

ABDUL R. JANMOHAMED

❖   ❖   ❖

T HE EXCELLENCE OF *Burger's Daughter*[1] is due to a judicious combination of the relative simplicity of its plot, the elegance and appro-
priateness of its style, and the integrity, acuteness, and courage of Rosa
Burger's attempt to define her "self." The novel is primarily concerned
with Rosa's examination of the priority of her own values, desires, and
needs against a nexus of values furnished by the apartheid society in South
Africa, by the bourgeois culture in Europe, and by the discipline, compassion, and political ideas inherited from her Communist Father. Given the
simplicity of the plot, the major movement of the novel—Rosa's exploration of her cultural inheritance—is a subjective journey that is perfectly
rendered through the bifurcation of the narrative, as in *The Conservationist*,
into objective and subjective components.

The skeletal plot of the novel is barely sufficient for a short story. Because the death of her parents (her father's in a South African prison) has
released Rosa from the burdens of the struggle against apartheid, she finds
herself free to reconsider her life. Upon the encouragement of her lover
she begins to examine the conflict between the self-sacrificial creed of her
Communist inheritance and her desire for self-fulfillment which stems
partly from her own human needs but which is strongly advocated by her
lover, Conrad, a champion of bourgeois values. After some soul searching

she decides that she can no longer sustain the self-sacrifice and anguish entailed by her predicament in South Africa and leaves to join her father's former wife, who has also deserted the self-imposed rigors of the Communist Party in order to live a blissful life on the Mediterranean coast of France. There Rosa falls in love, is blissfully, obliviously happy, but upon meeting her "brother" Baasie, a young black man who had grown up with her in the Burger household, she decides that the pursuit of self-satisfaction is an illusory charade and that because one is never free from human suffering, it would be more meaningful for her to suffer on behalf of a self-transcendent cause in South Africa than for selfish reasons in Europe. She returns to Africa, becomes involved in the fight against apartheid, and ends up in prison.

This simple plot is rescued from banality by the narrative style and structure and by the rigor and delicacy of Rosa's self-scrutiny. Unlike the disjunction relation of the objective and subjective narratives in *The Conservationist*, the two narratives in *Burger's Daughter* are complementary: the objective representation provides a fuller context which perfectly clarifies the subjective story. The proportional relationship between the two also accurately reflects Rosa's mood and preoccupation: the subjective narrative predominates in the first part of the novel which contains the bulk of her self-analysis, whereas the objective narrative overwhelms the subjective one in the second part when Rosa is less preoccupied with herself because she is in love, and the two narratives are more balanced in the third part when she has resolved her conflict.[2]

Within the objective narrative the omniscient powers of the narrator are carefully limited. In addition to confining itself to fairly factual information about the motives, desires, and mental processes of the various characters, the objective narrative adopts a calm, sober, neutral, and unobtrusive tone that, by contrast, highlights the lyric intensity of the subjective narrative. The former further enhances this effect by including within itself the mechanistic perspectives of the Communist Party and the South African Bureau of State Security (BOSS), both of which treat Rosa as an object in a large impersonal game, as well as various factual documentary material such as newspaper reports and a pamphlet from the Soweto Students Representative Council. In contrast to the blandness of the objective narrative, the subjective one has a powerful and controlled lyric intensity that is able to win the reader's complete sympathy. This is primarily due to a major change in the dramatic monologues, for unlike Mehring's, which are antagonistic, rambling, and subconscious, those of Rosa are carefully modulated conscious confessions to specific absent individuals. All the monologues in part one of the novel are addressed to Rosa's lover, those in the third part to her father, Lionel. Because all three individuals form a very sympathetic audience for Rosa, her monologues are never forced to become defensive, belligerent, or sentimental—thus she constantly strives for accuracy, intricacy, and honesty. The tone of her confessions varies in keeping with their content: at times it is objective, intelligent, and analytic, at times vulnerable and demanding genuine sympathy, at times angry and hurt, but never self-indulgent, self-righteous, or moralistic. As she is careful to point out, her monologues are neither apologias nor accusations. This strategy that combines the assumption of the audience's, and therefore the reader's, sympathies with the systematic variation of the tone produces a candor in her confessions that becomes absolutely irresistible: no matter how indifferent or hostile the reader may be, he cannot help being won over by Rosa's predicament and her attempt to find a way out of it. Thus seduced into entering the labyrinth of Rosa's life, the reader is able to experience almost at firsthand her hopes, frustrations, desires, and resentments, as well as her intellectual analyses of self and society.

Gordimer renders the stylistic bifurcation of the novel even more complex by making the subjective narrative, which contains Rosa's entire self-examination, in turn oscillate between a subjective and an objective pole and by endowing her heroine with an intricate and ironic awareness of this fluctuation. Rosa's attempt to avoid self-delusion is emphasized by the fact that the first subjective chapter of the novel consists entirely of a single sentence stressing the objective imperative of her self-analysis: "When they saw me outside the prison, what did they see?" (*BD*, 13). Her endeavor to see herself through the eyes of others is balanced by her narcissistic gaze at herself in a mirror. In fact she realizes that an original (subjective) and a mediated (quasi-objective) version of herself have been internalized in the very manner of her perception: "it is impossible to filter free of what I have learnt, felt, thought, the subjective presence of the schoolgirl. She's a stranger about whom some intimate facts are known to me, that's all" (*BD*, 14). That the tension between the presence and absence of self and her awareness of the polarity are products of her mode of existence is revealed during her recollection of the day when, at the age of fourteen, her first menstrual cycle began while she was waiting outside the prison in order to visit her mother: "But outside the prison the internal landscape of my mysterious body turns me inside out, so that in that public place on that public occasion . . . I am within that monthly crisis of destruction, the purging, tearing, draining of my own structure. I am my womb, and a year ago I wasn't aware—physically—I had one" (*BD*, 15–16). On this day too begins the lifelong surveillance of Rosa by BOSS. Thus her simultaneous yet unconnected existence as an object of public scrutiny and as a locus of private experience reflects her predicament as a bifurcated social being.

The very existence of the subjective and objective narratives in Gordimer's fiction reflects the burden of contradictions generated by the manichean South African environment. In a society replete with contradictions the Gordimerian self, hating apartheid culture, living in the sparse black-and-white society, yet unable to change social institutions to suit its own values and beliefs, is repeatedly forced to retreat from the divisive society in order to examine its own consciousness, values, and priorities. In this process the self is obliged to consider the socially enforced bifurcation between the subjective and objective as a fundamental ontological condition that permeates the very process of perception and conception. The complementarity of the two narratives in *Burger's Daughter* is a stylistic improvement compared to the previous novel, but the technique and its implication remain the same. Thus in this novel Rosa's awareness of the division and oscillation of self between the subjective and objective poles of existence and the anguish and frustration of her attempt to define herself are mirrored by the tension, the electrically charged gap, of the stylistic bifurcation. Yet in a sense she is able to transcend the disjunctive polarity because she realizes that both the private and public versions of herself are equally concocted, that no one perspective or set of signifiers can represent her completely.

Rosa's self-analysis is inspired by her lover, Conrad, whose self-centered bourgeois values and experiences provoke her to examine her own Communist heritage, which in its suppression of personal desires in favor of altruism is profoundly other-oriented. However, the most fundamental stimulus for Rosa's self-analysis is not Conrad but the mystery of death. Her ambivalence about Lionel Burger's death ("to exult and to sorrow were the same thing for me" [*BD*, 63]), which frees her yet leaves her with a moral burden, is supplanted by her encounter with the death of an alcoholic, who quietly expires on a park bench while Rosa is having lunch there. Unlike the death of her brother and parents, the meaning of which is obscured by personal emotions and circumstances, the stranger's demise provokes her to contemplate the ontological nature and meaning of death and, therefore, of life, which no political or social ideological inheritance is capable of explaining. This ontological mystery forces Rosa to examine and reconstruct her life. Her exploration of the labyrinth of "self" thus centers around two major propositions: the often-repeated "now you are free" and the fundamental question that pervades the novel, "What else was I?" (*BD*,

40, 65). Gordimer focuses these two related questions about the nature of freedom and being through Rosa's analysis of her Communist inheritance and the "good life" of bourgeois society. It is the *manner* in which she inherits her father's ethos, rather than the Communist theory or praxis per se, which becomes the main cause of her anguish. Her parents' concern for others is experienced by Rosa as an extension of their love for her; the needs of Baasie, of other unknown black children, or of oppressed people in general are as important as those of Rosa. Although their compassion and love is deep and boundless, Rosa does not occupy a privileged position in their affection. Thus because she has not learned the distinction between privileged love and a general sense of affection, her own feeling of moral obligation is not an abstract idea that she can easily discard whenever she wishes: rejection of the generalized obligation would necessarily entail an equivalent rejection of her parents' love for her as an individual. After her father's death she is theoretically free to abandon the burden of her concern for others, but it is so deeply ingrained in her emotions that she cannot do so without tearing apart her own personality.

The anguish caused by Rosa's attempt to renounce her sense of obligation and to overcome the habit of suppressing her own desires permeates the first part of the novel. It is brilliantly epitomized by her recollection of Noel de Witt, a young Communist who has been imprisoned. Because he has no family and because it is vital for the Communist Party network that someone communicate with him, Rosa's parents encourage her to visit him as his fiancée. Rosa, however, really is in love with Noel, but because she is afraid to jeopardize any aspect of the party's cause she refuses to admit this to her parents or to Noel while she continues to visit him for years. Thus she stoically plays this charade, pretending to be something that she would in fact like to be but afraid that expression of the real desire would be detrimental to the functional value of the role. Her recollection of this episode is full of pathos and irony. In her bitterness she accuses herself of having prostituted herself to political necessity, but she soon realizes that in the Burger house prostitutes, considered to be products of economic necessity, are not despised. Thus her father's ethos even deprives her of self-contempt. The major drawback of such a life is that it has robbed her of personally valid experiences and a distinct identity.

Rosa's attempt to renounce her heritage and define her identity through her own choices produces the novel's climactic moral and psychological paradox which is specifically Rosa's but which, in its general validity, also demonstrates the ontological depth of her self-analysis: "To be free is to become a stranger to oneself" (*BD*, 81). She would like to use

her newfound freedom to become herself, that is, to gratify her most intimate repressed desires. Yet in order to do so she would have to discard her
past, her parents, and her values; that is, she would have to reject herself as
she is. Rosa's analysis even leads her to consider how the nature of perception itself may affect her self-definition. Proceeding once more through
a dialectic of subjectivity and objectivity, she opposes secrecy, the exclusively personal perception of self, to the mediated, public view of her being.
Because she has been brought up in a Communist household, constantly
watched and harassed by the police, secrecy has become second nature for
Rosa, but she realizes that this deeply ingrained habit eventually makes it
impossible for her to acknowledge or identify her real motives and desires.
Conversely, when she tries to define herself through the perception of
others, she finds that most of them do not see her as Rosa but as Burger's
daughter, that is, as part of a family, class, or political group: she becomes
the object of various categories that do great injustice to her particular
subjectivity. Thus she always remains in danger of losing herself either in a
narcissistic or sociopolitical labyrinth: once more she oscillates between
the poles of self-presence (-interest) and self-absence (-denial).

Although Rosa is critical of the bondage imposed by her parents' radicalism, she does not rush over to the apparent freedom of bourgeois society which she knows has its own forms of solipsism and ideological imprisonment. She is critical of Conrad's idea of freedom because she is aware of
its essentially narcissistic nature; his preoccupation with his own desires
and emotions precludes all consideration for others. She feels that con-
sumer society imprisons the individual in his own desires—he can only escape the object of his desire by acquiring it, but desire then fastens itself on
another object. However, Gordimer's main criticism of bourgeois society is
reserved for Rosa's visit to France. In the meantime Rosa finds little to
choose between Communism and capitalism. Both are hoarding for the
future in their different ways and both are equally cruel and violent; the
domestic and colonial violence of European bourgeois society is no different for Rosa than the brutality of Stalinist Communism.

Thus hemmed in by various unresolved dialectic oppositions, Rosa
is strongly tempted to escape through the fundamental South African
alterity: the blacks. But she knows that white South Africans use blackness
as a way either "of perceiving sensual redemption, as romantics do, or of
perceiving fears, as racialists do" (*BD*, 135), and she realizes that her Communist colleagues often use blacks in the former manner: the overthrow
of apartheid and the freedom of Africans is their sacred goal. Even though
she knows that her parents' relationships with black individuals are based

invariably on genuine personal bonds that transcend their redemptive usage, she distrusts her own motives and therefore avoids the temptation to continue working against apartheid under the leadership of Marisa, a dynamic and charismatic black woman. She is also afraid that by working with Marisa she would be choosing an acolyte destiny once more and putting herself in a different kind of bondage.

Unable to resolve the various contradictions in which she finds herself or unable to escape through an African alterity, Rosa finally decides that perhaps she can resolve her problems more easily if she leaves South Africa. Her hesitation in leaving is overcome by an epiphanic experience of cruelty, a merciless beating of a donkey, which uniquely brings the disjunct subjective and objective worlds together for a moment:

> I didn't see the whip. I saw the agony. Agony that came from some terrible centre seized within the group of donkey, cart, driver and people behind him. They made a single object that contracted against itself in the desperation of a hideous final energy. Not seeing the whip, I saw the infliction of pain broken away from the will that creates it; broken loose, a force existing of itself, ravishment without the ravisher, torture without the torturer, rampage, pure cruelty gone beyond control of the humans who have spent thousands of years devising it. (*BD*, 208)

Rosa is perfectly aware that she could easily stop this violence; the black man would easily succumb to her white authority. Yet she refuses to do so because she feels that this specific instance of pain is a product of a whole chain of torture, that the man's cruelty is a translation of his own suffering and frustration produced by the apartheid system of South Africa. Her dilemma is twofold: first, she does not know at what point it is appropriate to intercede in this ecology of suffering; second, she herself, as a product of that ecology, is responsible for the ordeal: "If somebody's going to be brought to account, I am accountable for him, to him, as he is for the donkey. Yet the suffering—while I saw it it was the sum of suffering to me" (*BD*, 210). This epiphany is produced by the only moment in the novel where the objective and subjective worlds coincide. Not only is all the personal anguish of Rosa reflected by the pain of the donkey, but also her awareness of the complex psychic, familial, and historical "ecology" that defines her own identity is mirrored by her similar knowledge of the complex racial, economic, and political ecology that produces this specific objective instance of agony. Through her assumption of responsibility for the donkey's pain the two worlds coalesce. South Africa becomes the embodiment of human grief, and Rosa cannot bear the burden of that responsibility. She decides to leave: "After the donkey I couldn't stop myself. I don't know how to live in Lionel's country" (*BD*, 210). Thus she leaves Lionel's country, that is, South Africa, as well as the world of moral responsibility for others.

In the south of France, where she stays with another apostate, her father's former wife, Katya, Rosa is transformed. Away from the secretive, antagonistic, and precarious social environment of South Africa, Rosa becomes livelier, happier, and more carefree among people who have dedicated their lives to an honest, but nonpredatory enjoyment of their desires—people whose only imperatives are pleasure, loyalty to friends, and the avoidance of taxes. For Rosa the major merit of this life is tolerance: in Antibes no one expects her to be more than what she is or seems to be, whereas her comrades in South Africa expected her to be "equal to everything." If she were not, she would be a traitor to humanity. Her transformation is symbolized by the new name the French have imposed on her. Rosa, named after Rosa Luxemburg, becomes "La petite Rose": the moral heritage is abandoned for an existentialism that is exclusively aesthetic. Rosa's preoccupations with the Communist Party, her father, and her own apostasy are supplanted by her passionate love for a married man, Bernard Chabalier. Her reaction against her father's other-oriented ethos reaches its logical conclusion in the pleasure she takes in being Bernard's mistress, which, unlike the position of the wife, has no public obligations.

Rosa's reluctant decision to stay in this bourgeois paradise is suddenly shattered by her meeting with Baasie, her black "brother." Baasie, whose real given name, Zwelinzima, means "suffering land," is now a physical and emotional embodiment of the plight of his race and country: his body and face show signs of physical torture and all his emotions have coalesced into an overwhelming bitterness. His vehement rejection of Rosa's attempt to revive their personal, sibling intimacy is based on counterracism. In this specific instance, he resents what he considers to be the inordinate praise of Lionel Burger's heroism in contrast to the neglect of innumerable Africans, including his own father, who take similar stands and suffer similar fates. Rosa's repeated efforts to reestablish a subjective, personal bond between them is met by Baasie's insistence on severing such ties because of the objective, racial difference between them. A belligerent argument between them descends to insults that verge on racism.

Rosa's immediate reaction to this quarrel and severance of relations is emotional; having learned to express her feelings through her love for Bernard, Rosa now weeps for the apparent end of her personal ties with Africans. In trying to escape the moral burdens inherited from Lionel, she had not intended to abandon her personal relations with her black friends, but she now realizes that in the increasing antagonism in South Africa, black-white relationships cannot remain apolitical. Further reflection reveals to Rosa facts that become an important part of her decision to return to South Africa. The fight with Baasie makes her realize in a personal manner the truth of Lionel Burger's prediction that unless a substantial number of whites support the African demand for majority rule the blacks' reaction would transcend their political demands and become increasingly and exclusively racist. The second reason for her return, she insists, is not concerned with ideology or politics but only with suffering. She had believed that by being an ordinary person, by shedding the moral burden of her heritage, she could alleviate her anguish. But in Antibes she sees that ordinary people are as tormented as she, or Baasie, or Lionel. Because no one is immune from pain, she sees no virtue in being an ordinary person: suffering for a particular cause seems better to her than suffering for no reason. Thus her compassion for others is revived: soon after her return to South Africa she begins practicing physiotherapy again—teaching crippled children how to walk.

However, the most important reason for her return is one that Rosa does not recognize consciously. While contemplating her quarrel with Baasie, Rosa sees that "[in] one night we succeeded in manoeuvering ourselves into the position their history books back home [in South Africa] have ready for us—him bitter; me guilty. What other meeting place could there have been for us?" (*BD*, 330). The last sentence recalls one of Nadine Gordimer's first short stories, "Is There Nowhere Else Where We Can Meet?" *Burger's Daughter*, then, circles or rather spirals around to the point of departure. Rosa does not possess the fear of the unnamed heroine of the short story, but the search for that other location where blacks can possess equality and dignity and control their own destiny and where the two races can meet as equals remains the same in both cases. Rosa, however, is politically and ideologically more sophisticated and committed than her earlier avatar. The main purpose and goal of Gordimer's fiction have remained the same while her style and technique have been refined. It is clear, then, that Rosa returns to South Africa in order to continue her search for that other location and that now both Rosa and Gordimer are perfectly aware that it is situated in the future, on the other side of a revolution that will overthrow apartheid.

Rosa's return to South Africa coincides with two significant radical events that signal the beginning of a cataclysmic revolt. The first is the treason trial of Orde Greer, a young Afrikaner journalist who is indicted for inciting violence and rebellion, for reading General Giap's theories of guerrilla warfare, and for attempting to procure information about South African defense installations and equipment. His involvement in radical activity is somewhat of a surprise for Rosa and the reader because earlier in the novel he is depicted, in contrast to Rosa, as a rather inept romantic desperately searching for a cause. The second even more surprising action is that of Marie Nel, Rosa's cousin. Marie, who has only been mentioned in the novel as a young spoiled brat and who has been working in Paris for the South African government, captures the newspaper headlines when she is arrested for harboring one of the leaders of NAPAP, an international terrorist organization connected with the Baader-Meinhof gang and the Japanese Red Army. A journalist's discovery of her family relation with the Burgers further fuels the right-wing outrage in South Africa. Gordimer provides us with no further information about Marie's character, motives, or drastic political transformation: this incident, along with many others toward the end of the novel, is deliberately shrouded in mystery.

These two events are closely followed by and symbolically linked with the actual series of riots by young African students that are collectively referred to as the Soweto riots. Gordimer depicts this rebellion, quite accurately on the whole, it seems to me, as a spontaneous uprising of black children who are frustrated with poor educational facilities and generally aroused by the rather vague Black Consciousness movement, which in turn is inspired by the victories of Frelimo and Movimento Popular de Libertação de Angola (Popular Movement for the Liberation of Angola). She stresses the fact that the rebellion is by *children* who, unconcerned with any elaborate Communist theories of proletarian revolution, burst forth in a popular movement that surprises everyone. The initiative belongs entirely to the students. Blacks who had avoided political parties "have begun to see themselves at last as they are; as their children see them. They have been radicalized—as the faithful would say—by their children; they act accordingly; they are being arrested and detained" (*BD*, 348). Those who had already committed themselves to political action are invigorated by their children's revolt.[3]

Rosa too becomes involved in what Gordimer implies is a general unexpected revolt of the young against the apartheid regime in South Africa as well as against the moribund bourgeois and Communist cultures. However, the nature of Rosa's participation remains extremely mysterious. BOSS suspects that part of her stay in London was devoted to activities that culminated in the Soweto riots, and the novel is pointedly mute about various messages that Rosa receives prior to her arrest. Rosa, now imprisoned with Marisa Kgosana, her old friend Clare Terblanche, and other comrades, immediately busies herself with establishing a system of communication within the prison and with those on the outside. She is depicted as being livelier and less reserved than before: she is, in fact, quite happily reconciled to her destiny. She, along with the other rebels, is depicted as being very young: her new short prison haircut makes her look fourteen—the age at which we see her at the beginning of the novel, waiting outside the prison in order to visit her mother.

Rosa's renaissance traces a circle in Gordimer's work. Like Helen Shaw at the end of *The Lying Days*, who imagines herself reemerging like a phoenix from the ashes of disillusionment, Rosa reemerges with renewed vitality from the despair that is caused by her predicament. She also traces another circle. Whereas at the beginning of the novel she is angry and bitter toward her father, at the end she is reconciled with him: her respect and acceptance are indicated by the fact that her confessions in the last part of the novel are addressed directly to him. She understands him now as a man who was motivated primarily by compassion and not by dogma: she feels that he is more like Christ than Stalin. By the end of the novel, Rosa, like Lionel Burger, comes to accept a militant form of compassion as the overruling priority of her life and faces the consequences with equanimity. Rosa compares Lionel's sublime lucidity and elation to that of the black children marching arm in arm toward the rifles of the police.

Thus Gordimer ascribes the whole imminent revolution at the end of the novel to children. Rosa feels that the impending revolution is a vindication of the theories of her namesake, Rosa Luxemburg, who believed that the initiative for the revolution would come from the people, that theory would chase events. In this specific South African case revolt comes not from the people but from their children. (It is probably no coincidence that Gordimer published this novel in 1979, the Year of the Child.) What Gordimer is anxious to emphasize here is that the Soweto riots, or a later more cataclysmic revolution, are not or will not be a product of some diabolic plot masterminded in Moscow or Beijing, but that they are in indigenous rebellion by people who can no longer tolerate being treated as subhuman, evil slaves. The stress on children and spontaneity is designed to disarm the criticism of those liberals, inside South Africa and elsewhere, who would like to condemn the African recourse to violence as a Communist plot. In this novel Gordimer is quite trenchant in her criticism of the liberal position. The motto of the second part of the novel, a quotation from Weng Yeng-Ming, "To know and not to act is not to know," and the fact that for the first time all her major white characters are Afrikaners, not Anglo-Saxon South Africans, clearly indict those who ritualistically grumble about apartheid but who are really quite acquiescent. By choosing her heroes from among the Afrikaners, perhaps Gordimer is also attempting to urge them to rebel against their own government. If so, one suspects that she may be indulging in a little wishful thinking.

If Gordimer's insistence on children and spontaneity seems somewhat sentimental, her depiction of Rosa's and Lionel's compassion, which is the substantial moral center around which the novel coalesces at the end, is anything but sentimental. Lionel's love for Rosa is impersonal, and she resents his failure to recognize her personal, individual needs. Yet the pattern of relationships in the novel consistently valorizes generalized and public compassion rather than private and egocentric love. Rosa's quasi-familial relations verify this pattern: her affair with Conrad, a pseudobrother, is alienating and ultimately incestuous; her relation to her pseudomother, Katya, remains perfunctory; her love for Bernard is unable to compete with the demands of generalized compassion and political obligation; and her attempt to establish a personal relationship with Baasie, another pseudobrother, is rejected by the latter. Rosa is equally compassionate toward all these people, but none of them are able to claim a personal, privileged position in her life, just as she is unable to do in Baasie's life. The bonds of the biological family are replaced in *Burger's Daughter* by the cohesiveness of the political "family." Throughout the novel members of the Communist Party form an extended family that *does* look after its members, and at the end of the novel the same function is fulfilled by the sisterhood of Rosa, Marisa, Clare, and Leela Govinda in prison and Flora Donaldson, who is their contact with the outside world. Thus in spite of criticizing some aspects of the Communist Party praxis, Gordimer valorizes the power and efficacy of a compassionate political brotherhood. This form of deep sympathy is indirectly a product and a reflection of the apartheid system that attempts to prevent personal relationships across the color line and that therefore progressively forces those who resist apartheid to choose political alliances over personal friendships with people who may tacitly support apartheid.

Rosa's decision to choose impersonal compassion over the indulgence of personal desire is paralleled by the resolution of the dialectic of staying and leaving. *Burger's Daughter* contains the clearest and the most emphatic statement about that recurrent dialectic. Quite obviously, Rosa leaves South Africa in order to escape the burden of self-abnegating political obligations, and, even though in Europe she experiences the world of self-satisfaction, she returns because her acceptance of the universality of suffering enables her to bear the wretchedness of South Africa and thus once more to undertake her moral burden. However, in *Burger's Daughter* Gordimer compresses this dialectic into a shorter but morally more significant and powerful spatial movement. The novel begins with a fourteen-year-old Rosa waiting outside the prison walls and ends with Rosa, who looks fourteen, inside the prison walls. The dialectic has been reduced to a choice between staying out of prison or being willing to risk incarceration for one's beliefs and actions. The short spatial movement from one side of the wall to the other and the symbolic arrest of time signify a narrowing of Gordimer's black-and-white frontier society to the short spaces on either side of the moral dilemma. The choice is now entirely a *moral* one; neither time, that is, the belief that somehow "time" itself will provide a solution for the problems of apartheid, nor place, that is, being in South Africa or elsewhere, is a relevant criterion. Either one acquiescently accepts apartheid by staying or leaving or one actively fights against it and accedes to the inevitable imprisonment. Just as Rosa willingly faces the consequences of her actions, so too Nadine Gordimer, by the very act of publishing *Burger's Daughter*, shows her willingness to accept, in addition to the certain banning of her novel, her own banning, house arrest, or even imprisonment.

Gordimer's novel is not only a fictitious resolution of a real moral problem, but the publication of *Burger's Daughter* constitutes an actual sociopolitical act which could have relatively harsh consequences for the author. The novel is also a political act to the extent that it is Gordimer's reply to the questions raised by the Black Consciousness movement. The latter's rejection of white liberal-cum-radical sympathies and aid is rationally though not personally and emotionally acceptable for Gordimer because she feels that racial privilege has fundamentally altered the white South African psyche. The way forward for the white population lies through a radical self-examination:

> If we declare an intention to identify fully with the struggle for a single, common South African consciousness, if there is such a thing as white consciousness as a way to human justice and honest self-realisation, whites will have to take their attitudes apart and assemble afresh their ideas of themselves. We shall have to accept the black premise that the entire standpoint of *being white* will have to shift, whether it is under the feet of those who loathe racialism and have opposed it all their lives, or those to whom race discrimination is holy writ. . . . Could white consciousness—once you have decided what it is and how to put it into practice—provide a means for

whites to participate in the legal and economic and spiritual liberation of blacks? Will it find a way in which whites themselves may at the same time be liberated from the image of the Janus Oppressor, the two archetypal stereofaces, grinning racialist or weeping liberal, of the same tyrant?[4]

Burger's Daughter can be seen as Gordimer's post-Soweto examination of white consciousness, as a reply to the Black Consciousness movement and as the beginning of a dual attempt to arrive at the common South African post-apartheid consciousness.

Notes

1. Nadine Gordimer, *Burger's Daughter* (New York: Viking, 1979). All further references to this novel will be abbreviated as *BD* and incorporated in the text.

2. The ratio of pages devoted to objective and subjective narratives gives a rough indication of the shifting emphasis: part one, 8:11; part two, 8:2; part three, 8:4.

3. Nadine Gordimer's stress on the spontaneity of the children causes her to overlook the implication of the major reason that led to the Soweto riots. The efficient cause of the rebellion was the attempt by the South African government to substitute Afrikaans for English as the medium of instruction in African primary and secondary schools. Because Afrikaans is an entirely local language, it would effectively cut off future generations of blacks from the rest of the world, and thus make them entirely dependent on the white South Africans. The students' recognition of this ingeniously diabolical move demonstrates that sophistication rather than naiveté underlay their spontaneity.

4. These quotations are parts of a speech that Nadine Gordimer delivered to the University of Cape Town students after the Soweto riots. See "What Being a South African Means to Me," *South African Outlook,* June 1977, pp. 87–89, 92.

Burger's Daughter

The Synthesis of Revelation

MARGOT HEINEMANN

S PEAKING SOME YEARS AGO about African writing (including in that term writing about Africa *not* by black Africans), Nadine Gordimer noted that its themes are very different from those that have preoccupied modern European and American writers:

> European writers from Beckett to Marguerite Duras are obsessed with human alienation and its consequent problem of communication. . . . In Africa, it seems, the lines are still clear. The possibility of communication between man and man is taken for granted, it is what is conveyed that matters. Human beings still clash, rather than near-miss, in African writing.[1]

Although her subject matter and her perception of it as a white radical intellectual is inevitably different from that of black African writers, Nadine Gordimer is at one with them in rejecting "hyperintrospection" and the impossibility of communication as major themes. One can't, however, consider her simply in specialist terms as a South African writer, still less as one whose best work timelessly transcends the setting from which it comes. It's because she has remained obstinately rooted in the tragic situation of her own country that hers has become a major voice in world literature.

Her novel *Burger's Daughter* (1979) is the outcome of a long process of development in her art, in her way of seeing, and in the world she writes
about. This development becomes very striking if one reads her own selection of her short stories, *No Place Like* (1978), in the order in which they
were written. As she says in her preface to that collection:

> I had wanted to arrange the selection in sequence from the earliest story
> collection to the latest simply because when reading story collections I my-
> self enjoy following the development of a writer. Then I found that this
> order had another logic to which my first was complementary. The chrono-
> logical order turns out to be an historical one. The change in social attitudes
> unconsciously reflected in the stories represents both that of the people in
> my society—that is to say, history—and my apprehension of it; in the writ-
> ing, I am acting upon my society, and in the manner of my apprehension,
> all the time history is acting upon me. (p. 13)

"Politics is about people"—it's a truism. But the political situation in
South Africa, and hence its effect on people, is very different now from
what it was thirty years ago. The white girl in an early Gordimer story like
"The Smell of Earth and Flowers," experiencing "her generation's equivalent of religious ecstasy" through the unity of black and white in the passive civil disobedience campaign belongs to the early 1950s. In later stories
like "Africa Emergent" or "Open House" of the 1970s, white liberalism itself
is collapsing. White sympathizers with the African cause now may often be
regarded with suspicion (not without reason) as possible BOSS agents,
rather than be welcomed by black radicals with open arms.

With a great part of the African continent now independent of white
rule, directly as a result of military action by black guerrillas and independence armies, civil rights in South Africa have been yet more drastically
curtailed. Political campaigning has been driven underground, toward
armed resistance. Segregation is stricter, Black Consciousness more intense. In Gordimer's early stories we have humble black servants fatalisti-
cally bemoaning their lot (as the Burgers' servant Lily or old people in
Soweto still do in *Burger's Daughter*). In the later ones young black political
refugees awaiting military training or children demonstrating against
Bantu education in defiance of the guns become central to the fiction because they have become central to the consciousness of the time.

> In a certain sense the writer is "selected" by his subject—his subject being
> the consciousness of his era. How he deals with this is, to me, the funda-
> ment of commitment, although commitment is usually understood as

the reverse process: a writer's selection of a subject in conformity with the rationalisation of his own ideological and/or political beliefs. (*No Place Like*, p. 14)

The growth and complexity of *political* consciousness and involvement imposes changes in style and tone which are frankly disapproved and resented by some critics who greatly admired the earlier work. Thus the American critic Robert F. Haugh in his book-length treatment places Nadine Gordimer "among the masters" on the strength of a few "timeless" short stories like the very early "Is There Nowhere Else Where We Can Meet?"[2] But when it comes to the novels, and especially later ones like *A Guest of Honour* (1970), that deeply felt study of tension and conflict in an African state after independence, Haugh compares her blacks regretfully with Shakespeare's Othello and Conrad's James Wait, for him "the supreme creations of black men in literature" because they are "superb human beings," "authors of their woe." Gordimer's novels, he thinks, overemphasize race and sociology. "Frequently the trouble is that in seeking a more sustained story structure Miss Gordimer is drawn into the sort of direct racial confrontation that she avoided in her most successful short stories" (p. 161). Essentially it's the human and political implications of that "direct racial confrontation" that the critic can't take.

And in one sense Haugh is right. In a short story the social origins of action and pain can still be mysterious, inexplicit; as a reader one can fill in the blanks or not, as one wishes, and yet feel one's taking the central point. In the later novels this is no longer possible: they're not just accumulations of impressions, but contain within themselves the movements and connections of history.[3]

Most modern political novels, at least in English, have dealt with people concerned with politics only to the extent that seems "average." From E. M. Forster's *Passage to India* to Paul Scott's *Raj Quartet*, from Graham Greene's *The Third Man* to *Our Man in Havana* or *The Human Factor*, from Alan Sillitoe's *Saturday Night and Sunday Morning* to Raymond Williams's *Border Country*—the people don't *want* to be involved in politics, it happens to them. This has been the form in many of Nadine Gordimer's novels and stories too, from *Is There Nowhere Else* and *A World of Strangers* (1958) to *Livingstone's Companions* (1972) and *The Conservationist* (1974). But because in the increasingly polarized situation in South Africa "society is the political situation" and "politics is character,"[4] she now bases much of her fiction on people for whom political action to change society is at the center of their lives—like the Indian working mother duplicating leaflets and going to prison in the story "A Chip of Glass Ruby" (1965), or the heroes of novels like *The Late Bourgeois World* (1966), *A Guest of Honour* (1970), or now *Burger's Daughter* (1979) where she explores what it's like to be a Communist in a fiercely repressive capitalist society. And this is in some ways a rarer and more difficult achievement.

Nadine Gordimer is not a Communist. "Nonpolitical" is how she describes herself, in the sense that she has never joined a political party. But she's close enough to the subject to render her Communists, like her other characters, with that combination of "close identification and monstrous detachment" which she sees as crucial to the novelist's art. "The tension between standing apart and being fully involved; that is what makes the writer. . . . The validity of this dialectic is the synthesis of revelation; our achievement of, or even attempt at this is the moral, the human justification for what we do"[5]—the justification, that is, for using other people's lives and sufferings as raw material. She avoids presenting any kind of "typical Communist," whether romantic or steely-eyed. "The faithful" are identifiable by what they do—a practical stubbornness and courage—but are otherwise very different people. It's not a question of a particular psychological or personality type— fanatical, insecure, father-fixated, or whatever—being drawn to this kind of activity, though the activity itself, persisted in through the illegality and danger, may well bring out certain qualities in the activist.

The framework of *Burger's Daughter* is extremely simple. Plot in the ordinary sense in minimal; the underlying movement is in the mind of Rosa Burger. A child of two leading Communists—Lionel a doctor, Cathy a former organizer of a mixed-race trade union—brought up in an atmosphere of political struggle and through years of increasing defeat and repression of the Left, so long as her much-loved father is on trial or serving a life sentence Rosa feels she must unquestioningly bear her responsibility as the last survivor of his family and his sole link with the outside world. When he dies in prison, she is free for the first time to choose what to do with her life. She contrives to get herself a passport and leaves South Africa for Europe. There, staying in the south of France with her father's first wife, Katya—who, unlike her own parents, has chosen to live for the sensuous present—she meets a French academic with whom she falls in love and has an idyllic affair. She plans to take a flat and make a life near him in Paris: he has a wife and family whom he can't leave, but they might have a child. But visiting London, she comes into contact with South African political exiles who reject much of what her father stood for. Renouncing the happiness of the Paris plan, she returns to South Africa and at the end—inevitably—to prison. And that's about all.

It's the meaning of this movement that the novel explores, mainly through Rosa'a own consciousness (distinctly a "fine consciousness" in Henry James's sense, observed as well as delicately observing). Her memory recreates her own childhood, in slightly easier times: the open hospitality of "that house," the Burger house, where color wasn't divisive (the children sharing baths and games with the little black boy, Baasie, son of an absent comrade), and it was taken for granted that you "didn't belong to yourself" but to others, to the socialist and liberation movements, something you learned "as other children learn to wash their hands." The personal memories and flashbacks span also the historical and political changes of those years. As Rosa's driven to question and test old loyalties and principles, we're made to feel, as well as rationally to assess, the weight of the overpowering decision: can she, should she, how can she defect from the commitment and philosophy into which, without willing it, she was born?

Very little overtly happens or can happen in the novel, except the inner history of the heroine. Always in South Africa she's under surveillance, a "named person." Close friends are watched, in prison, or under house arrest. When she escapes, it's to a world where, by the terms of the understanding on which she's granted a passport, she can meet no one significant to the South African struggle. A similar focusing on the inner action is at the center of *Samson Agonistes*, another work about a revolutionary enduring the aftermath of disaster and the failure of the good old cause.

The narrative method is flexible, centered in Rosa's own observations, but shifting easily to other minds, to the impersonal reports of "surveillance," the hostile records of the political police—in the main quite unobtrusively. One notices these changes only when a particular contrast in the angle of vision is important to the story. Crucial moments are often represented not in narrative form but as scenes, in highly articulate conversation and discussion among the characters—the kind of thing which R. F. Haugh dismisses as "sociological," but which the intensity of the underlying conflict sustains and makes exciting

Strict adherence to a single point of view, whatever its formal and dramatic advantages, could have given only a linear version of what needs to be shown as a highly complex process. Nadine Gordimer deliberately uses a montage of different views and voices, integrated to represent a single action. She doesn't, in fact, allow point of view to get in the way of the human story she has to tell, but she does exploit it for dramatic and ironic effect. The cutting between different views places the central conscious-ness of Rosa (as of Bray in *A Guest of Honour*) within a society, while allowing the reader freedom to move and evaluate. Like the novelist, we're obliged to be both objective and involved.

Moreover, Rosa's first-person monologue—partly because of her isola-tion, there is unfashionably much of it—is itself subtly varied in presenta-tion. As she explains at the beginning:

> One is never talking to oneself, always one is addressed to someone. Sud-denly, without knowing the reason, at different stages of one's life, one is ad-dressing this person or that all the time, even dreams are performed before an audience. (*Burger's Daughter*, p. 16)[6]

What we call the self is, in fact, socially created. In the first part of the book, in South Africa, Rosa's inner speech is usually addressed to her drop-out friend Conrad. Later, in the French section, there's a good deal of straight talking to herself, but sometimes briefly she'll converse in her mind with Katya or with her lover, Bernard. Only in the final South African episodes are her thoughts addressed to her father: a connection is resumed.

The dominating consciousness remains Rosa's, and our sympathy with that sensitive, tough, self-mocking, occasionally bitchy voice organizes the novel. The other views distance the events, carry us quickly through his-torical time (in conversations with Burger's biographer), or allow us to see Rosa as well as see through her eyes. But the commentary on her thoughts and actions, the discovery of what she's really doing, has to be her own; and it's the absence of omniscient narrator here that makes the moments of inner climax dramatic and astounding.

Thus at the opening of the novel, when Rosa as a schoolgirl stands out-side the prison gates with comforts for her mother, the description we're offered is at first strictly external, the impersonal view of surveillance or of her headmistress. Fourteen years old, a "promising senior" in her brown and yellow school uniform, she's small for her age, "slightly bottle-legged (first hockey team)," with a strand of her hair "bleached lighter due to contact with chemicals in the school pool (second swimming team) and exposure to the sun." Such details imply the contrast between what might reasonably be her preoccupations at that age and what, for Burger's daughter, they have to be. At school, we're told:

> Her matter-of-fact and reserved manner made it unnecessary for anyone to have to say anything—anything sympathetic—indeed, positively forbade

it, and so saved awkwardness. She displayed "remarkable maturity"; that, at
least, without being specific, one could say in the report. (p. 9)

Contrasted with this, in the next brief shot, an emotional sympathizer
describes "little Rosa Burger . . . dry-eyed and composed . . . an example to us all of the way a detainee's family ought to behave" (p. 12). But
the ironic inner voice of Rosa herself immediately places this as the view of
a sentimental amateur, "a grown-up who made me feel older than she
was" (p. 15). For Rosa is by birth and training a professional revolutionary.
On her own initiative she brings a hot-water bottle, something her mother
never uses, so as to smuggle in a note twisted round the stopper. In
secret—neither surveillance nor sympathizers will know this—she's cop-
ing with bad adolescent menstrual pain: that's the extra suffering that
sticks in her memory. Here, as throughout the novel, we're reminded that
these highly articulate, intelligent activists live not only through the brain,
but like anyone else, physically and sexually from the waist downward.

Through Conrad, the hippie student she partly lives with in a casual in-
termittently sexual relationship during her father's trial and life sentence,
Rosa's inherited values are forced onto the defensive. Freedom, to him, is
wholly individual and asocial, the right to do your own thing. Parents and
their values are part of what you reject or escape from. (His own mother
had a lover: he hated and desired her.) As for Rosa, she's grown up entirely
through other people, he tells her, doing what they told her was appropriate: rationality, extraversion. "Life isn't there."

> Among you, the cause is what can't die. . . . It's immortality If you can
> accept it. Christian resignation's only one example. A cause more impor-
> tant than an individual is another. The same con, the future in place of the
> present. Lives you can't live, instead of your own. You didn't cry when your
> father was sentenced. I saw. People said how brave. Some people say, a cold
> fish. But it's conditioning, brainwashing: more like a trained seal, maybe.
> (p. 52)

Conrad, of course, speaks for many young radicals of his and Rosa's generation. And while she effectively answers him back, at deeper levels the
conflict goes on in her mind, fueled by the feelings of guilt that so often
goes with bereavement:

> When I was passive, in that cottage, if you had known—I was struggling
> with a monstrous resentment against the claim—not of the Communist
> Party!—of blood, shared genes, the semen from which I had issued and the
> body in which I had grown. . . . My mother is dead and there is only me,

there, for him. . . . Only me. My studies, my work, my love affairs must fit in with the twice-monthly visits to the prison, for life, as long as he lives—if he had lived. . . . And now he is dead! . . . I knew I must have wished him to die. (p. 62)

All her life has been geared, as she now sees it, to her parents' commitment. Before she'd ever had a real love affair she had to pretend to be engaged to a prisoner, a boy with Frelimo links, so that she could use the fiancée's privilege of letters and visits to keep him in touch with the movement. The pretended feelings became, on her side, desperately real: but if her mother realized Rosa's passionate involvement "she didn't choose to see." Released, the boy left South Africa at once; she didn't meet him again. Recalling that time, Rosa accuses both her mother and father.

At the initial crisis of the book she refuses—for the first time in her life—to do what "the faithful" expect of her. She has recently renewed contact, illicitly, with her father's old friends and comrades, the house-arrested Terblanches. Just afterward their daughter seeks Rosa out to ask her to borrow her firm's key to the photocopying room, so that they can get a duplicate made and print leaflets there. Rosa won't do it. Even more of a break with the tradition—she explains to Clare Terblanche *why* she won't. She's no longer prepared to conform, to sacrifice everything to The Future that never comes, and that might be unfree and repressive if it did. Dismissing Clare's arguments (which she knows already), Rosa notes her snuffling ungracefulness, her lack of sexual charm—irrelevant logically, but a kind of retaliation for her own sense of guilt.

The relationship with the older Terblanches is wonderfully done, and crucial for the novel. They are incontrovertibly good and heroic, in terms of action and selfless service to their cause (both have been in prison). They are also, as Rosa at this point sees them, ungraceful, uncharismatic physically aging, mentally inflexible, as parents demanding, as friends tactless. The mixture of feelings—love and admiration, fear and recoil, as from something threatening—permeates the precise physical observation which allows Rosa to see *the cause* separate from the deep emotional commitment to her own parents:

> Like many people who have high blood-pressure, Ivy Terblanche's emotions surfaced impressively: her voice was off-hand but her eyes glittered liquid glances and her big breast rose against abstract-patterned nylon. Lionel Burger once described how, when she was still permitted to speak at public meetings, she "circled beneath the discussion and then spouted like some magnificent female whale." (p. 107)

The passage implies more than it states. Ivy is aging and unattractive, her cloths cheap and ugly, her rhetoric out of date. Yet her courage and persistence are beyond praise. And the charming, civilized voice of Rosa's father—accepting and valuing her, yet able to place her with saving humor—is no longer there to distance her demands.

> In the enveloping acceptance of Ivy's motherly arms—she feels as if I were her own child—there is expectance, even authority. To her warm breast one can come home again and do as you said I would, go to prison. (p. 114)

Dick is even more touchingly heroic. An old sheet-metal worker, in solitary he couldn't remember poems as some prisoners could, to keep his mind occupied, so instead he carved in his imagination a whole dining-room suite, "barley-sugar uprights, with round knobs on top . . . man, it was craftsmanship" (p. 107). And it's he who hints of hope:

> Not long now, Rosa. Angola will go, Mozambique; they won't last another year. . . . Too late for Lionel, but you're here, Rosa. (p. 108)

But Rosa isn't with him (ironically, since the reader must know that Angola and Mozambique *did* "go"):

> Dick, with those ugly patches on his poor hands, said to me like a senile declaration of passion: we are still here to see it. He thought I was overcome at the thought of my father. But I was filled with the need to get away as from something obscene—and afraid to wound him—them—by showing it. (p. 111)

His still-passionate optimism seems grotesque to her because the world in which the unquestioning belief of these old Communists was formed the confidence that shines from their faces in Moscow peace conference photographs of the 1940s and 1950s—no longer exists. It's not only the bitterness of one defeat after another that makes it all seem obscene. Even more, it's the question from a girl brought up to feel public tragedies as acutely as personal ones—after Hungary and Prague, what can one still believe?

> When the Russians moved into Prague my father and mother and Dick and Ivy and all the faithful were still promising the blacks liberation through Communism, as they had always done. Bambata, Bulhoek, Bondelswart, Sharpeville; the set of horrors the faithful use in their secretely printed and circulated pamphlets. Stalin trials, Hungarian uprising, Czechoslovakian uprising—the other set that the Liberals and right-wing use to show it isn't

possible for humane people to be Communists. Both will appear in any biography of my father.

In 1956 when the Soviet tanks came into Budapest I was his little girl, dog-paddling to him with my black brother Baasie, the two of us reaching for him as a place where no fear, hurt or pain existed. And later, when he was in jail and I began to think back, even I, with my precocious talents for evading warders' comprehension now in full maturity, could not have found the way to ask him—in spite of all these things: do you still believe in the Future? The same Future? just as you always did? (p. 115)

The contradiction is unresolvable. Yet she does not find it easy to break her commitment to the Terblanches and her childhood, harder still to give up the sense of unity and solidarity directly with black militants. How hard, we feel when she embraces Marisa Kgosana, friend of her father and ANC leader, met by chance in a department store. Just back from visiting her jailed husband on Robben Island, Marisa is trying out the face cream "being rubbed on to her plum-dark skin with one white finger" by an admiring saleslady (who assumes the beautiful black woman must be a visitor from the *French* islands). Her dignity is complete and relaxed. She doesn't even need to be physically faithful like Penelope: one lives as one can. Restriction and surveillance are a different matter if one comes from Soweto:

> The comfort of black. The persistence, resurgence, daily continuity that is the mass of them. If one is not afraid, how can one not be attracted? . . . Marisa and Joe Kgosana have all this to draw on. . . . Behind *our* kind, who are confined to the magisterial areas of the white suburbs, are people who sent obscene letters calling my father a monster. (p. 143)

It wouldn't take much to draw Rosa into that orbit, as she realizes when she goes, illicitly, to a party in Soweto. "I felt a dangerous surge of feeling, a precipitation towards Marisa . . . a longing to let someone else use me, lend me passionate purpose, propelled by meaning other than my own." She's saved from that by the young Black Consciousness activists she meets at the same gathering, who are hostile to all whites, including herself. The sincerity and sacrifice of people like her father, so admired by the older generation of blacks there, is rudely ignored or rejected by the younger, who have no experience of any joint struggle with whites (the stricter apartheid laws have seen to that). Although theoretically Rosa understands their bitterness, emotionally their reaction makes it easier for her to apply secretly for a passport (something none of "the faithful" would ever do, except on orders) and to leave South Africa, perhaps only for a holiday, perhaps for good.

Everything experienced up to now contributes to this step. The kindness of well-off liberals like Flora Donaldson, who "fellow-travels beside suffering as a sports enthusiast in a car keeps pace alongside a marathon runner"; the complacency of the new African small-business people; the old man found insanely beating a donkey to death, whom Rosa dared not hand over to the police because he's black—after all this, "I don't know how to live in Lionel's country." In the end, she goes to Europe to defect from him.

The south of France scenes are perhaps less convincing. Katya and her friends—aging beauties, warm-hearted courtesans a little past it, homosexuals running gay bars, handsome young lovers bought by rich Americans—have charm enough, but scarcely the substance to sustain their part in the novel. They can't provide a strong enough image of what's attractive in European civilization, even a decaying civilization, to suggest that "whole world outside what Lionel lived for." And Katya herself, still in middle age living sensuously for sunshine and nightingales, is perhaps too directly the mirror opposite of Cathy Burger, a dream-alternative mother who makes no demands and only wants the child to be happy in the enjoyment of sex and French cuisine.

But the weakness, if it is one, is peripheral. For the love affair, for which this is only the setting, is admirably rendered in all its sexual delight and ambiguity. Bernard Chabalier, young, sympathetic, and sensitive, is distanced not only from Rosa's particular South African experience, but from the need to act one's convictions which is more hereditary and enduring than the unquestioning conviction itself. The curious recent relation of many near-Marxist European intellectuals to the untidy and tragic political struggle has never been better shown. It's delicately suggested by Bernard's flippant description of the thesis on French colonialism he's writing:

> You choose something you hope someone else isn't writing about already. That's the extent of the originality. . . . If you are too topical, the interest will have passed on to something else before you've finished. . . . But the influence of former French colonists who've come back to France since the colonial empire ended—I haven't got a working title yet—that's something that will go on for years. I don't have to worry. (p. 272)

And when Rosa, fascinated by the theme, asks why he can't write a book, rather than a thesis, he answers frankly that he needs the Ph.D., or he won't get out of school teaching into a university job: "You don't know how careful we are, we French Leftist bourgeoisie." The space between thought and action seems to Bernard normal and natural for his kind. He lives within it, signing amnesty petitions protesting against the abuse of psychiatry in the Soviet Union and censorship in Argentina, giving talks on *France Culture*—"usually the sociological consequences of political questions—that sort of programme." For him, disillusion with the Future assumed as inevitable by the faithful produces not as agonizing conflict—as it must for Rosa Burger—but a freedom from responsibility for any future at all.

The contrast defines itself during a cosmopolitan intellectual discussion where Bernard attacks "the new anti-Sovietism of the Left" as still not sharp enough in condemning socialist illusions. "Socialism is the horizon of the world, but it's a blackout." Following up, an English parliamentarian rejects the entire socialist vision as "evil utopia":

> When rationalism destroyed heaven and decided to set it up here on earth,
> that most terrible of all goals entered human ambition. It was clear there'd
> be no end to what people would be made to suffer for it. (p. 295)

Suddenly Rosa sees the whole group with amazement, and Bernard as one of them: "For a moment her presence went among them like an arm backing them away from something lost and trampled underfoot" (a poetic image that precisely conveys the emotional intensity of the political moment). She mocks their proposition—to her, absurd—that "you can't institutionalize happiness":

> There isn't the possibility of happiness without institutions to protect it.
> . . . I'm talking about people who need to have rights—*there* in a statute
> book, so that they can move about in their own country. (p. 295)

"Oh well, ordinary civil rights. That's hardly utopia." In conceding her point they dismiss it. But Rosa carries it further, as if seeing for a moment the relations of things:

> "But the struggle for change is based on the idea that freedom exists isn't it?
> That wild idea. People must be able to create institutions—institutions *must*
> *evolve* that will make it possible in practice. That utopia, it's inside
> . . . without it, how can you . . . act?"—The last word echoed among
> them as "live," the one she had unconsciously substituted it for. (p. 296)

But although the distance between the lovers, instinctive as well as rational, has been tellingly established, it's not at this point that the love affair gives out. (Gordimer is too subtle an observer for that.) Indeed Rosa is so much physically in love (as she never was with Conrad) that Bernard's honesty doesn't seem to break what's between them, even when he tells her:

> I want to say to you—you can't enter someone else's cause or salvation. Look at those idiots singing in the streets with shaved heads a few years ago. . . . They won't attain the Indian nirvana. . . .—The same with your father and the blacks—their freedom. You'll excuse me for saying . . . the same with you and the blacks. (p. 297)

The way out opens into the personal life. For the time being the flow of feeling carries her on toward it with a sense of release—the more that it does not even require the public status and obligation of marriage. Yet this conversation prepares the way for the decisive confrontation of the book—one which, in its violent and overwhelming discharge of accumulated tensions, is even more deeply related to Henry James than are the delicate elaborations of style.

Rosa has not reacted, at any conscious level at least, against Bernard's dismissal of her heritage. Awaiting him in London, she feels free to make contact with the anti-apartheid circles she has avoided so long as she intended to go back to South Africa. At a social gathering of political exiles, black and white, she is the center of sympathy and moving speeches, as Burger's daughter. Ironically, at the moment when she's being publicly acclaimed, she has already opted out. And it's exactly at that point that she recognizes the little black boy Baasie ("little master"), with whom she shared a bed, a bath, and a father, until her parents were taken to prison and the children were split up. The meeting after twenty years is awkward, strained, but she presses her phone number on him. Later that night he rings her—angry and insulting—and the whole thing explodes in her face as he attacks not only Rosa but the memory of her father:

> Everyone in the world must be told what a great hero he was and how much he suffered for the blacks. Everyone must cry over him and show his life on television and write in the papers. Listen, there are dozens of our fathers sick and dying like dogs, kicked out of the locations when they can't work any more. Getting old and dying in prison. Killed in prison. It's nothing, it's us, we must be used to it, it's not going to show on English television. (p. 319)

> Whatever you whites touch, it's a takeover. . . . Even when we get free they'll want us to remember to thank Lionel Burger. (p. 320)

For Baasie has moved on. He's no longer the "little black kid" she remembers. His father too has died in prison, reported hanged with his own prison pants. Why should he want to know her? In his need to make his future he, even more than she, has remade and devalued the past. Her reaction is an intense contradiction of feeling—rage, nausea, desire to defend her father, revulsion and hatred of Baasie. "Impulses of cruelty" come "exhilarating along her blood vessels" as she snaps out one insult after another, accusing him of wanting money, implying that he ought to be in the bush with the Freedom Fighters, denying that either of them has the right to judge her father, "unless you want to think being black is your right." When it's finished, she's left with the overwhelming awareness of a commitment from which she will *never* be able to escape.

It's in the shock after this experience that her thoughts, for the first time in the book, become conversation with Lionel Burger himself. The effect is startling and strangely moving. What she strives for above all is his cool rationality. Her father would have understood Baasie's anger as a phase in the growing movement, never retaliated in a way she herself now feels to be "filthy and ugly." And now, inevitably, she has to go back. The idyll with Bernard, perfection of a kind, is never mocked. Simply, she realizes that "no-one can defect."

The change we feel when she returns to South Africa, however, isn't only in Rosa but in the political situation itself. For the black people's movement, quiescent for years, suddenly bursts into action on a vast and unexpected scale. No longer fighting the bond of feeling she inherited from her father, Rosa passionately observes and interprets as if for him the Soweto school riots of 1976, where tens of thousands of black children protest against the inferior education (compulsorily in Afrikaans) that sums up their oppression by whites in their own country. In a way Lionel couldn't have foreseen, the children are radicalizing the parents; yet such unforeseeable transformations are the essence of his vision. As Rosa herself puts it, "the real Rosa [she means Rosa Luxemburg] believed the real revolutionary initiative was to come from the people: you named me for that."

The children's protest, even if it's still blindly antiwhite, in its courage recalls Lionel Burger. It liberates Rosa from the sense of futility and mere habit in continuing her parents' work. Whatever was mechanically copied from older generations has to be relearned; the role of whites in the movement can't be the same as in the past. Yet they have to be there: "Like everyone else, I do what I can."

As a physiotherapist Rosa helps to rehabilitate black children smashed up by the police. And secretly she renews contact with Marisa Kgosana and the black activists in Soweto. Before long continuity asserts itself in another way; she's arrested without charges, perhaps to be used in a big political trial of Marisa herself. Rosa, Clare Terblanche, and Marisa are all held in the same prison. The sympathizers standing outside the gates provide visits and parcels on her behalf, as she did for her mother at the beginning.

The ending is still in some degree open; for Nadine Gordimer deliberately presents the reader with a fine balance between despair and difficult hope. It would be possible to see what happens to Rosa as simply the working out of an Oedipal fixation, a tragic inability to free herself from her father's deluded shadow and to live. Yet we learn through indirect report that even in solitary confinement she's in touch with the others. Marisa sings hymns and pop songs that can be heard outside her cell: she develops a mysterious spinal ailment for which Rosa is allowed to give her physiotherapy: "Laughter escaped through the black diamond mesh and bars of Rosa's cell during these sessions." The symbolic sensual contact of black and white is reestablished. As for Rosa herself, her only permitted visitor, the maligned but loyal Flora Donaldson, testifies, "She's all right. In good shape. She looked like a little girl. . . . about fourteen. . . . except she's somehow livelier than she used to be. In a way. Less reserved." One would have to bring an irremovable set of responses (Conrad's perhaps?) not to feel some renewal of hope.

To represent a revolutionary hero is in some ways a particularly difficult thing for the novelist, and just painting in a few warts is no solution. For here the simple one-to-one equation of radical politics and immediate everyday human motive no longer operates. "I am not a politically-minded person by nature," says Nadine Gordimer." I have come to the abstractions of politics through the flesh and blood of individual behaviour, I didn't know what politics was about till I saw it happening to people."[7] But if the novel is to be a novel and not a tract, how does the writer depict a character who, as well as being a humanitarian activist, is a leader who has to deal with "the abstractions of politics"? For the fully committed revolutionary leader doesn't simply *experience* racial oppression and class conflict spontaneously, as personal material fact, on the time scale of his single human life. He must also perceive what's outside himself and analyze it rationally, conceptually, in the lives of others as in his own, in order to intervene in history, knowing that the time scale of change he must consider spans many generations. And it's this quality in her father to which Rosa finally and unsentimentally returns—the same habit of analysis of our kind," the "sweet lucidity" which gives him, in the face of all that can be done to him in the moment, a sublime calm.[8]

That people can rule their lives like this gives them, to outsiders like Conrad, Katya, or in the end Bernard, a chilling quality that's slightly unreal. For the reader living in a less extreme situation, the stance could easily seem priggish. Yet in a novel about this particular (and far from unique) history, it is, I think, convincing—and not only because of the known analogies between the heroism of Lionel Burger and that of real-life leaders like Bram Fischer or Nelson Mandela, on which it's partly based. What impresses in Burger's life, as in his speech from the dock (the only time we hear his voice), is not a blind faith, but a reasoned though fallible one based on the best available evidence; not a heroic adventurist gesture but a calculated risk; not the courage of one man alone but that of thousands. His daughter sums it up:

> Who among those who didn't like your vocabulary, your methods, has put
> it as honestly? Who are they to make you responsible for Stalin and deny
> you Christ? (p. 349)

Even on the Left different readings are possible. The oddest critical view of *Burger's Daughter* I have read is that it "has nothing to say," is not revolutionary, and hardly deserved the honor of being banned in South Africa. (The chairman of the censors, rescinding the ban, said almost the same thing.)[9] But of course a political novel, if it's any good, is not as a rule political in the same way as a pamphlet or a treatise. Its effect is diffused and tends to operate more slowly, at different levels and over a longer period. Nadine Gordimer herself said of this book, "I don't have any intention in the way [the censors] say I do. I'm not preaching, I'm exploring." To do that, in the fearless sense she understand it, is commitment enough.

Notes

1. *African Writing*, lectures given at the University of Cape Town's Public Summer School, Feb. 1972 (Cape Town: Board of Extra Mural Studies, University of Cape Town, 1972).

2. R. F. Haugh, *Nadine Gordimer* (New York: Twayne, 1974).

3. Indeed it could be argued that as novels they have almost *too* much unity: that *every* detail is relevant to the central meaning, as in the short story it must be, and we miss something of the randomness and oddness of the world we know, where some details matter and others are merely there, uninterpreted, relevant perhaps to some other story about different people—an effect which partly

depends on the sense of space and openness one gets from *War and Peace* or *Anna Karenina*.

4. Nadine Gordimer, "A Writer in South Africa," *London Magazine* 5, no. 2, May 1965.

5. Author's introduction to *No Place Like* (Harmondsworth, England: Penguin, 1975), p. 12.

6. This and subsequent quotations are taken from *Burger's Daughter* (London: Cape, 1979).

7. "A Writer in South Africa."

8. Bray, the hero in *A Guest of Honour*, achieves this kind of rationality, though it doesn't save his life. Max, the young saboteur-betrayer in *The Late Bourgeois World*, who lacks it, is consumed by a personal need for recognition which makes him a traitor and destroys him in the end.

9. The novel was banned by the South African censorship board in June 1979 on the grounds that "the authoress exploits the black-white dichotomy in South Africa for political ends. The negative is stressed; the positive ignored." In October 1979 the Publications Appeals Board lifted the ban, the chairman, a former judge, commenting afterward that the book was "very badly written. . . . this is why we eventually passed it. We knew our people wouldn't read it anyway" (from feature article in *Observer*, 23 Mar. 1980).

What the Book Is About

NADINE GORDIMER

◆　　◆　　◆

A.　The treatment of the theme is undesirable.—Publications Control Board

The theme of my novel is human conflict between the desire to live a personal, private life, and the rival claim of social responsibility to one's fellow men—human advancement. Through the personage of Rosa Burger, the question is posed and explored: What is a meaningful life? Is there a cause greater than the gift of life itself? Can one fulfill oneself simply by earning a living, falling in love, marrying, and producing the next generation, with no concern for anyone outside the family circle? Conversely, can one fulfill oneself while sacrificing personal emotional preoccupations, ambitions, joys, and sorrows— what is generally accepted as the pursuit of happiness— to the selflessness exacted by faith in a cause greater than oneself?

This conflict is central to civilized man's existence. It contains, for example, the essential challenge of Christ's teaching. It is basic to Freud's view of the problems of human existence.

The theme came to me as a question: What is it like to be the daughter of a hero, in a country where social strife still produces the hero figure, that is, the man/woman who has no regard for his/her personal fate and will endanger his/her life for what he/she believes is the good of others? Since fiction writers can only express what is already *there*, available to the creative imagination, in the substance of their society, it was as natural for this aspect of the theme to occur to me as it is for writers in other countries, where everyone has long had access to constitutional means to resolve social injustice, to deal with the theme in the person of the antihero *their* type of society has produced.

Rosa Burger (the principal character in my novel) is born to a white couple who are prepared to sacrifice personal freedom, safety, security, and the ordinary pleasures of life to change South Africa into a nonracial society where the color bar will be abolished. They accept unquestioningly that their daughter will inherit their values and make the same sacrifice; from the time she is a small child, they do not hesitate to make use of her in the service of their cause, whatever consequences this may have for her private needs and the development of her personal identity.

The form taken by the theme is the way in which the challenge of special responsibility is met, first by Lionel Burger and his wife, then by their daughter, Rosa. Lionel and Cathy Burger are Communists; —Lionel Burger dies in prison while serving a life sentence as a political prisoner, convicted for revolutionary activities in collaboration with the African National Congress. Part of Rosa's self-searching into the nature and worth of the identity that has been imposed upon her examines reasons why a young white Afrikaner of good family, such as her father, should, in the 1920s and 1930s, have felt it necessary to join the Communist Party. During that period it was a legal party among others; why should a white youngster whose ordinary daily experience, from childhood, had shown him that blacks were unjustly treated and humiliated and that he himself, in his white privilege, was party to that humiliation, have been unable to find another political home? Another political party where blacks would not merely be legislated *for* (even if with goodwill), but envisaged as equals entitled to take part in the lawmaking and governing process of the country?

There was at that period no political party other than the Communist Party whose policy reflected these requirements. By the time Rosa Burger grew up there was no legal party at all which did so.

Throughout the book Rosa probes critically the consequences of her father's decision, and its effect on his public and private morality. For example, she passes through a period of resentment against the way in which she was used to keep contact with a political prisoner by being sent to visit him in prison as his fiancée, while her own feelings, as a young girl in love with a man who saw her simply as an emissary, were not understood, or were ignored by her parents. She reflects on the obligation of her father and his associates, as party members during the 1930s, to accept the purges, liquidations, forced labor, and imprisonments in the Soviet Union, as contemporary South Africans are expected to accept the shooting at Sharpeville and in Soweto in 1976, the detentions without trial, and the forced removals of black communities under the Group Areas Act. She reflects on the inadequacy, for her, of her father's philosophy—presented to her since childhood as the complete answer to existential problems—to deal with the awesome fact of mortality, as she experiences it through the death of a tramp in a park. She seeks objectively to rediscover Lionel Burger for herself as a whole man, not merely a Communist leader, or her beloved father; as a complete human being—warts and all—whose contradictions and weaknesses do not need to be denied in order to grant him, as she does finally, nobility of character, measured against the extraordinary and terrible demands of his time and his country, and the various ways in which others, who revile him, have failed to meet them.

A political novel explicates the effect of politics on human lives and, unlike a political tract, does not propagate an ideology. Rosa's character, actions, and reactions have been shaped by the political choice of her parents, and the kind of life this inevitably implied; therefore this is a political novel from the point of view of the material it deals with. The society in which Rosa is shown growing up, and living as an adult, is one in which many different kinds of people interact according to a wide variety of private mores and public ideologies; therefore this is a novel of ideas. A romantic love story or an adventure story deals with a narrow, confined area of human existence; the novel of ideas seeks to explore concepts of the meaning of life and its social ordering—the ideas men live by. During her stay in France, Rosa Burger meets people who confront her with this world of ideas in art and philosophy, as well as politics—beyond the political obsessions of South Africa. She experiences an alternative life to the one she has known.

Rosa Burger is not drawn into the Black Consciousness movement "through the activities of her parents"; indeed, she is not "drawn into" the movement at all, and as a white, could not be accepted in it. Both parents were dead before the movement (as a matter of chronology) came into being, and, had they lived, it would have been ideologically inconsistent for them, as Communists, to espouse the movement. She leaves South Africa, having obtained a passport from an influential *verligte* Afrikaner (who sees her father as a hero figure, if, from his point of view a tragically mistaken one) in an attempt to defect—not only from radical political involvement, but from the necessity to face the fact of human suffering under political repression. Abroad, she finds evidence that another kind of suffering—

loneliness, old age, death (like the death of the tramp in the park)—is the inescapable end of those, like her father's first wife, who seek to hide away in the consolations of the wholly private life, absolving themselves of the imperatives of social responsibility. Ultimately her politics are that since suffering cannot be escaped, it must be fought where and how it can be. If she has to choose between passing the time pleasantly until she is forced to face the animal suffering of her own old age and death, or taking up the challenge of fighting the kind of suffering, imposed by man upon man, that one must believe (if one believes in man) can be overcome, the meaning of existence for her is in the latter choice. After a devastating telephone conversation with a black man who once was her childhood companion in her father's house—a confrontation in which each betrays the relationship of the past in the bitter deterioration of the contemporary situation between black and white which has been their inheritance—she returns to South Africa because that is *where she believes she is most fully alive.*

She goes back to her work as a physiotherapist in Baragwanath Hospital, teaching people how to walk again, and it is from there that she experiences the human consequences of the events in Soweto in 1976. She is detained in 1977 as many other people were whose history and associations made them suspect. When she is about to be brought to trial on a charge of complicity in the student revolt, it is with the wife of an ANC leader imprisoned on Robben Island. It is clear that she has taken some political action, but whether she succored and aided black students out of allegiance to her father's old ally, the ANC, or in support of the Black Consciousness movement, is not clear. What is certain is that in taking up the burden of other people's suffering through revolutionary political action, she has acted in her own name and her own identity, rather than the family tradition.

I make no apology for creating characters and situations that are as truthful an imaginative evocation of South African realities as my abilities can achieve. There are no "goodies" and "baddies" among the many characters; both blacks and whites represent a full range of human qualities, which are never unmixed within the individual. The facts of life in South Africa are the foundation of this novel: there is a Broederbond, there was a Communist Party. Both are part of our history and will be reflected in our literature. There always have been and still are people who, once having accepted social responsibility and its logical consequence, political action, are torn in deciding how best to change the South African way of life which all now admit, to one degree or another, is unjust to blacks and must be changed. A minister of the present government, Dr. Koornhof, has even anticipated the achievement by declaring, "Apartheid is dead." This novel is about some of the kinds of people who long believed it ought to die.

B. *Section 47 (2) (a). Parts of the book are indecent, as well as offensive and harmful to public morals.*—Publications Control Board

Quoted are:

P. 70. ". . . as little Baasie and I had long ago performed the child's black mass, tasting on a finger the gall of our own shit and the saline of our own pee." (Baasie is a black boy and the godchild of Lionel Burger.)

For the record, Baasie is not the godchild of Lionel Burger.

Any child psychologist—and any parent who observes the development of his own children and remembers with honesty his own childhood—will confirm that young children commonly make such experiments in the process of exploring the functions of their bodies.

Therefore one can only conclude that (see the committee's parenthesis) it is the fact that Baasie is a black child and Rosa, his companion, a white one, which constitutes the "indecency," "offense," and "harm to public morals."

P. 126. "She looked the way I must have, when you described to me watching your mother and her lover fucking in the spare bedroom."

In context, the incident is recalled as something that profoundly shocked the person concerned. That shock is matched to the shock received by the girl, Clare Terblanche, when Rosa ridicules the type of clandestine political act the two young women are expected to perform by their Communist parents. There is no description of the sexual act referred to, at this point or anywhere else in the book.

C. *Section 47 (2) (b). Parts of the book are offensive to the religious feelings or convictions of a section of the inhabitants of the Republic.*—Publications Control Board

Quoted are:

P. 47. "One day when he was a kid Jung imagined God sitting up in the clouds and shitting on the world below."

The quotation comes from Jung's *Memories, Dreams, Reflections.* That book is not banned.

P. 153. "Always the same story, Mandela, Sisulu, Kgosana on Robben Island . . . same as Christians telling you Christ died for them."

In the context from which this fragment of dialogue is lifted, an African National Congressman is being viciously attacked for setting up Robben Island heroes as martyrs, hence the reference to Christ.

Somewhere in the committee's nine-page dossier it is categorically stated that the author is responsible (as an expression of her personal opinions) for all views, pro and con, expressed by her fictional characters. Yet here, as throughout, she is condemned by the committee for views expressed by one character, while a counterview, expressed by another character—often refuting a statement made by the first—is totally ignored by the committee.

D. Section 47 (2) (c). Parts of the book bring a section of the inhabitants of the Republic into ridicule and contempt.—Publications Control Board

Quoted are:

P. 11. "Bloody Boers, dumb Dutchmen, thick Afrikaners . . . they would go and lock up your mom."

Another case of selective quoting. The irony of the passage is absolutely clear, in context: the racially prejudiced English-speaking children don't seem to realize that Rosa is herself an Afrikaner.

P. 161. "Whites, not blacks, are ultimately responsible for everything blacks suffer and hate, even at the hands of their own people; a white must accept this if he concedes any responsibility at all. If he feels guilty, he is a liberal; in that house where I grew up there was no guilt because it was believed it was as a ruling class and not a colour that whites resumed responsibility."

The passage is inaccurately quoted. "Resumed" is substituted for the original "assumed."

Spoken by the character Rosa Burger, the first sentence is not a statement but an ironic comment on the fact that blacks blame whites for everything; and whether the white likes this or not he has to accept the consequence of conquest and overlordship. The second sentence deals with the question of guilt versus responsibility, and restates the well-known difference between the viewpoint of Communists and liberals.

P. 163. "When he goes for fruit, the kaffir gets the half-rotten stuff the whites won't buy. That is black."

Spoken by a young Black Consciousness disciple in the course of a heated polemical discussion—he is expressing in high emotion the kind of concrete experience that is symbolic of and true to the daily humiliations all blacks will testify to. The use of "black clichés," here as elsewhere is intentional, for authenticity. As Rosa Burger says (p. 328), "I've heard all the black clichés before. I am aware that, like the ones the faithful use ["faithful" refers to her father's comrades], they are an attempt to habituate ordinary communication to overwhelming meanings in human existence. They rap out the mechanical chunter of a telex; the message has to be picked up and read. They become enormous lies incarcerating enormous truths, still extant, somewhere." The speaker is represented, in this scene, as aggressive and arrogant, and his statements are often contested by other blacks.

P. 322. "Why do you think you should be different from all the other whites who've been shitting on us ever since they came?"

The context from which this sentence is lifted is a crucial telephone call in London in the small hours of the morning, when Rosa Burger is confronted with the accusations of Zwelinzima Vulindlela, who was the small black boy (Baasie) who lived with the Burger family when he and she were children. His father, an African National Congressman was a friend of and worked closely in political action with Lionel Burger, her father. The two young people have not seen each other for twenty years or more; their fathers have both died in prison. Zwelinzima resents the recognition abroad of her father as a hero of the Left, while there are "plenty of blacks" who have made the same sacrifice but who remain nameless in the world outside South Africa. He insinuates that Rosa feels her father's way of life exempts her from the general situation of whites as people privileged under apartheid laws. She, in her turn, taunts him with his living in London while other blacks are risking their lives as freedom fighters. Later, she is appalled and sickened by her own behavior and his, but she says: "What other meeting-place could there have been for us? There have been so many arrests, trials, interrogations, fleeings." All of this stands between the two young people and their old natural bond. They are presented as tragic victims of circumstance.

E. *Section 47 (2) (d). The book, seen as a whole, is harmful to the relations between sections of the inhabitants of the Republic.*—Publications Control Board

The book reflects the reality of relations, good and bad, between people who are divided by the sectionalism of a color bar.

F. *Section 47 (2) (e). The book is prejudicial to the safety of the State, the general welfare and the peace and good order. . . . The writer uses the characters in her book to propagate Communism.*—Publications Control Board

Quoted are:

PP. 24–28. Three quotations from the statement made in court, at his trial, by Lionel Burger. He is explaining why he became a Communist, and inevitably puts the Marxist interpretation on the solution of South Africa's problems of social injustice. If a character is a Communist, he must speak in character.

In another section of the book (pp. 173–91), the Nationalist, Brandt Vermeulen, expresses views and speaks in character as an Afrikaner Nationalist. Does this mean the writer uses him to propagate Afrikaner Nationalism?

P. 32. "Everyone there was fiercely proud of Lionel" (an outspoken Communist).

"Everyone" refers to his fellow Communists and friends, meeting after his address from the dock and his dignified acceptance of a sentence of life imprisonment.

P. 72. "My father [Lionel Burger] often quoted that other Rosa [Rosa Luxemburg]; although he had no other choice but to act the Leninist role of the dominant professional revolutionary, he believed that her faith in elemental mass movement was the ideal approach in a country where the mass of people were black and the revolutionary elite disproportionately white."

This is an accurate reflection of the thinking that might be expected of a Communist in response to the facts of the South African situation.

P. 91. "Lionel Burger told the court the Communist Party stood for the unity of workers regardless of colour. Communists had served the workers' cause by organising unskilled and semiskilled Africans, Coloureds and Indians, the largest and most neglected sector of the labor force, and through this achievement the Communist Party had made a unique contribution to racial harmony in a country constantly threatened by racial unrest."

Again, this is an accurate reflection, based on relevant documents of the period, of how Communists saw their function in relation to the black labor force and to the incontestable fact that a huge black labor force had neither the organization nor the legislative protection associated with Western democracy, to which South Africa claimed to belong.

P. 126. "The huge strikes of black workers in Natal with which her mother will have become involved even if they were spontaneous to begin with, these are an example of Lenin's observation that the people sense sooner than the leaders the change in the objective conditions of struggle. But the necessity for political propaganda remains."

Inaccurately quoted. Should read, "these are an example of Lenin's observation that the people sense sooner than the leaders the change in the objective conditions of struggle, yes."

The passage is lifted from the same chapter of the book as that quoted under B. Section 47 (2) (a), where Rosa is confronting Clare Terblanche with objective criticism of and skepticism toward their Communist parents.

P. 135. "Through blackness is revealed the way to the future. The descendants of Chaka, Dingane, Hintsa, Sandile, Moshesh, Cetewayo, Msilekazi and Sekukuni are the only ones who can get us there; the spirit of Makana is on Robben Island as intercessor to Lenin."

The context from which this passage is lifted is Rosa's probing of her own personal relationship to black people and, in particular, her beautiful friend, Marisa Kgosana. She contrasts the romantics' way of perceiving a sensual redemption in blacks (as childlike "primitives" who live instinctually and give full rein to emotions the way "emotionally repressed" whites cannot do) and the racists' way of perceiving personal fears through blacks (blackness representing the uncontrollable id without the repressive white superego), with her parents' politically determined attitude to blacks. Her parents would have categorized both romantic and racist attitudes as aspects of "false consciousness." She concludes: "But even in that house [her parents'] blackness was a sensuous-redemptive means of perception.

Through blackness is revealed the way to the future. The descendants of Chaka, Dingane, Hintsa, Sandile, Moshesh, Cetewayo, Msilekazi and Sekukuni are the only ones who can get us there; the spirit of Makana is on Robben Island *as intercessor* to Lenin" (my italics). She is interpreting the role of blacks through her parents' eyes. The passage is an imaginative reconstruction, by her, of the attitude *they* would have had to blackness.

P. 313. "The great men who had not lived to see oppression in Southern Africa breached . . . Xuma, Luthuli, Mondlane, Fischer, and of course Lionel Burger . . . the callousness and cowardliness of the Vorster government, keeping an ageing and dying man in jail . . . who asked nothing of Vorster less than justice for the people. The white racist government has stolen his body but his spirit was everywhere . . . in Mocambique; in this room, to-night."

The context from which these disconnected fragments are lifted is a speech in memory of Lionel Burger made at a gathering in London to welcome a Frelimo government delegation seeking economic aid from the British government. The tone and choice of phrase, etc., is what would be expected of an elderly flamboyant left-wing orator honoring a dead comrade.

As for the facts, the real people referred to along with the fictional Burger—Xuma, Luthuli, Mondlane, Fischer—are indeed regarded in South Africa as great men, by thousands of people—including whites—who are not Communists. After the (proven) treatment of political prisoners during the Vorster government indicted it more than any fictional selection of such incidents could be accused of doing.

2. [There is no number one in the original.—Ed.] *The idea of a revolution in South Africa is found throughout the book. It creates a psychosis of revolution and rebellion.*

The *idea* of the danger of revolution, if apartheid is not abolished through peaceful change, is publicly debated at all levels, including that of Parliament, throughout South Africa. If this is a "psychosis" (*OED*: any kind of mental affection or derangement; especially one that cannot be ascribed to organic lesion or neurosis) it already exists in the South African people and does not require to be "created" by the influence of any work of fiction.

P. 26. "But what we as Communists black and white working in harmony with others who do not share our political philosophy have set our sights on is the national liberation of the African people."

Lifted from the context of Lionel Burger's statement to the court, at his trial. See F. Section 47(2)(e). Burger is explaining why he became a Communist and puts the Marxist interpretation on the solution of South Africa's problems of social injustice.

P. 28. "Amandhla, Awethu" (Power to the people).

In the context from which this cry has been isolated, it comes from the black spectators in court when Lionel Burger goes back down to the cells after having received a life sentence. Anyone who has ever attended a political trial in South Africa has heard it, as it is the customary salute from blacks, despite the presence of the police, when prisoners leave the dock.

P. 79. "The revolution we lived for in that house would change the lives of the blacks who left their hovels and compounds at four in the morning to swing picks, hold down jack-hammers, etc. . . . building shopping malls and office towers in which whites . . . moved in an "environment" without sweat or dust. It would change the days of labourers who slept off their exhaustion on the grass like dead men, while the man died."

In context, this passage (here garbled from sentences and phrases picked from the text) is part of Rosa Burger's philosophical soliloquy on the failure of the Communist philosophy to meet the existential anguish of the fact of death. This is prompted by the discovery of a tramp, bolt upright, dead on a bench in the park where she is eating her lunch.

P. 112. "The defeat of the Portuguese colonial armies in Angola and Mocambique; the collapse of white Rhodesia; the end of South Africa's occupation of Namibia brought about by SWAPO's fighters or international pressure; these are what they're waiting for, as Lionel was waiting, in jail. Signs that it will soon be over, at last. The future is coming. The only one that's ever existed for them, according to documentation. National liberation, phase one of the two-stage revolution that will begin with a black workers' and peasants' republic and complete itself with the achievement of socialism." (Here again the communistic pattern is clearly evident—initially a civilian revolution followed by socialistic revolution.)

Of course the "communistic pattern is clearly evident." It could scarcely be otherwise, in the context from which this passage is lifted. Rosa has just visited the Terblanches, close associates of her father and veterans of the pattern of detention, imprisonment, banning orders, which dominates the lives of the Terblanche and Burger families. She is marveling, with some mixture of fear and distaste (they want to draw her back into political activism), at the way in which the Terblanches continue to live, giving up the present—which is all a human being can count on experiencing—for the future they believe in. She repeats to herself the revolutionary litany of which she is currently being reminded in a series of interviews, probing her father's life, by a writer who is researching a biography of Burger.

P. 124. "I began to recite a quiet liturgy. The people will no longer tolerate. The people's birthright. The day has come when the people demand."

In context, Rosa is taunting Clare Terblanche with the catch phrases of Communist rhetoric. See B. Section 47 (2) (a).

P. 126. "It is just as impossible to conceive of workers' power separated from national libera-tion as it is to conceive of true national liberation separated from the destruction of capitalism. The future he was living for until the day he died can be achieved only by black people with the involvement of the small group of white revolutionaries who have solved the contradiction between black consciousness and class consciousness, and qualify to make unconditional com-mon cause with the struggle for full liberation. . . . It is necessary for these few to come into the country secretly." An attempt is made here to reconcile the communists (who are con-cerned with the class war) with the Pan-Africanists (who are more concerned with the libera-tion of the Black race). Also refer to the reasoning on pages 163 and 164 where the entire rea-soning is subtle propaganda to reconcile Black consciousness with communism.

Again, the quotation is lifted from the context of Rosa's confrontation with Clare Terblanche. (See above note referring to p. 124, and also B. Sec-tion 47 (2) (a) when she taunts her with the "conformism" to the Left which is expected of them both, by their parents.) Again, she is repeating a litany of political orthodoxy, the policy the Communists worked out, over many years, in response to the South African situation both while theirs was a legal party and when it operated clandestinely. This policy has been published in political histories of South Africa. She repeats it by rote, so to speak. Beginning with the last sentence quoted, there is a change of tone in her monologue; it becomes derisory of the kind of activities expected to be performed by Clare and herself as (I quote Rosa) "the instruments of the struggle appropriate to this phase" (the 1970s). The portion not quoted by the committee continues as follows: "It is necessary for these few to come into the country secretly or be recruited within it from among the bad risks, romantic journalists and students, as well as the good risks, the chil-dren, lovers and friends of the old guard, and for them to be pinched off between the fingers of the Special Branch one by one, in full possession of their invisible ink, their clandestine funds. . . . Such things are ridiculous (like a child's 'rude' drawing of the primal mystery of the mating act) . . . only if one steps aside out of one's historically-determined role and cannot read their meaning." Rosa's entire monologue is torn, in a complex fashion that cannot be conveyed in brief excerpts, between skepticism and belief.

Pages 163 and 164 referred to are part of a long polemical argument, in Soweto, between middle-aged veterans of the African National Congress, young proponents of Black Consciousness, and a white journalist putting forward the Communist viewpoint.

As a novelist I am not interested in "reconciling" political ideologies, only with writing about human beings and representing through my characters as faithfully as possible their beliefs and concerns as, living among them, I observe these. If reconciliation of differing beliefs is the concern of anyone, this is given expression as a matter of fact.

Pp. 348–49. "The real Rosa [Rosa Luxemburg] believed the real revolutionary initiative was to come from the people. . . . This time it's coming from the children of the people, teaching the fathers . . . the ANC, BPC, PAC. . . . Who are they [the whites] to make you responsible for Stalin and deny you Christ?" Here revolution is stirred up.

In context, Rosa is speaking to her dead father on her return to South Africa after a period in Europe when she opted for a private life, eschewing social responsibility. The time is just after the Soweto Riots of June 1976. The uprising of students and schoolchildren was incontestably revolutionary, in that it demanded radical change, in the form of abolition of "Bantu education," which would mean that black children would have the same standard of education as whites. The uprising was put down by methods used to suppress an incipient revolution: the police shot, killing and injuring many people.

In the original, the final sentence does not follow on the first part of the quote, but comes from another paragraph. Rosa recalls how her father prophetically understood in his lifetime, long before the children rioted, what it was they were really asking for during the riots: "You know how it is they understand what it is they want. You know how to put it. Rights, no concessions. Their country, not ghettoes alloted within it, or tribal 'homelands' parcelled out. The wealth created with their fathers' and mothers' labour and transformed into the white man's dividends. Power over their own lives instead of a destiny invented, decreed and enforced by white governments." And she challenges those who condemned *him*—who surely lived with Christian compassion—for being a Communist, while they themselves did nothing to improve the lot of blacks, although they call themselves Christians: "Well, who among those who didn't like your vocabulary, your methods, has put it as honestly? Who are they to make you responsible for Stalin and deny you Christ?"

3. The standpoint of an unlawful organisation, the Soweto Students' Representative Council, is propagated. This is done through the document published on pages 346 and 347.

P. 347. "We the students shall continue to shoulder the wagon of liberation irrespective of these racist maneouvers to delay the inevitable liberation of the Black masses."

This pamphlet (p. 77/6/208) was declared to be undesirable within the meaning of section 47(2)(d) and (e) on 6 July 1977 (Government Gazette 5655 of 15 July 1977: Notice No. 1336).

Possession was also prohibited under section 9(3), and the prohibition was confirmed by the Appeal Board under section 9(5).

On 19 October 1977 the SSRC was declared to be an unlawful organization in terms of section 2 of the Internal Security Act, 1950 (Act 44 of 1950).

I reproduced this document because my stylistic integrity as a writer demanded it: it is a necessary part of the book as a whole. I reproduced it because it is sometimes essential, for the total concept of a work of fiction, to incorporate blunt documentary evidence in contrast to the fuller, fictive version of events. Rosa says of the document (speaking to her dead father), "The kind of education the children've rebelled against is evident enough; they can't spell and they can't formulate their elation and anguish. But they know why they're dying."

I reproduced the document exactly as it was, in all its naïveté, leaving spelling mistakes and grammatical errors uncorrected, because I felt it expressed more eloquently and honestly than any pamphlet I could have invented the spirit of the young people who wrote it.

4. The book contains several unbridled attacks against the authority entrusted with the maintenance of law and order and the safety of the State. P. 37. "His life sentence was served but the State claimed his body."

This refers to the fictional funeral of Lionel Burger, but it has happened in fact in the case of the death of at least one political prisoner. The family of

Abram Fischer was refused permission to bury him and his body was claimed by the state.

P. 337. "Christ! Apartheid is the dirtiest social swindle the world has ever known. . . . The chap had every right to use his compulsory service to take any information he could that would contribute to destroying that army and all it stands for." Such dissemination (even though by mouth of a character) contravenes the Defence Act.

Daily, in journals and newspapers and in the forums of the world, apartheid is called far worse things than the remark quoted above.

The second part of the quote is another example of selective quoting. The context is a dinner-table argument when a political trial involving a journalist turned activist, who is alleged to have tried to recruit a young national serviceman as a spy, is being discussed. The quote is a response to someone who suggests that "the proper course for that young man, if he was so repelled by the idea of serving in 'that army,' if it went so strongly against his principles, was to become a conscientious objector. . . . Not a spy. The liberal position was to oppose the present regime openly, not betray the right of the people of the country to defend themselves against foreign powers who wanted to take advantage of this situation." The academic argument ends as such things tend to, with the host offering a choice of liqueurs with the coffee.

5. The South African Police are placed in an extremely unfavourable light.

Once again, it has not needed any fiction writer to bring this about; it is the light in which many of their actions, testified to in the South African courts, have placed them.

P. 44. "Sipho said how when the police were loading the dead into vans he had to ask them to take the brains as well."

Refers to brains spilled from a man's smashed head. This fact was part of the sworn evidence at the Commission of Enquiry held after Sharpeville. See *Shooting at Sharpeville,* by Ambrose Reeves, published by Gollancz, 1960. Robert Maja being examined by Sydney Kentridge, p. 115.

P. 51. "When blacks were shot by the police, when people were detained, when leaders went to jail, when new laws shifted populations you'd never even, seen banned and outlawed people, those were your mournings and your wakes."

Black people shot by the police, detentions, imprisonments, the uprooting and removal of communities, bannings which outlaw people from normal concourse—all these are true facts of life in South Africa.

P. 133. "Bloody white bastard. Bloody police bastard."

Commonly used epithets in South Africa. Suppressing them in print will not unsay them.

P. 208. "The entire ingenuity from thumbscrew and rack to electric shock, the infinite variety and gradation of suffering by lash, by fear, by hunger, by solitary confinement . . . the camps, concentration, labour, resettlement, the Siberias of snow and sun, the lives of Mandela, Sisulu, Mbeki, Kathrada, Kgosana, gull-picked on the Island, Lionel propped wasting to his skull between two warders, the deaths by questioning, bodies fallen from the height of John Vorster Square."

Rosa has just encountered a drunken black man beating a donkey brutally and the image suddenly catalyzes all the other forms of suffering—the suffering that man inflicts on man—into an intense awareness of the problem of suffering itself, the pure phenomenon, gathering up in her mind the atrocities committed by East and West. Her contemplation of the central human fact of suffering—and possible responses to it other than her father's chosen one—preoccupies her throughout the book.

P. 342. "[The Police] also wounded anyone else who happened to be within the random of their fire." "At each successive burial black people were shot while gathered to pay homage to their dead or at the washing of hands at the house of the bereaved that is their custom."

These things are to be read in confirmed newspaper reports of the period; they occurred.

P. 344. "I can tell you . . . when it's dark I'm afraid to go across my yard to the lavatory. I never know when I'm going to get a bullet in my head from the police."

The quote is incomplete. The text continues: "or a knife in me from someone else." A Soweto resident is describing to Rosa the combination of lawlessness and police zeal that made Soweto doubly dangerous during the Soweto Riots.

P. 346. "Remember Hector Peterson . . . fell victim to Kruger's uncompromising and un-controllable gangsters of the riot squad." "Remember our crippled brothers and sisters who have been disabled deliberately by people who have been trained to disrespect and disregard a black man as a human being? Remember the blood that flowed continuously caused by wounds inflicted by Vorster's gangsters upon the innocent mass demonstrating peacefully."

These two pieces of student rhetoric are lifted from the context of the SSRC document I reproduced. See my response to item 3.

Since the minority report, asking that my novel be banned for possession in addition to sale and distribution, was not successful, I shall not trouble to answer the points made there. I leave the tenor of that report to speak for itself.

Still Waiting for the Great Feminist Novel

SUSAN GARDNER

✦   ✦   ✦

IN JULY 1979, Nadine Gordimer's novel *Burger's Daughter*—the story of a young Afrikaner woman from a Communist family, focussing on her personal and ideological rebellion after her father's death during life imprisonment—was banned for import and distribution in the author's country, South Africa. The Publications Control Board's accusations declared the book "undesirable" on every count under section 47(2) of the Publications Act of 1974.[1] Although a barrage of criticisms was fired at *Burger's Daughter* under each count, it was particularly damned under Section E, concerned with "the safety of the state, the general welfare, or the peace and good order." The director of publications commented:

> The writer uses the characters in her book to propagate communism. . . .
> The idea of a revolution in South Africa is found throughout the book. It
> creates a psychosis of revolution and rebellion. . . . The standpoint of an
> unlawful organisation, the "Soweto Students' Representative Council"
> is propagated. . . . The South African Police are placed in an extremely
> unfavourable light.[2]

Yet, three months later, *Burger's Daughter* was the first of several books by white writers selectively unbanned while most banned books by black writers (and many of these writers themselves) remained so. The director of publications had appealed against the decisions of his own committee; the Publications Appeal Board appointed three literary experts, one of them a professor of English at an Afrikaans-speaking university and one an expert on state security, to reassess the novel's potential impact or threat. In summary, the Publications Appeal Board concluded:

> Limited readership and considerable literary merit are extenuating circumstances in considering possible prejudice to the safety of the state. . . . No real possibility of harm to safety of state. . . . Book's effect rather counterproductive than subversive.[3]

The literary "experts" defended *Burger's Daughter* with rationalizations familiar in other literary and sociopolitical contexts where "literary quality" has been invoked on behalf of "obscene" or "subversive" material. The expert on state security (also from an Afrikaans-speaking university) reached these conclusions:

> Although I am no specialist in the field of English literature I can with reasonable certainty make two statements . . . firstly that this book definitely has a considerable amount of literary value and secondly that in this area it isn't totally above criticism. . . .
>
> Because of its nature and its degree of difficulty this book will be limited on the one hand to literary critics and on the other hand to people with a specific interest in subversive movements in South Africa.[4]

In view of *Burger's Daughter*'s radical theme, and such ham-fisted state intervention, it might be expected that many South African militant or left-wing groups would have welcomed *Burger's Daughter* and rallied to its defense. But its publication/reception history is conflict ridden and fascinating sociologically. International and domestic acclaim were also countered by hostility. Some reactions were crude personal attacks on Gordimer which, in their most sophisticated form, ignored or disregarded the crucial distinction between narratives that record specific fact and those which represent *what resembles* specific fact.[5] *Burger's Daughter* was thus deplored as a distortion of South African Communist Party history, which also profits from the sufferings of some of the prototypes (members of the Fischer, Roux, Bunting, and Simons families). This is a politicized, but still reductive, version of criticism Gordimer has encountered and countered before about fictional characters with some recognizable biographical features (see the preface to her *Selected Stories* [1975]).

Since accounts of the publishing history of *Burger's Daughter* have appeared elsewhere, however, and Gordimer's unceasing, uncompromising opposition to South African censorship as applied to *all* South African writers, black and white, is abundantly recorded,[6] I will discuss here a previously understated issue: the relevance of *Burger's Daughter* from a feminist perspective.

It is tempting to suspect that the South African state's suppression of numerous feminist books and articles—*Our Bodies, Ourselves, The Second Sex, Fear of Flying,* many lesbian novels—indicates an awareness of feminism's revolutionary challenge: that a transformation of sociosexual divisions and roles would result in and from a reordering of the political, economic, ideological, and psychological structures and relations of patriarchal capitalism. Some gender and class-related implications were, I believe, partially recognized during the 1960 prosecution of Allen Lane in England for releasing an unexpurgated Penguin edition of *Lady Chatterley's Lover* (only recently unbanned in South Africa). Such famous phrases as "Would you let your wife or servant read it?" "Would you leave it lying around the house?" point toward a feared breakdown in the social control of sexuality. Fiction, no longer dismissed as an ivory tower or leisure-time pursuit, can become a material, effective force when it presents alternatives to compulsory, monogamous, domesticated heterosexuality—especially if the work, mass-produced and therefore cheaper, becomes accessible to a wide reading public.

The banning of *Burger's Daughter* shared several features with the *Lady Chatterley's Lover* trial.[7] The novel was read as a transparent duplication of reality rather than as an imaginary probing of experience; investigation of a text changed to, in effect, putting author and characters on trial; elitist and classist presumptions prevailed that experts must advise a jury or panel of "normal, balanced, right-thinking and reasonable people" on what they can safely read.[8] Occasionally, a South African censor has discerned the radical significance of a feminist argument, as when a "Women in Focus" article in *Varsity,* a University of Cape Town students' magazine, was quoted as partial justification for banning the whole magazine in perpetuity. The article, "following the customary but somewhat extreme line adopted by militant women, claiming liberation in sexual matters, from the dominant role hitherto played by the male," was deemed "undesirable under the law" because it expressed controversial views in a manner "offensive, repugnant, painful or mortifying to the average standard of morality in South Africa."[9] In December 1981 Marilyn French's *The Women's Room* was the first book unbanned under the provisional imposition of an age restriction (over eighteen) on the sale and library lending of previously or potentially suspect material. *The Women's Room* was originally banned be-

cause of "extensive sex descriptions, a rape scene, and crude language"—
criteria hardly applied to the mass-circulating "mercenary" and "antiterrorist" pulp novels in South Africa.[10] Professor Van Rooyen, chairman of
the Publications Appeal Board, qualified this "liberalization":

> [*The Women's Room*] had literary merit and was "an uncompromising attempt
> at depicting the realities of the lives of married women in their relationships
> with men."
>
> Because of its "sombre and bitter tone," it would require "a concentra
> tion and perseverance that the average reader is not likely to give it." . . .
> The age restriction would be applied only to books "with a popular likely
> readership which have substantial literary or other merit."[11]

Gordimer, spotting as usual the contradictions and evasions inherent
in censorship policy, downplayed this latest relaxation, dubious about
whether it would mean greatly decreased censorship:

> I doubt this, especially regarding political books. If it means only that
> slightly sexy popular novels may be read by more people, then I don't think
> it is anything to get excited about.[12]

But in the case of *Burger's Daughter*, can we assume that the furore and
state action it aroused were due to a subversive feminist message or style,
however latent or realized in the author's intention, the text, and its reception? What is *Burger's Daughter*'s significance for feminists, whether writers or
readers?

To date, no feminist critique of *Burger's Daughter* has appeared.[13] But it is an
irritating, inspirational novel for feminist readers. Of obvious interest is the
heroine's attempt to differentiate herself from her patriarchal identity as
"Burger's daughter"—to become self-determining when her previous individual and social existences have been massively overdetermined by political factors (from both the Communist Party and the South African state).
By the end of the novel, however—as her mother is when it begins—she is
a political prisoner herself, and Gordimer has clearly indicated that this ending should not be read as a circular or passive development:

> It is clear that [Rosa] has taken some political action, but whether she suc
> coured and aided black students out of allegiance to her father's old ally the
> ANC, or in support of the Black Consciousness movement, is not clear.
> What is certain is that in taking up the burden of other people's suffering
> through revolutionary political action, she has acted in her own name and
> her own identity, rather than the family tradition.[14]

Another of *Burger's Daughter*'s major themes—Rosa's attempt to evolve a language to convey suffering and represent reality more adequately than any accepted rhetoric can encompass—is also of engrossing concern to feminists. A considerable body of speculation and investigation has now accumulated on the vexed question of gender-specific styles, themes, and forms. Virginia Woolf was one of the first feminist critics to entertain the possibility, in relationship to Dorothy Richardson's writing, of the "psychological sentence of the feminine gender." From a more strident position, Tillie Olsen and Adrienne Rich have criticized the "oppressor's language": an institutionalized set of largely male-created literary codes and conventions mastered by women but not originating from their specific experience and, therefore, not suitable to express their situation, or the forms of consciousness it fosters.[15] Rosa's search for a more comprehensive, flexible, and sensitive language has affinities with these currents.

An equally central concern for Gordimer has also been how to become an "Afrocentric" writer. From the beginning, her work has probed the double binds of her own class, race, and (to a more limited extent) gender marginality: the torment of not belonging to the country of one's birth, being rejected by the majority of its inhabitants and many of her own class, and not wishing to escape into exile. Here, however, I am considering *Burger's Daughter*'s interest for feminist fiction and criticism, formally and in their consciousness-raising aspects. Does *Burger's Daughter* increase women's understanding of their objective condition under patriarchal controls (over women's fertility, sexuality, children, property, persons)? Enable us to glimpse possibilities for changing it? In short, is Nadine Gordimer one of "our" writers?

THERE IS NO DOUBT that Gordimer does not regard feminist criticism as paramount for discussion of her work. She has consistently resisted categorization as a "woman writer" and has, instead, used "writer who happens to be a woman" (the way most women writers would like to be regarded but this remains utopian).[16] Acceding, it would seem, to what Tillie Olsen calls the "patriarchal injunction" ("If you are going to practice literature . . . divest yourself of what might identify you as a woman"),[17] Gordimer apparently regards "woman writer" as implying special but subordinate and segregated status. Nonetheless, Olsen has situated Gordimer's work in two important contexts: the characteristic antislavery tradition in women's writing and those few (but increasingly numerous) women with children who have achieved significant distinction in their craft. (Olsen does not emphasize enough—as any account of a white South African woman writer must—the enabling of time for writing by the institution of black women's domestic servitude.) Gordimer has claimed:

> My femininity has never constituted any special kind of solitude for me. Indeed, in that small town, walled up among the mine dumps . . . exiled from the European world of ideas, ignorant that such a world existed among Africans, my only genuine and innocent connection with the social life of the town (in the sense that I was not pretending to be what I was not, forever hiding the activities of mind and imagination which must be suspect, must be concealed) was through my femaleness. . . . Rapunzel's hair is the right metaphor for this femininity. . . . I was able to let myself out and live in the body, with others, as well as—alone—in the mind.[18]

In her review of Ruth First and Ann Scott's 1980 biography of Olive Schreiner, Gordimer reiterated her conviction that feminism (which she seems to regard as an exclusive, elitist movement) is marginal rather than central in the struggle for South African liberation. Schreiner's own "strongest motivation" is therefore discounted as insignificant to the fight against apartheid ideology and the racial capitalism it seeks to legitimate and perpetuate:

> The fact is that in South Africa, now as then, feminism is regarded by people whose thinking on race, class and colour Schreiner anticipated, as a question of no relevance to the actual problem of the country . . . to free the black majority from white minority rule. . . . in the South African context . . . the woman issue withers in comparison with the issue of the voteless, powerless state of South African blacks, irrespective of sex. It was bizarre then . . . as now . . . to regard a campaign for women's rights—black or white—as relevant. . . . Schreiner seems not to have seen that her wronged sense of self, as a woman, that her liberation, was a secondary matter within her historical situation.[19]

No politically concerned person could dispute that the majority of South Africa's oppressed peoples are African, Indian, and Colored, or that white women have been complicit in the exploitation of women and men from other groups.[20] Simultaneously, however, it is indisputable (as the pamphlet "Working Women in South Africa," published by the South African Congress of Trade Unions in London suggests) that gender saturates and exacerbates other forms of oppression:

> As the most oppressed and exploited section of the black population, the black woman worker is the lowest paid, works under the worst conditions,

carries out the menial and unskilled jobs, and has minimal opportunities to jobs, training and education. (p. 2)

A dialectical rather than polarizing awareness is needed to perceive the interrelatedness of women's and other liberation struggles, an issue fully discussed in Adrienne Rich's essay "Disloyal to Civilization: Racism, Feminism and Gynephobia" (1978). It is interesting also that Simone de Beauvoir's consideration of the same issue—Which should come first, national or women's liberation? Are they in fact separable? Should women be content to wait until "after the revolution"?—led her to an opposite conclusion from that of Gordimer: "Later means never." It is particularly important, in South Africa, *not* to reiterate, however unwittingly, the polarizing modes of thought which fragment perception of a society artificially divided and stratified.

But assuming that a feminist critic can only agree to disagree with Gordimer about the priorities of national and feminist liberation,[21] I shall now turn to aspects of *Burger's Daughter* for indications of a potential feminist awareness obscured by more conventional patriarchal writing codes. After looking at devices and assumptions which, rather than subverting these codes, tend to reinforce them, I shall suggest that the novel nonetheless has a discernible woman-concerned subtext which makes it a novel impossible for feminists to dismiss or ignore.

WHEN WOMEN HOPE for "the great feminist novel," they may be calling for a *Bildungsroman* with different thematic options to those the form (closely tied to the development of Western, bourgeois male subjectivity) has traditionally offered women: falling in love, going crazy, becoming a revolutionary. In the traditional *Bildungsroman*, the male protagonist defines himself over and against the public world of work and the emotional world signified by women, initially protesting against the dictates of bourgeois vocation and marriage. But Hegel concluded that while the hero might aspire to be "a new knight . . . who aims to punch a hole in [the] order of things," he ends with "getting the corners knocked off him. . . . In the last analysis he usually gets his girl and some kind of job, marries and becomes a philistine just like the others."[22]

Earlier experimental work by and about women such as Dorothy Richardson's *Pilgrimage* or Doris Lessing's *The Golden Notebook* and *Children of Violence*, embody various rejections and refusals: portraying women as stages and objects in the unfolding of male destiny (women as sign, representing qualities a male must suppress or conquer to attain social masculinity); producing female accounts imitating male experience; having their experience become the subject of case histories (therefore designated as pathological or deviant) written by others instead of the raw material of their own creative exploration.[23] Contemporary readers want depictions of women authoring their own destiny (insofar as anyone, male or female, can)—certainly without primary or sole reference to and identification with men—and writing their own stories. This demand may be realized in various literary forms, some of which have been feminist socialist realism and the *Tendenzroman* of the Marilyn French type; there has also been a resurgence of the *Bildungsroman* with markedly different aims of self-realization, as with the intriguing mix of confessional and picaresque in Lisa Alther's *Kinflicks.*

Burger's Daughter has the special interest for feminists of being—as Gordimer has said she discovered *after* writing it[24]—the *Bildungsroman* of a young woman who dissociates herself from a revolutionary political heritage that other fictional heroines strive to acquire: she then critically reclaims it, with all the implications and consequences of such a choice. Many abandoned storerooms, houses, and lovers' hideouts symbolize (as does the sign Streng Privaat on the door of one of them) her desire to lead a private life, especially after her father dies. This theme recurs in numerous female novels and (auto)biographies: What shall a woman do when she is "no longer the woman of my father's house"? (p. 85). But the final room Rosa inhabits is a prison cell, demonstrating that in her country (and elsewhere as well) there can be *no* separation of individual fate and social destiny. *Burger's Daughter* shows a woman rather passively accepting her familial and political inheritance after considerable resistance throughout most of the book's action. Her ultimate acquiescence is a renunciation (symbolized by cutting her hair, which she had allowed to grow during her escapist period in the south of France)—giving up a heterosexual love affair in a foreign country. This seems a stereotyped "alternative," but it is functional within the novel's terms: "I really do not know if I want any form of public statement, status, code; such as marriage. There's nothing more private and personal than the life of a mistress, is there? . . . Bernard Chabalier's mistress isn't Lionel Burger's daughter; she's certainly not accountable to the future" (p. 304).

But is Gordimer's portrayal of Rosa's life cycle and the phases in her coming to self-knowledge particularly innovative, a feminist-inspired or influential reworking of the *Bildungsroman* pattern? My general contention is that *Burger's Daughter* provides some change in the representation of female subjectivity, but hardly its subversion. A more definitive conclusion is difficult because of the novel's many narrators and implied addressees. A very close reading is essential to discern who speaks and who is the implied listener. Indeed, this is not always clear because of the *form* of *Burger's Daughter*: the purposes of such narrative strategies as Joycean punctuation; the usually unidentified (but identifiable) quotation and insertion of historical material; and the satirizing of South African society's abuses of language (radio reports, schoolmistresses' assessments, political jargon). The structural difficulty is compounded by the mode, vacillating between irony and inspiration. Nonetheless, and although confusing or equating the biographical author with signs of the author's presence in the text is one of the first pitfalls we learn to avoid, wielding the various ploys and stratagems we can only find Gordimer herself. So, although it would be reductive and futile to deduce Gordimer's personal consciousness from the novel's representational devices, I think it can be fairly asserted that her very choice of material and narrative resources is not accidental and is significant sociologically. To some extent she could have written otherwise (especially, I shall contend, in the representation of Rosa's own consciousness). And if it were unimaginable to her to do so in some circumstances, then *Burger's Daughter* can be read as an example of the sociocultural possibilities and limitations conditioning its author.

Connecting biological, psychological, historical, and mythical time has been a fascination for feminist cultural workers, as films such as *Amy!* and *Sigmund Freud's "Dora"* demonstrate. Markers such as maps, time lines, and titles superimposed on images relate the heroines' personal trajectory to the course of contemporary history. In *Burger's Daughter*, Rosa's coming of age is correlated with the increasing exploitation of Nationalist government policy. She is born in the month and year when it comes to power. Her painful early menstrual periods occur at approximately the time of the protest and massacre at Sharpeville. Her adolescence is marked by the treason trials. Her flight from South Africa takes place at the time of the fall of Mozambique. She comes to terms with her destiny as Cathy and Lionel Burger's daughter after the Soweto uprising of 1976.

The very title *Burger's Daughter* alerts us to double binds in Rosa's quest for self-definition. It indicates that she is a "named" person in more than the South African political sense because she is her father's daughter (a phrase she resentfully repeats five times in one paragraph). Not only is her psychology therefore patriarchal-incestuous, she is also the daughter and sole inheritor of a hero. Thus, when she considers ideological betrayal, she conceives of it as a defection from her father: personal and political are indeed at one here. She rebels in wholly typical fashion by embarking on several narcissistic and solipsistic love affairs. The first is with Conrad, who convinces her, after her father's death, that she is finally free to define herself without reference to social commitments (in the process, she begins to learn to "read," to "decode," and to "speak" on her own). The second is with Bernard Chabalier, a foreigner from the remote place ("Paris is a place far away in England," p. 56), which even as a child, Rosa associated with privacy and escape.

But Rosa is not only Lionel Burger's daughter. She is also the daughter of Cathy, "the true revolutionary," a relationship frequently alluded to but not developed. (In this structural and thematic aspect, *Burger's Daughter* is strikingly like Margaret Atwood's *Surfacing*, where the heroine is presented as searching for her father but achieves a greater self-knowledge when she imagines an encounter with her dead mother.) There are hints throughout that Rosa is not only seeking the signification of her father's life but also the meaning of her mother's. She is strongly and sensuously attracted to figures such as Marisa, the wife of a black political leader in life imprisonment, and Katya, her father's first wife, who *did* defect from Stalinist interference in personal relationships. There is a shared world of female experience, almost a subculture, sometimes present in the novel. But it is presented dismissively ("a harmless political activity" describes the interracial women's meeting at the home of the fellow traveler Flora Donaldson, a recurrent figure in Gordimer's fiction), unhopefully (black and white female interchanges at cross-purposes in Soweto), or—when it is a matter of potential sexual competition between Rosa and her childhood friend Clare—antagonistically. An exception is Rosa's seraglio-like exchange of information and confidence with Katya; perhaps the most compassionate passage in the book, from a feminist point of view, is about her: "When I saw you plucking the cruel beard from your soft chin, I should have come to you and kissed you and put my arms around you against the prospect of decay and death" (p. 304). The passages where Rosa and Clare quarrel about their ideological patrimony typifies the kind of writing Rich would say offers little threat to patriarchal norms and images concerning women. Rosa's triumph is symbolized by her sexual appeal to men: she has "a body with the assurance of embraces, as cultivated intelligence forms a mind. Men would recognize it at a glance as the other can be recognized at a word" (p. 121). Clare's flesh, however, is "dumb. . . . A body that had no signals; it would grow larger and at once more self-effacing. Few men would find their way, seek her through it" (pp. 121–22). Their confrontation culminates with a typical Gordimer motif as Clare disgustedly disposes of an ancient, used sanitary towel. Malaise before the physical fact and evidence of menstruation (more obviously a reproductive than a sexual function) occurs again in Gordimer's novel *July's People.*

Female sexuality is presented somewhat more positively in the sense that Rosa can obtain a kind of calisthenic gratification, but this is with the help of skilled male lovers. Her confidence to Bernard ("You are the only man I've loved that I've made love with," p. 308) is a telling comment on what heterosexual permissiveness has signified for her. Her sexual psychology prior to this affair is an extraordinary Aristotelian mishmash: she refers to "the semen from which I had issued and the body in which I had grown" (p. 62); "Why could not Noel de Witt and I have gone away to farm, to breed babies from me that would look like him" (p. 68); even during her mature affair with Bernard, a more objective narrator refers to "a child of his in her" (p. 289). The point here is not that Gordimer undoubtedly knows better, but that this is how she chooses to represent the sexual mentality of an adolescent girl from a socialist (and medical) family.

Rosa's female and sexual consciousness highlights what I view as the novel's implicit, structuring question and obsession. *Burger's Daughter* seems to me to be a development of Gordimer's first *Bildungsroman* and first novel, *The Lying Days* (1953), and to be asking, "What would it have been like if someone in my position—a woman from a white, middle-class, politically unconcerned family—had instead been the daughter of people like the Burgers?" As Gordimer has said in an interview with Ronald Hayman, "I was approaching a mystery. I know people who've lived that life [of political commitment and sacrifice] but I'm not one myself. . . . Rosa's being such a withdrawn person . . . It's been a slow process of moving towards the centre of someone like that. It's really an attempt from the outside, more than in any other book I've written."[25] Thus, while *The Lying Days* can be considered fictionalized autobiography, *Burger's Daughter* is speculative, fictionalized biography, a bourgeois fantasy about what it would have meant to be *that* kind of burger's daughter. The result is that a "foreign" female psychology has been injected into Rosa; it is probably more typical of women of Gordimer's class and generation, and is concentrated in Rosa's aspiration to be "ordinary," "a girl like any other" (again, a recurring phrase in Gordimer's work).

But what *is* "a girl like any other"? Can one conceive of "a man like any other"? (The nonequivalence of *girl* and *man* is no accident here, but typical of gender inequalities embedded within the English language.) The novel concludes that Rosa cannot allow herself a life of psychobiological immanence because of the political demands of her totalitarian society. But does this imply that, in less stringent circumstances, an innate, normally inescapable "femininity" would be available to her, and preferable? Has Gordimer universalized and abstracted sex in a way that she would not do with race, leaving her vulnerable to suspicions of sexual determinism? Does she confuse sex (a biological category) and gender (a social construct)? More positively, I should mention one very powerful image which translates an awareness of South African society's extreme objectification of women, black and white. An Afrikaner official possesses a plastic objet d'art which signifies "woman" by gross exaggeration of, and reduction to, her sexual parts. But the reiteration at all narrative levels (albeit with different degrees of ironic detachment) of sexist clichés suggests that Gordimer uses culturally pregiven stereotypes concerning sex and gender less critically and more carelessly than she would racial ones. Again, I am not suggesting that Gordimer endorses these, but that combating them was not her primary concern in *Burger's Daughter*. It does not ask about women what Tillie Olsen has called "the writer's question: Is this true? Is this all?" Otherwise some of its narrators—certainly Rosa herself—would use them with more discrimination and distance. Examples of such sexist *idées reçues* (here cited cautiously, because a mere listing cannot convey their different functions within the narrative) include the south of France section, which abounds in clichés about lesbians, homosexuals, gigolos, impotent men, and aging women (the intention is clearly to show that some aspects of the "alternative" private life which Rosa seeks are *no* alternative, little better than "the bourgeois fate, alternate to Lionel's: to eat without hunger, mate without desire," p. 117); one narrator's assurance that Rosa and Cathy, however revolutionary and committed, are beautiful and sexy; the bleak possibilities for female solidarity; the heightened valuation of heterosexual romance, presented as the most appropriate way for a "girl" of Rosa's socialist background to recover individual subjectivity (what Carolyn Heilbrun has referred to as "the exploration of experience *only* through sexuality, which is exactly where men have always told [women] that such an exploration should take place";[26] the assumptions that a woman needs a man to feel womanly and that a woman in love obviously can no longer spend much time with women; and that aging women, as their sexual attractiveness declines, are pitiable, and the frequent recourse to their biological disintegration as an image to convey that historical, as opposed to biological, suffering can and must be fought.

Burger's Daughter, I have argued, merits and repays feminist readings not only because of the fascination of its story, but because of its concern to reappropriate/renew language as a self-reflective means of investigating "reality" ("The old phrases crack and meaning shakes out wet and new," p. 348), but also because of the conservatism of so many of its techniques describing women's situational consciousness, conforming only too well to the processes described by Tillie Olsen in "Some Effects of Having to Counter and Encounter Harmful Treatment and Circumstances as a Writer Who Is Female."[27]

Moreover, the very element that some South Africans deplore—*Burger's Daughter*'s subjecting selected factual materials to fictive methods—could prove to be a valuable direction and technique for feminist (and other) writers. To be more precise, it travels an old road: one need only think of George Eliot's *Middlemarch* "quarry," Mrs. Gaskell's notebooks, and Charlotte Brontë's research for *Shirley*, to realize that Gordimer is renewing, not inventing, a typical storytelling process.

Equally important, Gordimer is extending the *Bildungsroman* further than the form has traditionally permitted. For the classical *Bildungsroman* of apprenticeship and adjustment, as Kaplan has shown with reference to a writer parallel to Gordimer in origin and development, Doris Lessing, has not only been an uncongenial form for women, but perhaps less flexible and relevant than it initially seems:

> If *Children of Violence* is really a *Bildungsroman* (and Doris Lessing defines it as such at the very end), Martha, its heroine, has always differed from the typical focus of that genre—the sensitive youth discovering individuality—in that her search was always associated with larger issues, such as racism, class conflict, and war. . . . Martha reaches the limits of self-concern: she discovers a social world, a political world, and a communal consciousness. Her individualism is tempered by worldwide movements, historical changes, and the coming end of known civilization. Long before her death, she is aware of her insignificance. And the very struggle for some kind of identity that is specifically female is left far behind.[28]

If, as Lessing and to some extent Gordimer have concluded, individual consciousness cannot be explored apart from its "relations with the collective" (Lessing's phrase), and the individual and society cannot be reconciled, the *Bildungsroman* becomes self-destroying. Gordimer's recognition of its inadequacy is signaled by the epigraph to *Burger's Daughter*—"I am the place where something has occurred" (Lévi-Strauss)—and by many of Rosa's reflections about the difficulties and indulgences of self-knowledge.

But if this is the case, a more inclusive and inventive form is needed. Daughters of the bourgeoisie as many feminists are, by birth and/or education, we must be concerned with any attempts to diversify and surpass culturally encoded narrative genres: as Michel Zeraffa has postulated, the "best" writers are betrayers of the bourgeoisie because the forms they work out translate their questioning or denial of its values. In some respects, the structure of *Burger's Daughter* reminds me of the explicitly feminist Cuban film, *One Way or Another*. This depicts the problems of socialist-feminist romance and links these to the social factors shaping the protagonists. Unabashedly presenting itself as "a film about real people, and some fictitious ones," it quotes historical documents, resorts to "intrusive" voice-overs, and allows some of the "real people" to play themselves and to improve, all while getting on with the open-ended story.

The difference is that *Burger's Daughter*, however discontinuous, is still seamless. It does not deliberately reveal the research and direct borrowings which entered into its final construction. Gordimer has never sought to hide how aspects of the novel were assembled and, in one interview about *Burger's Daughter*, she defined fiction as "fragments of fact recombined . . . and the essence of events, rather than the events themselves."[29] This is a far more subtle view than the criticisms mentioned at the beginning of this paper, for Gordimer is undoubtedly aware of the fictive/feigning qualities of all narrative—even manifestos, broadsheets, polemic. Any novel, however obliquely, is an imaginary transposition and projection of some immediate materials which were "always already" ideological, and then refashioned. From this perspective, Gordimer's representation and exploration of post-1948 South Africa is no more ideological, partial, or deceptive than anyone else's; perhaps less so precisely because it wrestles with the problems of knowledge and language. But her novel *July's People*, by taking place in the near future, frees her from the necessity to acknowledge fact while telling a story. Fantasy, allegory, and science fiction can resolve the tension between history and story that unbalances *Burger's Daughter* by simply dissolving one of the terms (thus it is engrossing to observe that several South African novelists—Lessing, Jacobson, Gordimer, and Peter Wilhelm—are now writing "in" as well as "for" the future). But further evaluation of the synthesis of fact and fiction in *Burger's Daughter*, and a more insistent probing of the function or necessity for its feminine rather than feminist values, should lead readers to ask how else the fictions that feminists crave could tell the stories waiting to be told in our time. What would a consciously feminist Rosa have been like? How would her story then have been told differently? Would she have made such an absolute distinction between the decadence of private life and the conformism of Communist politics, or conceived of either in such terms? Meanwhile, we are faced with the paradox that this novel written by a nonfeminist without a feminist audience in mind remains one of the most important and provocative yet produced and, in this sense, Nadine Gordimer is very definitely "our writer."

Notes

All references to *Burger's Daughter* are to the hardcover edition published by Cape, London, 1979.

1. According to this, "a publication, object, film or public entertainment is . . . undesirable if it: (a) is indecent or obscene or is offensive or harmful to public morals, (b) is blasphemous or is offensive to the religious convictions or feelings of any section of the inhabitants of the Republic [of South Africa]; (c) brings any section of the inhabitants of the Republic into ridicule or contempt; (d) is harmful to the relations between any sections of the inhabitants of the Republic; (e) is prejudicial to the safety of the State, the general welfare or the peace and good order" (John Dugard, "Censorship in South Africa: The Legal Framework," in Nadine Gordimer, John Dugard, et al., *What Happened to* Burger's Daughter; *or, How South African Censorship Works* [Emmarentia, Johannesburg, South Africa: Taurus, 1980], 69). For other explanations of how South African censorship works, see the journal *Index on Censorship*, London; John Jackson, *Justice in South Africa* (London: Penguin, 1980); and Louise Silver, ed., *Publications Appeal Board: Digest of Decisions* (Johannesburg, South Africa: Center for Applied Legal Studies, University of the Witwatrstrand, recurring).

2. Letter from E. G. Malan, director of publications, to Raymond Tucker (Nadine Gordimer's lawyer), 16 July 1979, in *What Happened*, 8–12. Queensland readers will probably note similarities in rationales for the Queensland state government's banning of federally produced materials and other publications.

3. Report of the Publications Appeal Board, 3 October 1979, ibid., 36.

4. C. J. van der Merwe, "Report on 'Burger's Daughter' of Nadine Gordimer," ibid., 59.

5. See Robert Scholes and Robert Kellogg, *The Nature of Narrative* (Oxford: Oxford University Press, 1976), 57.

6. In addition to *What Happened*, see Sheila Roberts, "South African Censorship and the Case of *Burger's Daughter*," *World Literature Written in English* 20, no. 1 (Spring 1981): 41–48. For only a few of Gordimer's clear and unremitting statements opposing censorship see her "Censorship and the Word," *The Bloody Horse* 1 (Sept.–Oct. 1981): 20–24, and "New Forms of Strategy—No Change of Heart," *Critical Arts* 1, no. 2 (June 1980): 27–33, since reprinted in *Index on Censorship*.

7. *Burger's Daughter* cannot be said to have had a trial, because of the nature and operation of South African censorship committees, for which see *What Happened*, 5.

8. J. C. W. van Rooyen, then acting chairman, Publications Appeal Board, Decision on *Burger's Daughter*, 25 Oct. 1979, ibid., 40.

9. Letter from Director of Publications to President of the Students' Union, University of Cape Town, 16 Sept. 1977.

10. "Two Cheers for South Africa's Adults-Only Books," *Rand Daily Mail*, Johannesburg, 29 Dec. 1981, p. 1. For a discussion of the sexist and racist ideologies in popular fiction spawned by the wars for liberation in Kenya and Zimbabwe, see David Maughan Brown, "Myths on the March," presented to the Conference on Literature and Society in Southern Africa, University of York, Centre for Southern African Studies, 8–11 Sept. 1981.

11. Ibid.

12. Ibid. Even more recently (Jan. 1982) the film of Doris Lessing's *The Grass Is Singing* has been unbanned. Originally the Publications Control Board had decided, in Oct. 1981, that it was "detrimental to the security of the State" because its central theme was regarded as "a confrontation between Black and White." The theme is now said to be "the effects of isolation and alienation" and (distorting Lessing's own view expressed in the novel's epigraphs) "the study of the gradual marital disintegration and descent into insanity of a woman who cannot come to terms with Africa and dislikes rubbing shoulders with the Black workers whom she treats with a misguided severity." The appeal board, using the familiar "considerable artistic merit" rationalization, further decided that the film was unlikely to attract a wide popular interest: "It lacks the emotive power to influence the revolutionary or potential revolutionary." Nonetheless, some sexual scenes were cut (presumably those discreetly implying the relationship between Mary and her black servant, Moses, though these are more suggestive than blatant), and a 2–18 age restriction has been imposed. The basic challenge of the novel—its exploration of the sexual roots of racism, and the taboos between white women and black men—seems not to have been recognized or discussed by the control and appeal boards. See Ann Palmer, "Ban Lifted on Film Accused of Causing Race Conflict," *Sunday Express*, Johannesburg, 10 Jan. 1982, p. 8.

13. In a file of approximately three dozen reviews of *Burger's Daughter* read at Jonathan Cape's London office in Oct. 1980, I found only two indicating awareness of feminist implications. Brian Firth in the *Tablet* (the oldest Roman Catholic magazine in England) called it a novel "about the restrictions of being a woman. . . . [Rosa] is as doomed as Antigone to fulfill the family pieties" (18 Aug. 1979); while M. M., in *Newsagent and Bookshop*, asserted, "where this book would stand in any canon of

'women's literature' is by no means clear, but its excellence as a portrait of one woman's self-determination cannot be questioned" (24 May 1979).

14. "What the Book Is About," in *What Happened*, 20.

15. In addition to her essays in *On Lies, Secrets and Silence,* see also talks Rich gave at Conway Hall and the Institute for Contemporary Arts, London, Oct. 1980.

16. "Women Who Take the Literary Lead," *Rand Daily Mail,* 14 May 1981.

17. Tillie Olsen, *Silences* (London: Virago, 1980), 250.

18. Preface to *Selected Stories* (London: Jonathan Cape, 1975), 10–11.

19. "The Prison-House of Colonialism," *Times Literary Supplement*, 15 Aug. 1980, p. 918. This biography of Olive Schreiner is banned to all practical purposes in South Africa because one of the authors, Ruth First, is a political exile, and nothing that she writes can therefore be quoted in South Africa. See Susan Gardner, "No 'Story,' No Script, Only the Struggle: First and Scott's *Olive Schreiner,*" *Hecate* 7, no. 1 (1981), 40–61.

20. See Jacklyn Cock, *Maids and Madams: A Study in the Politics of Exploitation* (Johannesburg, South Africa: Ravan, 1980), reviewed by Deborah Gaitskell in *Hecate* (no. 8, 1982).

21. In an interview with me in July 1980, Gordimer stated: "I feel that if the real battle for human rights is won the kingdom of . . . feminine liberation follows. Because if we are all free individuals, that's all we need, we don't need to have any special feeling because we are women." See *Kunapipi* 3, no. 2 (1981) for this interview.

22. Quoted by Bonnie Hoover Braendlin, "Lisa Alther's *Kinflicks*," in Janet Todd, ed., *Gender and Literary Voice* (London: Holmes and Merer, 1980), 162.

23. See Susan Gardner, "Dora and Nadja: Two Women in the Early Days of Psychoanalysis and Surrealism," *Hecate* 2, no. 1 (1976): 23–40.

24. Interview in *Kunapipi.*

25. *Books and Bookmen,* July 1979, p. 37.

26. Cited in Olsen, *Silences* (London: Virago, 1980), 255.

27. See especially Olsen's examples of "Writing Like a Man" and "Writing Like a Woman," in *Silences.*

28. "The Limits of Consciousness in the Novels of Doris Lessing," *Contemporary Literature* 14, no. 4 (Autumn 1973): 537–38.

29. Ronald Hayman, "Nadine Gordimer in Interview," *Books and Bookmen,* July 1979, p. 34. Gordimer has acknowledged consulting H. J. Simons and R. E. Simons, *Class and Colour in South Africa, 1850–1950* (London: Penguin, 1969); Mofika Pascal Gwala, B. A. Khoapa, and Thoko Mbanjwa, eds., "The Black Community Programmes." Other sources very plausibly include Hilda Bernstein's *The World That Was Ours* (London: Heinemann, 1967); Mary Benson, ed., *The Sun Will Rise: Statements from the Dock by Southern African Political Prisoners,* rev. ed. (London: International Defence

and Aid Fund, 1981); Bettie du Toit, *Ukubamba Amadolo: Workers' Struggles in the South African Textile Industry* (London: Clerkenwell Workshops, Onyx 1978); Helen Joseph, *If This Be Treason* (London: Deutsch, 1963) and *Tomorrow's Sun: A Smuggled Journal from South Africa* (London: Hutchinson, 1966); Naomi Mitchison, *A Life for Africa: The Story of Bram Fischer* (London: Merlin, 1973); and Eddie Roux and Win Roux, *Rebel Pity: The Life of Eddie Roux* (London: Collings, 1970).

Burger's Daughter

Lighting a Torch in the Heart of Darkness

LORRAINE LISCIO

◆　◆　◆

Here they are, returning, arriving over and again,
because the unconscious is impregnable. They have
wandered around in circles, confined to the narrow
room in which they've been given a deadly brain-
washing. You can incarcerate them, slow them
down, get away with the old Apartheid routine, but
for a time only. As soon as they begin to speak, at
the same time as they're taught their name, they
can be taught that their territory is black: because
you are Africa, you are black. Your continent is
dark. Dark is dangerous. You can't see anything in
the dark, you're afraid. Don't move, you might fall.
Most of all, don't go into the forest. And so we have
internalized this horror of the dark.

　　Hélène Cixous, "The Laugh of the Medusa"

I N   N A D I N E   G O R D I M E R ' S   F I R S T   N O V E L, *The Lying Days*, the
protagonist, Helen Shaw, lists the writers who shaped her literary heritage: Auden, T. S. Eliot, Donne, Hemingway, D. H. Lawrence, Chekhov,
Smollett, and Pepys. She is puzzled to find that "in nothing that I read
could I find anything that approximated to my own life; to our life on a
gold mine in South Africa." If she failed to recognize her world in European narratives, Helen felt equally alienated from the pictures of Africa
portrayed by books she read: "What did the great rivers, the savage tribes,
the jungles and the hunt for huge palm-eared elephants have to do with
the sixty miles of Witwatersrand veld that was our Africa?" (96–97).

　　Helen's dilemma is paradigmatic to South Africa as well as to women
writers and, as this essay argues, to the plight of Rosa Burger in *Burger's Daugh-*

ter. Following Rosa's cue in her desire to break through the surface of a given political ideology to sound the depths of her female origins, I will begin by briefly placing Gordimer within the context of colonized, contemporary South African writers. I will then show how Gordimer's preoccupation with "the personal life" places her in a female literary tradition. These preliminary steps will lead to a discussion of Rosa Burger, a female "place where something has occurred" (*Burger's Daughter*, opening epigraph).

As a South African writer, Gordimer knows the difficulty of writing out of a colonial past and finding little to identify as a tradition. Living in a country where censorship has banned political writers—and as Gordimer herself says, in South Africa the political filters through every level of experience—Africans have only two alternative forms of representation available to them: government-approved art and literature or artistic depictions of themselves by foreigners. This, of course, is only one facet of the problem. If Africans had freedom of self-expression, the next question to be addressed is one of identity: Who are we? As Dan Jacobson said of his own culture, "A colonial culture is one which has no memory. Blankness rules; blankness perpetuates itself" (Schreiner 7–8).

This blankness or lack of identity stems partially from having had a European tradition imposed on South African culture. It was the Nationalists' hope that the native way of life would evolve or be assimilated into the colonizers' and thereby the Africans come to enjoy the "fullness" of Western civilization. For the writer, approval by Europe and America meant acceptance into the literary community. The imperative to conform to an established and recognized literary standard was what led writers like Jacobson to excuse himself for not being "universal," or Alan Paton to extol cooperation between races through Christian liberalism rather than miscegenation. Here again the value and significance of how and what one writes came from outside rather than from within.

In her fiction Gordimer has consistently alluded to the inadequacy of cloaking one culture in another. She deems this liberalism a failure because it precludes real dialogue and exchange among radically diverse groups— blacks, colored, Indians, Afrikaners, and English-speaking Africans—a dialogue that would uncover a totally new form of community, unimaginable under apartheid rule.

Gordimer's first novel in 1953 had already exposed the need that Guy Butler formulated at the 1956 Witwatersrand Conference on the state of literature in South Africa. He implored writers "to explore, to measure, and to name the Africa of the senses and the mind" (quoted in Cooke 3). Butler's words echo those of Mira in Marilyn French's *The Women's Room* when she claims that dulling women's minds, senses, and ability to articulate themselves has estranged women from their bodies and self-knowledge.[1] Although Gordimer disclaims any association with feminism—she believes writers are androgynous—her literary enterprise resembles that of feminist writers: she is writing about a country where the native subdominant group is forced to accommodate itself to the dominant. It is powerless, invisible, speechless, without a history, and alienated from itself. Just as Hélène Cixous exhorts women to undermine Freud's concept of woman as a dark continent by voicing their real selves and desires, Gordimer says the same to the country in which that metaphor originated.

Added to this fact is the recurrent emphasis in her fiction on the personal sphere of experience as the necessary core of all responsible public action. In this sense she is the daughter of Austen and the female tradition whose fine observation of manners and the private life informs their portrayals of the fabric of society. Except for chance, Gordimer would have been vulnerable to the facile exhortations of narrow-minded critics to women to stop writing about domestic matters and write about "the world"—as if the two were mutually exclusive and unrelated. Gordimer admits that had she been born anywhere else her work would not have been as political as it is. It is the personal that is important to her, and in South Africa, where whites and blacks have not been allowed in each others's homes or where until recently interracial marriages were illegal, the personal *is* political. Like Austen, Gordimer values seeing the larger social fabric through the lens of the personal, an understanding that typifies the complicated, unresolved textural quality of her novels.

Despite the fact that in her more recent novels the protagonists have moved further into the public arena, it in no way reduces the centrality she ascribes to the inner struggle. Her book *July's People* reverses the order of domestic servant and paternalistic protector, relegating full power and control to those who were previously insignificant and invisible, revealing the difficulties of altering a self-definition that has been publicly codified. In *Guest of Honour* Bray enters history in a decisively personal way and in so doing relinquishes a liberal political ideology that left him free but unaccountable for a radicalism that engages him fatally. The personal for Gordimer is in some ways like the unconscious. It refuses to behave or line up congruently with the public order. Instead it continues to disrupt the status quo, just as the black man's corpse in *The Conservationist* defies burial and returns to plague the racist Mehring.[2]

In *Burger's Daughter*, the double disclosure of the private, disruptive voice and the public, conventional one informs both the narrative structure and the story of a woman's search for identity. More specifically, it is the dialogue between the maternal and paternal sides of Rosa. The narrative alternates between first and third person, but lest this duality be too easily reduced to clearly defined binary oppositions, Rosa's voice is addressed to three different people: Conrad, Colette Swan, also known as Katya, her father's first wife, and her father, Lionel, all of whom are important to her, but none of whom are present as real listeners—a literary crystallization of a female reality. Hence the complexity of Rosa's voice and shifting identity is set up in a structure that typifies Gordimer's style.

Born into a politically active Afrikaner family, Rosa had assimilated Marx and Lenin as other children do their parents' religion. For her the given conditions of responsible, adult life were living under surveillance, being named, censored, and repeatedly imprisoned, a norm reinforced by her parents' periodic detentions. After their deaths—her mother, Cathy, succumbs quietly to multiple sclerosis while her father, Lionel, dies a hero serving a life sentence for anti-apartheid activities—Rosa is faced with the problem of what to do with her life.

Her impulse to defect from her father and his liberal ideology draws Rosa into a series of relationships that give space to her private life of individual needs, emotions, conflicts, and pleasures. It was her family's belief that this personal sphere of experience would fall into place once capitalist values of power and possession were resolved. The two influential presences that chart her course toward maturity validate her need for a temporary period of self-preoccupation and exploration apart from the exigencies of the larger human community. The first is Conrad, a student of literature, and the second, Colette Swan, her father's first wife, an ex-dancer, and former member of the Communist Party. As the literary names suggest, Rosa is headed for a world quite foreign to the public life of collective responsibility and action.

Having inherited a well-defined, paternal, public role of commitment, Rosa seeks to fill in the present form with meaning, that is, the feminine, the personal, the maternal, the concealed life. She must get in touch with her self, body, voice, and modes of perception in ways that are similar to a child who learns how to walk before crawling. She must at some time regress to go through that step. For full coordination it is necessary to return to the feminine/maternal, which coincides not surprisingly with childhood.

Rosa unconsciously embarks, then, on a search for her mother, who, although mentioned often, seems subsumed in the political ideals and image of the father. The names alone—Cathy, childlike and familiar; Lionel, grand and heroic—convey the degrees of public presence each one enjoys. Cathy is curiously absent in a narrative that *does* allude to her. She slips away and fades despite the fact that she is named —and we feel that this is the point. Being "named" Cathy Burger makes her anonymous, somewhat invisible. It would be telling to note how many readers ignore the fact that in the title, *Burger's Daughter,* Burger can apply equally to Cathy and to Lionel. Being "named" in this context, however, offers Cathy a form of cover that deflects attention from her to a publicly activist husband, enabling her to be more mobile, secretive, and effective.

In a 1980 interview with Susan Gardner, Gordimer tells of politically active Afrikaner families she knew in which the husband was traditionally considered the official head and leader and, therefore, the one to be watched closely by surveillance. The woman, on the other hand, seen as less dangerous and needed at home, was often dealt with leniently by the court. This gave her more opportunity for underground operations. "The question of who was the more important person in Party work would very often be covered up, in the eyes of the world, with the facade of marriage" (101).

Gordimer goes on to elaborate the role women have played in South African politics. On the one hand, there were the middle-class Flora Donaldsons who had the leisure time to devote to charitable activities and who consequently became involved in efforts to bring about social reforms. These women understood the inequity of black oppression and tried to effect some change. Their class status and protective husbands impeded them from undertaking more radical, dangerous methods of protest, but the wives did recognize a need for action. (Their action, of course, did not preclude problematic dealings with working-class women of color whose specific life circumstances were foreign to them—shortcomings in evidence at Flora Donaldson's meeting.) Citing women's organizations like the Black Sash as one to which Flora might belong, Gordimer asks: Where are their husbands, why do the *women* have "the guts" to defy public opinion, and the police, and to demonstrate for social reform in Vorster Square or outside the university? (104–5).

In Cathy's case, both Ivy Terblanche and Colette see her as the real revolutionary. If this is so, then we must conclude that there is a very definite relationship among female silence, absence, and what we understand by revolution. For Rosa, her mother's story has more gaps than narrative line. Is it Cathy who was lacking or Rosa's perception of her? Part of Rosa's desire is to fill in the blank space of what has been lost. She defects from paternally formulated family expectations in order to separate herself from the prescribed role of revolutionary and to coax to the surface forgotten pockets—defects?—of connectedness and warmth she believes did exist in her family. Hers is a defection from the male/public form of action to the female/private sphere of silence, absence, defects. It seems that Rosa's capacity to do this was lacking in her mother. Cathy did not fill up (w)holes of experience. She never "fill[ed] up that hole" (128), that is, the swimming pool where Rosa's brother Tony drowned, and the depression she suffered at that loss appears somehow related to the paralysis that finally killed her. The sleeping pill Lionel gave her was a quick fix for pain symptoms but did not effect a cure. As Rosa says, "my father—as a doctor—put her to sleep" (83), and we suspect that this unconsciousness—dulling the mind and senses—was fatal.[3]

It is as if Cathy's public self had no real center in her body or emotions, but instead existed as an unnoticed, enclosed space that housed and sheltered others for the time they needed to grow. The Burger swimming pool is an appropriate metaphor for Cathy. It is the place where Tony, Baasie, and Rosa learn to swim under the "official" protection of Lionel, "the privileged signifier" (Lescan 287). Cathy provides the uterine opening for significant events to happen. She is the background on which action/meaning is imposed. Rosa's pursuit of the female as a place that needs to be understood and known—she leaves Africa to "know somewhere else" (187)—does not chart a linear journey from "here to there." The Lévi-Strauss epigraph that opens the story suggests this inner journey: "I am the place in which something has occurred." Cathy's loss of self, then, is the reverse side of the disoriented, wandering, bourgeois woman Rosa later meets in Paris who is like "a hamster turning her female treadmill" (332). Both versions are equally self-destructive.

When Rosa notices her mother's attractiveness in a photo, she remembers Cathy as "a woman who is unaware of her good looks, but . . . literally *does not inhabit them*" (82). Her mother's split from her body is a defect that Rosa recognizes subliminally as unhealthy. Later when she instinctively travels to Nice to visit Colette, it is a desire for psychic health and survival that unconsciously prompts her. Cathy was, after all, approved by the Communist Party, a sign of her self-effacement, whereas Colette could not tolerate an ideology that sacrificed her private self for the collective welfare.[4]

Rosa's attentiveness to a lost mother as a silent, unheralded place resembles feminists' attempts to validate female, maternal experience, which corresponds to the pre-Oedipal, prelinguistic stage of development. They challenge the given convention of phallocentric value: that the male is the producer of language and meaning. Instead they point to the mother as primary caretaker and the place where much communication occurs through visceral and sensual "conversation" between her body impulses and the infant's. This conversation between mother and child duplicates a female sexuality or, as Luce Irigaray suggests, "fills the gaps in a repressed female sexuality" that if free of taboos is "that contact of *at least two* (lips) which keeps woman in touch with herself" (26–27). The problem for Cathy was not having ever enjoyed the conversation with a mixed, plural self, a multiple Otherness, not having used a language in which "'she' sets off in all directions leaving 'him' [in this case we might insert Lionel] unable to discern the coherence of any meaning" (Irigaray 29). Being "named" Burger, she surrendered to the male logic of synecdochical meaning (the part for the whole) and pared away parts of herself to become a stable, unified Other.

For Cathy, being "named" has debilitating effects. It makes her a curious absence. Is this naming, however, any more debilitating than Lionel's fate of being a presence circumscribed in a public voice?[5] Rosa understands his danger in becoming a central signifying voice, an understanding that grows through her encounter with Conrad, a friend whose literary name coincidentally recalls another tragically central signifying voice, Kurtz's in *Heart of Darkness*.[6]

Conrad's influence in the process of Rosa's emerging self is similar to the knowledge Helen Shaw gains from reading the male tradition of writers. He initiates her into the journey toward self-knowledge. However, his self-centeredness and impersonal fascination with others' lives is unsettling to Rosa. Uninterested in personal commitments, Conrad travels to places he has read about in novels. Overcome with guilt from Oedipal conflicts and fearful of his subsequent suicidal tendencies, he reductively defines the only real human realities as sex and death. Conrad's secure self-absorption inoculates him from others' pain. His curiosity, excised from real human demands, is a personally disengaged one that makes people objects of observation. It recalls the way in which Marlow's amazement and fascination work to distance him from emotional involvement with Kurtz even when he dies: "Anything approaching the change that came over his features I have never seen before, and hope never to see again. Oh, I wasn't touched. I was fascinated" (117).

Whereas Conrad tries to blunt the realities of sex and death by invoking "fascinating" theories and abstractions about them, Rosa's experience of them opens her more fully to empathize with others. Once, while in a park square, she discovers that a man apparently dozing on a bench is really dead. The mystery and significance affect her existentially so that she transfers the personally felt meaning of death to the memory of her father, whose death she did not witness and whose body the state has claimed. Unlike Marlow she *admits* to being deeply touched; hence there are real possibilities that, for Rosa, Lionel can become more than simply a symbol or a remembered voice. He can become more than a mere hero, a full-bodied person in her memory.

Inhabiting one's body, being alive to the mind and senses, is an underlying theme throughout the novel. For Rosa it is intimately bound to public action. From the very beginning of the story we learn that she is endowed with an unacknowledged but nonetheless intense emotional acuity that informs her perception of reality. Remembering a scene when she was fourteen, waiting outside the prison to visit her mother, the adult Rosa wonders about the busload of passengers who watched her as they passed: "When they saw me outside the prison, what did they see?" (13). She distinguishes between seeing and real awareness that takes into account the integrated forces of mind and body. She says that at fourteen "real awareness," next to which public or political awareness pales, is identified with "the peculiar, fierce concentration of the body's forces in the menstruation of early puberty" (15). It is these forces that when accepted and respected will provide her with the understanding of human suffering that moves her to action. Rosa will eventually come to politics, not through abstract ideological doctrines but through the body, that is, through others' needs that elicit in her an emotional, physical response. To respond fully, though, requires a strong presence of self.

An example of how this functions in her life is seen in her chosen work as a physiotherapist, which she leaves temporarily but returns to in the end. It is a job in which she helps others learn to "put one foot before the other" (332). Not only is it reminiscent of maternal care for toddlers, but it is also a personal version of surveillance, the public form of which is rigid and threatening in its attempt to penetrate Rosa's motives for action.

During the course of Rosa's growth into womanhood, she moves in the orbit of women who awaken in her a deeper sense of being female. As she sorts through different gender models, she takes away from each different versions of connectedness with self. The Terblanche family offers three women. Ivy, the mother, went to prison for two years rather than talk to the authorities about Lionel's activities. Ivy, like the other rebel women, is well trained in silence. Unlike Cathy, though, Ivy's body is a strong, assertive, physical, colorful presence; she wears bright print dresses, and her hair is wild like Einstein's. Her two daughters are also revolutionaries. Gloria's husband "has a cover job teaching in Tanzania" (109). Like Cathy, Gloria disappears behind her front/husband. Clare Terblanche is the revolutionary Rosa might have become had she not resisted the family ideology in search of the missing feminine. Rosa sees in Clare a servitude to her father's cause and the high price Clare has paid:

> Her flesh was dumb. She lived inside there, usefully employing now tall, dependable legs that carried one haunch before the other until she found the flat. A poor circulation (showing itself in the pallor and flush of the face), breasts folded over against themselves, a soft expanse of belly to shelter children. A body that had no signals; it would grow larger and at once more self-effacing. (121–22)

These two young women never connect. What has been *thrust* between them is a male ideology that prevents intimacy, interrupts the contact of "two lips which keeps women in touch with herself." The intimacy manqué is burlesqued during the visit with an intermittent background voice of the radio disc jockey who ironically announces with cliches of intimacy records played for loved ones. Clare has opted for the cause, but in so doing renounces her body in much the same way that she hurriedly and shamefully disposes of the sanitary napkin she finds in the empty flat.

Marisa Kgosana, on the other hand, attracts Rosa as much as Clare repels her. A black woman, banned and under house arrest, and whose husband has been imprisoned on Robben Island for years, Marisa moves about comfortably in her body. She does not stutter or shift tones when speaking of prisoners while in public. Her ordinary speech, free and unfettered, is a natural double discourse that communicates information to Rosa while leading others to think her husband is vacationing on an island somewhere. Marisa's splashy-colored dress, her clear, unhesitating voice, her lovers, and the fact that she and Rosa meet over the cosmetics counter make her a character link between Ivy Terblanche and Colette Swan. Rosa's description of the pull Marisa exerts on her reveals the strong, sensuous nature of the attraction:

> To touch in women's token embrace against the live, night cheek of Marisa, seeing huge for a second the lake-flash of her eye, the lilac-pink of her inner lip against translucent-edged teeth, to enter for a moment the invisible magnetic field of the body of a beautiful creature and receive on oneself its

imprint—breath misting and quickly fading on a glass pane—this was to immerse in another mode of perception. As near as a woman can get to the transformation of the world a man seeks in the beauty of a woman. (134–35)

Rosa says this while consciously resisting the temptation to transform Marisa simplistically into a romantic symbol of redemption.

However, although Rosa acknowledges this attraction, she learns that Marisa's blackness is something that separates them, interrupts the commonality of their female bonds. Rosa distinguishes in ways her father could not. She feels the complexities of racial problems in the closeness of her relationship with Marisa, whereas Lionel invited blacks into his white suburban home without realizing the contradictions they felt there. The inkling Rosa has of this inherent incongruence will later be literally "brought to light" in her prone conversation with Baasie, an exchange that will make her physically ill and convince her to leave Europe for Africa.

Her recognition of such ambiguities is the result of being what she calls a "kaffir [nigger]-boetie [Afrikaans] girl" (135), a woman where opposites collapse into each other in shifting relations and plural selves: Cathy/Lionel; kaffir/boetie; Rosa (for activist Rosa Luxemburg)/Marie (for her Afrikaner grandmother whose motto was "Peace, Land, Bread"); woman/revolutionary.

What makes the last of the paired terms indecipherable and slippery is the value afforded Rosa's stepmother, Colette Swan. Without any predetermined plan, Rosa finds herself seeking out Lionel's first wife, whose home in Nice—the English meaning enhances its significance—evokes multiple variations of the theme of romance, not commitment. Colette lives in a small house, dominated by a castle, overlooking an old monastery, fronted by a secret wood, and opening out to the sea. This is a veritable fairytale setting where Rosa is introduced to the bourgeois life of personal desires. It recalls the writer Colette in approximating her residence in southern France as well as the sensual appetite for which she was famous. The third-person narrator in part Two of the novel is reminiscent of Colette's style:

> The silk tent of morning sea tilted, pegged to keyhole harbours where boats nosed domestically like animals at a trough; Vauban's ancient fort squatted out to the water; two S-shaped buildings towered, were foreshortened, leaned this side and that of the wing, rose again. Lavender mountains with a snail-trail spittle of last winter's snow swung a diagonal horizon across the fish-bowl windows. Down to earth, the plane laid itself on the runway as

the seagulls (through convex glass under flak of droplets) breasted the sea beside it. (214)

What is worth noticing in Nice is the profusion of color, scents, exotic foods, and stories Rosa hears from Colette's friends. They provide her with the joy of viscerally felt pleasures associated with early child development and connectedness with the mother. This childhood sensuality was absent or forgotten for Rosa. We observe her regression to a self-centered greediness typical of infancy: "The food was delicious and roused a new pleasure, of greed. Rosa Burger had not known she could want to eat so much" (224). Among the members of Colette's entourage, all desires are openly expressed and satisfied. The group consists of artists, drifters, homosexuals, European hedonists of mixed origins whom society stereotypically deems irresponsible for their choice of and indulgence in private affairs. When they tell their personal stories, Rosa questions them as a child would: "What happened to Vaki-the Greek? I pipe up from time to time, like a child listening to folk-lore" (238). Names are richly allusive: in Nice, Rosa becomes Rôse; Didier is a clownish Bacchus; a Manx cat that has wandered in—perhaps from Oxbridge?—is constantly under Colette's feet and reminds us of the original Colette's story "La Chatte"; Gaby Grosbois points to the gabbing, not silent nature of this society as well as the atmosphere of romance that permeates it (Grosbois meaning large wood). Colette's naming herself Katya, like a Russian dancer, and Rosa's eventual love affair in Paris with Bernard Chabalier (cavalier) both serve to reinforce the storybook quality of Nice. Other factors that add to this atmosphere are the pastimes of Colette's acquaintances. They spend their time traveling, having picnics, and going to the beach. They float capriciously from one activity to another and are never pinned down to specific, accountable positions of responsibility.

Colette shares their freedom of movement. Unlike the stable, "committed"—with all the possible connotations—Cathy, Colette dabbles in as many jobs as she has names. Her maiden name is reminiscent of literature's most famous dilettante, Proust's Swann. Like the real Colette, she was initially a music-hall dancer who wrote plays and songs. As Mme. Bagnelli—an invention in itself because she and Bagnelli were never married—she gives English lessons, dancing lessons, tends shop for vacationing owners, does housekeeping, and works as a secretary and editor for a Russian writer. As Colette Burger, she did political work for the Communist Party, taught classes in Marx and Lenin in a cold warehouse but hated it so much that she used her art—songs and plays—as a vehicle to foster change. Katya, a Russian form of Cathy, is the name she designates for her relationship with Rosa.

If Cathy is swallowed up into the darkness of the "committed," prison-associated Burger name, Colette emerges in the brightly sunlit Mediterranean landscape bearing as many identities as Renoir's diverse colors, creating the impression of an object under the changing effects of light. This place called Nice stands for the world of art—it was Renoir's home, and Picasso's museum is there, Colette reminds Rosa. It is a place where personal lives are exposed to the light. Colette/Nice, then, is Cathy-mother-place-where-something-has-happened turned inside out, baring Cathy to the curious, loving scrutiny of her daughter. Cathy's disappearance behind the cover "Burger" is the inversion of Colette's externally fragmented plural self. Cathy dies under the predictable straightness of patriarchal ideals, whereas Colette survives in the sinuous unevenness of changing occupations. She embodies "the personal," dodging definition and constantly upsetting "the public," given order. For Rosa this unsettling impulse reveals unexpected snags in the fabric of Lionel's ideology. She learns from Colette's friends that while Communist Party members in South Africa were horrified by Nationalists' attacks on innocent people in the Sharpeville massacre, Communist troops were moving into Prague, there were uprisings in Hungary, and knowledge of the Stalin trials was spreading. Rosa's newly acquired information about the collective consequences of ideological incongruities is eventually coupled with an understanding of the private tragedies as well: Baasie's phone call in the middle of the night informs her of the personal gaps that liberalism fails to address in its movement toward a Nice picture of "the Future." Baasie has no "place" on the world map where he can fit. In a symbolic gesture, he tells Rosa to turn on the light before he explains this to her.

In plotting the course of Rosa's self-knowledge, it is impossible to measure the distance she has covered. She has "advanced" in sounding a place: the feminine, the maternal. Her journey is one of traveling all the while remaining at home. The timelessness of Nice is where pleasure and appetite—some feminists would call it *jouissance*—take precedence over action and responsibility. It is a self-enclosed, womblike space outside time and sequence. There is an almost eternal quality in Colette's account of Nice's history where the feudal structure of the robber barons and serfs remains constant despite centuries of new actors playing those roles. After the French Revolution, industrialists and businessmen replaced the noble lords. During World War II the Resistance was based in the cellars. The castle, now a hotel, is owned by an arms dealer, and an elderly couple maintains the garden. "The suzerain changes his nationality. . . . Japanese are the ones buying up big properties here now. North Africans are the serfs making roads and living in their *bidonville*—squatters" (221). The dominant and subdominant groups reproduce themselves, with a form of "resistance" always ready to escape from the cellar and act as the personal or feminine does in this narrative. Colette is aware of the essentially static nature of an ostensibly "advancing" society.

Rosa's temporary stay in this timeless place enables her to tease apart the fabric of her self, moving inward and backward through the mother, as Woolf recommended.[7] For her it takes the form alternately of allowing her body the freedom of feeling and expression, of questioning other women, of measuring herself alongside them, of probing the commonality of their experience. This is new territory for Rosa. As she tells Colette, "I've never talked with anyone as I do with you, incontinently, femininely" (262). "You tell me anecdotes of your youth that could transform my own" (263).[8]

Colette's nurturing, then, allows Rosa to grant full scope to her sensuality and emotions, an indulgence noticeably lacking from her inherited familial experience of obligation and responsibility. It is an important stage of development because without pleasure and appetite, part of the self is still left unsatisfied and, therefore, is incapable of giving to others disinterestedly. Pleasure in the self is what enlarges the capacity to move freely toward a real Other rather than one who will be unconsciously sought to fill one's lack. (This point is central to the theory of feminists like Cixous and Irigaray.)

Rosa's growth opens her to the Other as Other, rather than as reflection of self. The simultaneous plotting of these two coordinates, self and Other, expands into a nourishing fullness. Her first affair happens soon after Lionel's death. The mate is a Swede writing a biography of her father, and his sexual expertise reimburses Rosa for the information he gets about Lionel. The public, economic nature of the exchange makes this a sterile encounter because Rosa is targeted as an informer for profit. Her shared life with Conrad in the small cottage designates, on the other hand, a private arena for self-expression; it is a refuge from public institutions—courts, prisons, the hospital where she works as a physiotherapist—that had hitherto defined her life. This relationship is inadequate too, however, because Conrad's Marlow-type, self-absorbed stupor blocks him from others. Rosa finally recognizes this relationship for what it is, namely, incest, and thus formulates in heterosexual terms the drawback of traveling while never leaving home.

With Bernard Chabalier she has an emotionally and sexually fulfilling love affair. However, romance threatens to put her inborn sensitivity to sleep just as Lionel's pill did to her mother. Their self-enclosed desire can have hurtful consequences for others: "A wild, strong, brazen, narrow-eyed resoluteness, cast in desire, treading on the fingers of restraint, knocking aside whatever makes the passage of the will improbable and even impossible" (306). Bernard's political sympathies approximate Lionel's: a history teacher aspiring to a university professorship, he is aware of and signs petitions for political prisoners all over the world. He also, however, belongs to the leftist bourgeoisie; he has a wife and children and is saving for his house and a plot of land. Although Bernard satisfies Rosa's desire for a companion and a lover, he lacks the empathy for others that flows naturally in her. She knows that Bernard, like Conrad, would not have recognized the poor black family's agony that she remembers having seen in the donkey-drawn cart on the South African backroads. For her the hidden backroads contain people whose oppression and suffering she recognizes, not sees. The experience entails "know[ing] somewhere else" (187) not through one sense but through the integration of many, to constitute a female sensuality. It also affirms an underlying separateness-in-commonality-with-others that allows for recognition. She learns the meaning of the epigraph of chapter 2, "To know and not to act is not to know" (213).

Rosa's return to South Africa leads to her eventual imprisonment with other women revolutionaries: Marisa, Clare, and an Indian. She is not *inside* the prison walls where her mother, Cathy, was at the beginning of the story. Consequently the narrative focuses on the interior of the prison, which is described as a combination cloister—the chief matron is like an "abbess of an Order" (354)—and a "dance hall in a nineteenth-century painting" (359). The female wardens' attire evokes memories of Colette and her friends, and the Nice castle in Rosa's drawings bespeaks a fairytale reversal of what is outwardly recognized as female/prison life. All these elements give breadth to the female/Nice landscape and experience, incorporating it, bodying it forth to round out the story.

When Cathy was in prison, we readers saw it only from the outside. Rosa's commitment, however, is different, a fact reinforced by her messages to those outside, sent not through public speech conventions—a form Rosa used strategically to communicate with her detained mother—but through art. Her personally drawn Christmas cards portray Marisa, Clare, the Indian woman, and herself as carolers and assure those outside of their well-being. Despite their isolation from one another they remain connected through the song and laughter that escape from their cells. Having internalized Colette's, or Mme. Bagnelli's—*bagnelli* is the Italian word for little baths or pools—version of womanhood, Rosa has filled in the swimming pool/(w)hole of her mother, Cathy. It is for this reason that Flora Donaldson, Rosa's only visitor, says that "she's somehow livelier than she used to be. In a way. Less reserved" (360).

The narrative structure of the novel is divided into three parts, each comprising a third-person narrator and Rosa's first-person address to Conrad, Colette, and Lionel successively. Her voice is never public—although she does come close to it when she speaks about South African politics to Colette and her friends, but this is in a private group. Her impulse to withdraw from an audience is so strong in the beginning that she writes to Conrad, her imagined addressee, "If you knew I was talking to you I wouldn't be able to talk" (17). Rosa innately knows the danger of public display through acts—her brother Tony drowned showing off in the pool—and through speech, which can carry fatal life "sentences" like Lionel's.

In Lionel's final, eloquent courtroom speech, he twice refers to Marxism as a solution "based on the elimination of contradiction" (25). The reduction of ambiguities to a direct ideological line to "the Future" produces heroes and victims but leaves few flesh-and-blood fighting survivors. Those who do remain are like Marisa; they have the agility to move around in a double discourse as one dances through a mine field.

Public speech often metonymically misses the mark. It is perhaps for this reason that the third-person narrator weaves a fabric of varying public and private modes of perception. This shifting point of view takes its cue from the subject of each section as the narrative moves in and out of indirect discourse. The account of Rosa's interview with the Swedish biographer, for example, never aspires to go beyond publicly knowable facts: "Lionel Burger had been born in 1905. . . . He began his medical studies at Cape Town" (88). The public mode of perception has multiple voices, however. When Rosa seeks a passport form Brandt Vermeulen, the narration sounds like surveillance: "She was known to have driven to town. . . . Perhaps it was a favour she wanted" (173). When the narrator tells of Orde Greer's trial, she alludes to newspapers and adopts a press style: "The State had almost concluded its evidence when Rosa attended a session" (333).

The narrator is also privy to the inner life. She has access to personal knowledge about Conrad—"He was not looking for personal commitment" (17)—as well as Rosa: "she felt a strange embarrassment" (18). During Rosa's love affair with Bernard, the narrator describes the intense pitch of sensation she feels: "In the presence of a creature so contained, Rosa came to awareness of her own being like the rising tick of a clock in an empty room" (272). When Rosa is invited to Brandt's house to discuss the possibilities of acquiring a passport, the narrator scrutinizes Brandt's strategies to win her sexual favors in exchange for it: "He did not evade her gaze; his grin deepened and the skin at the side of his left eye was tweaked by some nerve; he got up suddenly and stood as if he had forgotten what for" (185). Uncovering personal motives here poses a sharp contrast to the surveillance tone calculated to penetrate Rosa's reasons for action in the previous section. The narrator is trying to get it all in, from as many angles as is possible.

Colette, Conrad, and Lionel provide points of stylistic reference for the third-person narration: a sensually rich, poetic perception of events; a tenacious "fascination" with and interrogation of people, events, places, and their meanings; and an analytic clarity that allows for unfettered actions. Colette and Lionel are two extremes, female and male, with Conrad poised in between because his style partakes of the interrupting, questioning, feminine, open textuality, along with the male, quest-oriented, clearly shaped ending (as is demonstrated in *Heart of Darkness*). We detect these same traits in the character Conrad. In his fascination with possible meanings about experience, he gets caught up in meditative wanderings that lead to his disappearance at sea in a lost pleasure craft.

These three figures also point to different forms of knowledge to which Rosa is naturally predisposed and that inform her voice: Colette, an intuitive knowing without reasons, essentially connected with her female body; Conrad, a questioning suspicion of concocted truth; and Lionel, a self-assured lucidity that leads to action. An example of the first style resonating in Rosa's voice approximates the earlier citation of Colette: "Sweat of wet wool heating up in sun through glass and scent of apples baking with cinnamon" (109). Rosa's consciousness of alternative versions of "truth" reminds us of the vague language that characterizes Marlow's ambivalent search for truth, as well as his decision to fix it in a final version. Like him Rosa says, "My version and theirs. And if this were being written down, both would seem equally concocted when read over" (16). Finally, in her last personal address to her father, Rosa debunks the slogans of Lenin and Lionel's political liberalism, affirming the only true action as a radical/personal one. She says:

> The real Rosa believed the real revolutionary initiative was to come from the people; you named me for that? This time it's coming from the children

of the people, teaching the fathers—the ANC, BPC, PAC, all of them, all the acronyms hastening to claim, to catch up, the theory chasing events. (348–49)

Through Rosa's voice, then, the paternal theory catches up with the forgotten, invisible, maternal qualities; poetry and revolution are brought to the surface and made accessible and useful. Poetry and revolution in this sense are like the chaotic, preverbal, unarticulated semiotics of bodily sensations and messages that Julia Kristeva associates with the mother during the pre-Oedipal stage of child development. In the last quote, it takes the form of the radically political Soweto riots of 1976, action that came not from organized liberal parties but from the black and colored children following their instincts to revolt, survive, and express their desires.

The alternation of Rosa's personal narrative with the third-person narrator provides the double discourse (which more precisely is multiple) necessary to sustain life and to change the existing order. It reflects living meaning and significance as process, rather than the deathly finality of inhabiting the sentence. Rosa's personal impulse is to resist linear, finite meaning. She discovers instead a new version of commitment, one that must constantly be renewed and revised:

No one can defect. I don't know the ideology: It's about suffering. How to end suffering. And it ends in suffering. Yes, it's strange to live in a country where there are sill heroes. Like anyone else, I do what I can. I am teaching them to walk again, at Baragwanath Hospital. They put one foot before the other. (332)

Having internalized Colette's opinion about heroes and put it to use in the form of action that she has taken from her patriarchal inheritance, Rosa has become a place of ongoing double discourse. She has become a separate-while-connected woman able to engage others fully and yet disinterestedly. Luxuriating in knowing who she is—a knowledge that is always changing—gives her a center from which to extend herself to those in need. As she says, "That utopia, its inside. . . . without it, how can you act?" (296).

Notes

My title anticipates the subject of the essay by alluding to two important literary parents of Gordimer: Virginia Woolf and Joseph Conrad. As in *Burger's Daughter*, the more obvious influence will appear to be paternal, that is, Conrad's *Heart of Darkness*.

Those conscious of their maternal literary inheritance will recognize Woolf's phrase "lighting a torch" and will understand its relevance to Rosa's story. Woolf writes in *A Room of One's Own:* "For if Chloe likes Olivia and Mary Carmichael knows how to express it she will light a torch in that vast chamber where nobody has yet been" (88).

1. Mira says that for women, survival "requires the dulling of the mind and the senses, and a delicate attunement to waiting, without insisting on precision about just what it is you are waiting for" (59).

2. Having identified the personal with the female tradition, I now suggest a parallel between the personal and the unconscious. Luce Irigaray makes the connection between the feminine and the unconscious by asking, "whether the feminine does not, in part, consist of what is operating in the name of the unconscious? Whether a certain 'specificity' of woman is not repressed/censured under cover of what is designated as the unconscious? Thus many of the characteristics attributed to the unconscious may evoke an economy of desire that would be, perhaps, 'feminine'" (123).

3. A recurrent theme in Doris Lessing's *The Golden Notebook* is the subtle undermining of women's intuitive sense of themselves by the language men use to define them: "Paul gave birth to Ella, the naive Ella. He destroyed in her the knowing, doubting, sophisticated Ella and again and again he put her intelligence to sleep, and with her willing connivance, so that she floated darkly on her love for him, on her naivety, which is another word for a spontaneous creative faith" (211). In Cathy, we find the consequences of such unquestioned molding by male ideology.

4. Jean Baker Miller has convincingly argued in *Toward a New Psychology of Women* that women have for too long used their energies and resources to abet the welfare and growth of children and husbands to the neglect of their own development. There are signs, however, that women are changing: "Women are the people struggling to create for themselves a new concept of personhood; they are attempting to restructure the central tenets of their lives. This effort extends to the deepest inner reaches" (44). This personal growth, Miller believes, will enhance and beneficially restructure community life. Cathy subordinated individual goals to her "responsibility to others." Colette, on the other hand, is the model Rosa needs in her struggle for self-fulfillment and a new form of service to others.

5. Irigaray elaborates the impoverishment of men whose self-expression is confined to a phallocratic model of speech: "So long as men claim to say everything and define everything, how can anyone know what the language of the male sex might be? So long as the logic of discourse is modeled on sexual indifference, on the submission of one sex to the other, how can anything be known about the 'masculine'?" (128).

6. Unlike Rosa, who seeks to expand her memory of her father to find the man behind the voice, Marlow defensively insists on the eloquence and moral victory of Kurtz's "summing-up" utterance. "The horror! The horror!" (118). "Better his cry—much better. It was an affirmation, a moral victory paid for by innumerable defeats, by abominable terrors, by abominable satisfactions. But it was a victory. That is why I have remained loyal to Kurtz to the last, and even beyond, when a long time after I heard once more, not his own voice, but the echo of his magnificent eloquence thrown to me from a soul as translucently pure as a cliff of crystal" (120).

7. In *A Room of One's Own* Woolf asks why literary production by women had been so sparse. After examining the circumstances in which they wrote and which posed impediments to consistently good writing, she marvels at their success, meager though it seems vis-à-vis men's imposing output. The greatest obstacle she finds to women's literary careers was the lack of a female tradition, "for we think back through our mothers if we are women" (79). This is the process in which Woolf herself is engaged as she imagines the psychic and momentary deprivation suffered by her maternal literary ancestors.

8. In her essay "(E)Merging Identities: The Dynamics of Female Friendship in Contemporary Fiction by Women," Elizabeth Abel expands Chodorow's theory of female psychology based on mother/daughter relationships to include female friendships. She signals the centrality of this theme in contemporary fiction, stating that commonality rather than complementarity between female friends allows for transference and countertransference to occur, leading to greater emotional growth and psychic wholeness on both parts.

Works Cited

Abel, Elizabeth. "(E)Merging Identities: The Dynamics of Female Friendship in Contemporary Fiction by Women." *Signs* 6 (1981): 413–35.

Cixous, Hélène. "The Laugh of the Medusa." *Signs* 1 (1976): 875–93.

Conrad, Joseph. *"Heart of Darkness" and "The Secret Sharer."* New York: Bantam, 1902.

Cooke, John Wharton. *The Novels of Nadine Gordimer. DAI* 37 (7) (1977): 4346A. Northwestern University.

French, Marilyn. *The Women's Room.* New York: Berkley, 1978.

Gardner, Susan. "A Story for This Place and Time: An Interview with Nadine Gordimer about *Burger's Daughter.*" *Kunapipi* 3 (1981): 99–112.

Gordimer, Nadine. *Burger's Daughter.* London: Cape, 1979.

———. *The Lying Days.* London: Cape, 1978.

Irigaray, Luce. *This Sex Which Is Not One.* Trans. Catherine Porter. Ithaca, N.Y.: Cornell University Press, 1985.

Lacan, Jacques. *Ecrits.* Trans. Alan Sheridan. London: Norton, 1977.

Lessing, Doris. *The Golden Notebook.* New York: Simon, 1962.

Miller, Jean Baker. *Toward a New Psychology of Women.* Boston: Beacon, 1977.

Schreiner, Olive. *The Story of an African Farm.* London: Penguin, 1971.

Woolf, Virginia. *A Room of One's Own.* New York: Harcourt, 1929.

Exiled In and Exiled From

The Politics and Poetics of *Burger's Daughter*

LOUISE YELIN

◆　◆　◆

I N   A   F A M O U S   P A S S A G E in *A Room of One's Own*, Virginia Woolf identifies the position of women as simultaneously inside and outside patriarchal cultural hegemony: "If one is a woman one is often surprised by a sudden splitting off of consciousness, say in walking down Whitehall, when
from being the natural inheritor of that civilisation, she becomes, on the
contrary, outside of it, alien and critical" (101). Woolf offers a way of con-
ceiving the question of women and exile. To be exiled is to be "outside,
. . . alien and critical": on one hand, to be displaced by that culture
("outside" or exiled from); on the other, to be engaged in trans-
forming/displacing it ("alien and critical"). Paradoxically, the most dis-
abling version of exile may be a consequence of women's position as inheritors of a civilization, for a condition of their inheritance—their position
"inside"—is acquiescence in a cultural or political set that subordinates
them, displaces them, or exiles them to the outside. Woolf defines the
stance of much recent feminist criticism and theory—a stance that Joan
Kelly identifies as the "doubled vision of feminist theory" and Rachel Blau
DuPlessis calls the "both/and" vision of female modernism and implicitly
of feminist criticism ("For the Etruscans"). But in this passage, at least,
Woolf's privileging of gender occludes other crucial aspects of the
social/cultural ensemble. What does it mean, for example, to be the inher-

itor of the civilization symbolized (figured) by Whitehall? Surely not all women can claim such an inheritance. To define feminism with reference to the particular group of women Woolf sees as inside/outside "that civilisation" yields an elitist, ethnocentric vision of both feminism and exile.

In this essay, I will examine Nadine Gordimer's *Burger's Daughter* as a text that opens up—multiplies—the both/and vision of Woolf, Kelly, and DuPlessis and of U.S./European feminism in general. Gordimer writes from a position both inside and outside the dominant European cultural tradition ("Conversation," 30–31). Her frame of reference is defined by a literary tradition that runs from Plato to Conrad and Proust and by her situation in South Africa: she is a white, English-speaking woman actively opposed to apartheid and its regime. For Gordimer, then, the African context as well as the female one constitutes a version of exile in and from— displacement from/of—the European cultural tradition. That is, for Gordimer, the reality of apartheid mandates a politics of active opposition that inflects gender, exile, and feminism.[1]

In the first part of this essay I discuss the deployment of the both/and vision in the narrative discourse of *Burger's Daughter*. Like any number of novels, *Burger's Daughter* plays off a public/political narrative and a private/ personal one. But the way Gordimer does this, I suggest, destabilizes the opposition between the political and the personal. In the second part, I examine the novel's plot and argue that Gordimer revises the conventions of the female *Bildungsroman* and thereby forces the reader to confront the cultural specificity of the values, codes, and genres of the dominant cultural tradition—European, bourgeois, patriarchal, and feminist. Thus I suggest that the politics and poetics of *Burger's Daughter* redefine the meaning of exile.

Destabilizing Narrative Discourse

The opening sequence of *Burger's Daughter* calls in question the nature of representation and, therefore, the status of its own narrative discourse. Even before the beginning, the status of the bourgeois self or subject—and its avatars, the subject of first-person narration or the protagonist of a ("the") novel—is thrown into relief by the epigraph from Claude Lévi-Strauss: "I am the place in which something has occurred." In this sentence, *I* occupies the place of the grammatical subject, but the sentence identifies *I* not as a person, a Cartesian subject of consciousness, but as a place, a site of activity. Because readers open the novel aware that it is about South Africa, the sentence invites us to identify I, the speaking subject, with (South) Africa, the place where something—the events that the novel describes?—occurs. Thus the epigraph evokes both the structuralist decentering of the subject and the poststructuralist displacement of humanism and with it of European ethnocentrism. This displacement, made from within European discourse about Africa, is itself displaced by the epigraph to part 3, an epigraph spoken by as well as for South Africa, the slogan of the African National Congress, "Peace. Land. Bread." This sequence represents the postmodern decentering of bourgeois subjectivity as part of a larger political project, which dislodges the imperial(ist) self and empowers formerly colonized Others in and through the struggle against apartheid. The sequence of epigraphs, moreover, cautions us to read *Burger's Daughter* as a novel made from both inside and outside the European political and cultural hegemony that constitutes colonial others as Other, from both inside and outside the liberation struggle in Africa.

This double perspective connects Gordimer with the stance of feminist theory and criticism, with feminism as it is at once part of and critical of— inside and outside—the dominant cultural tradition. Gordimer's particular position as a white woman opposed to the white racist regime opens up or further multiplies the double perspective of U.S./European feminism. This multiple perspective governs the way we read *Burger's Daughter* as the story of a particular woman in a particular family and also as the story of a place in which something occurs.

The opening sequence of *Burger's Daughter* calls in question the nature of representation and, therefore, the status of its own narration. The novel begins in 1962 with a group of people standing outside a prison waiting to bring parcels to those who are only later revealed as having been detained for participating in the struggle against the regime.[2] Among the group is the novel's protagonist, identified first as "a schoolgirl in a brown and yellow uniform," subsequently as "Lionel Burger's daughter . . . fourteen years old, bringing an eiderdown quilt and hot-water bottle for her mother," and then given a name and a detailed description of her physical appearance (9–10). The three ways that Rosa Burger is designated in the opening sequence seem initially to be synonymous or complementary ways of describing the same person, but the three designations—schoolgirl, Lionel Burger's daughter, Rosa Burger—are hieroglyphs, signifiers of the relationship of the perceiver (narrator) and the persons/things described. How Rosa is seen depends on who is seeing her and from where, and who and where are not neutral terms but politically charged, like everything else in this novel about a country in which "society *is* the political situation" and "politics is character" (Gordimer, "A Writer in South Africa," 23).[3]

Throughout the novel, the terms that designate Rosa represent the different perspectives, the ideologically charged languages, of different groups in South African society.[4] The schoolgirl in uniform is the product of a journalistic view of the anti-apartheid movement, one that purports to "humanize" it by packaging it for consumers of the mass media. (The novel as a whole works to defamiliarize this perspective and the view it produces of South Africa.) Lionel Burger's daughter is the object (person) seen by those Rosa calls "the faithful," the activists in the struggle against apartheid and her parents' comrades in the South African Communist Party. The faithful have their own narratives of the novel's events. One of these, an account of Rosa's participation in the movement, is given just after the opening sequence. In this account, party rhetoric appears as a hodgepodge of contending clichés that present Rosa as a heroine at once revolutionary and domestic: "Already she had taken on her mother's role in the household, giving loving support to her father, who was all too soon to be detained as well. On that day he had put others' plight before his own" (12). That white radicals in the anti-apartheid struggle legitimize their movement with the rhetoric of bourgeois domesticity is a sign of the continuing hegemony of bourgeois, patriarchal ideology and, thus, of a contradiction that defines Rosa, especially for U.S. or European feminist readers, a contradiction between feminism (Rosa's liberation as a woman) and the struggle for justice in South Africa. The novel's treatment of this conflict distinguishes it from many novels written by women and suggests that female experience and indeed feminism are not universal but historically and geographically—politically—specific.

If the schoolgirl is the product of the mass media and Lionel Burger's daughter is Rosa as seen by the faithful, who gives us "Rosa Burger, about fourteen years old"? The obvious answer is the third-person narrator, but as Stephen Clingman points out (189–90), there are several third-person narrators. At least one of these presents events as if writing a surveillance report for the government: one of the ways that *Burger's Daughter* calls narration into question is by linking it with spying and surveillance, with an organization of knowledge that is also an organization of power. Each narrator (narrative voice) represents a different perspective, point of view, position. Thus the third-person narration is the site of contending narratives, a place in which something—a contention of narratives—occurs. This narration and these contending narratives are also placed in dialogue with the narrative of Rosa herself.

Burger's Daughter plays off a third-person narration that attempts to name, capture, or represent—contain—a social totality against the more personal first-person narration of the protagonist.[5] Rosa's narrative emerges in part as a response to the question posed by the opening sequence, a question she also asks herself: "When they saw me outside the prison, what did they see?" (13). Rosa embraces narrative complexity and indeterminacy. She begins her story with a disclaimer: "I shall never know. It's all concocted. I saw—see—that profile in a hand-held mirror directed towards another mirror" (14). The two mirrors yield a series of reflections, each of which renders reality as representation. Each image in this series is like an element in a signifying chain; there is no absolute referent or transcendental signified, no original or authoritative master code.[6]

Rosa eschews not only the convention, whereby the author has authority over her (usually his) text, but also other versions of authority in first-person narration, in particular the idea that the narrating self can ever know the self-as-narrated or that the relationship between the self-as-narrated and the narrating self is one of continuity: "It's impossible to filter free of what I have learnt, felt, thought, the subjective presence of the schoolgirl. She's a stranger about whom some intimate facts are known to me, that's all" (14). Despite Rosa's repudiation of the idea that she is privy to her past self, her narration apparently privileges the personal, individual, private dimensions of experience. Thus she re-presents (reinterprets) the inaugural event of the novel: she tells us that she was carrying a hot-water bottle because she was suffering "the leaden, dragging, wringing pain, . . . the peculiar fierce concentration of the body's forces in the menstruation of early puberty" (14–15). The hot-water bottle now appears to signify menarche and therefore to inscribe *Burger's Daughter* in the subgenre of the female *Bildungsroman*, where menarche so often encodes the protagonist's initiation into maturity, her subjection to the female destiny of anatomy and the constraints of the feminine gender. (I am thinking here of the "pungent suffering" that Jane Eyre experiences when her cousin John Reed throws a book at her and sends her to the Red Room [chapter 1]; of Catherine Earnshaw's wound when she is bitten by the dog Skulker as she escapes from Wuthering Heights and goes with Heathcliff to Thrushcross Grange, from which she emerges a "lady" [chapter 6]; and of Maggie Tulliver's encounter with Philip Wakem in the Red Deeps [*The Mill on the Floss*, book 5, chapter 1].)

But Rosa—or Gordimer or *Burger's Daughter*—also discredits this code, or at least treats it as lacking the special authority of a novelistic master code. For Rosa now says that she carried the hot-water bottle to convey a message to her mother in jail: "*Dear Mom, Hope you are all right.* Then this in-nocently unsuitable tone became the perfect vehicle for the important thing I needed to convey. *Dad and I are fine and looking after everything. Lots of love from both.* She would know at once I was telling her my father had not been taken since she had gone" (16). This is the first and most innocuous of many instances in the novel when white anti-apartheid activists use the language of domesticity, family values, or romance—"private life"—as a cover for their political activities.[7] Indeed, the milestones of Rosa's life are not—or rather they are and are not—the developmental crises defined by psychoanalytic theories of personality but events in the modern history of South Africa. She is born on 1 May 1948, the year the first Afrikaner gov-ernment took office (her birthdate, of course, identifies her with Commu-nism), and her life is punctuated by the treason trials during which her parents are imprisoned (1956–57), the Sharpeville massacre (1960), the ban-ning and jailing of activists in the 1960s, and the movement sparked by the Soweto students' school boycott (1976–77). As a young woman, Rosa is "engaged" to activist Noel de Witt so that she can visit him in prison. A trip she takes during her subsequent affair with a Swede who is making a film about her father gives her the opportunity to smuggle a passport to a black comrade in a remote area. Throughout the novel, but especially in the opening sequence, the use of domesticity or the personal as a cover for po-litical activity frames that ideological ensemble. The frame—irony—ap-parently distinguishes the self-conscious deployment of the personal/domestic from the unselfconscious rehearsal of domestic pieties, in either the annals of the faithful or the propaganda of the Afrikaner regime. But whether self-conscious or unselfconscious, ironic or straight, the deploy-ment of domestic codes in *Burger's Daughter* makes it clear that private life—and its chief literary representation, the classic European novel—is among other things a sign of white privilege.

The third-person narration is structured synchronically: each of the contending narratives signifies the stance of the observer(s) toward Rosa or the place where something occurs. Rosa's narrative is structured di-achronically. It is divided into three sections (the three parts of the novel), which are distinguished by Rosa's narratees: in part 1, her hippie lover; in part 2, her father's first wife (her surrogate mother); in part 3, her father himself. Like the multiple perspectives of the third-person narration, this structure implies that the narrating subject is not the only influence or authority over narrative discourse; unlike the organization of the third-person narration, it implies a plot, a sequence of development.

Difference and Plot: Rewriting the *Bildungsroman*

Rosa addresses her narrative first to her lover, next to her surrogate mother, and finally to her father. This sequence inscribes a movement toward the father; in other words, it rewrites the generic conventions of the *Bildungsroman*, which tends to take its protagonist ever further from his parents in his quest for whatever the novel or the culture he inhabits defines as maturity (Buckley, 17–19). As Elizabeth Abel et al. have noted (8), the ends of *Bildung* and therefore of the *Bildungsroman* are often gender-specific: autonomy (work) for men, marriage, romance, or sexual fulfillment for women. Of course some novels—*To the Lighthouse*, for example, or Christina Stead's *The Man Who Loved Children*—depart from these gender-marked norms in defining work or art, not love, as the object of women's quest. I argue here that *Burger's Daughter* revises even these female or feminist revisions of *Bildung*, since Rosa's quest is defined primarily neither by love nor work but by political activity, and it takes her toward as well as away from her father, and that this difference is among other things a sign or product of the African context of the novel, Gordimer's "responsibility toward the situation to which I was born" ("A Writer in South Africa," 22).[8]

If the inaugural event of the novel is Rosa's appearance outside the prison with a hot-water bottle for (alternately) herself and her mother, its real plot motivator is the death in prison of Lionel Burger. Like the lives of so many novels' protagonists, Rosa's early life is punctuated by a series of deaths: her brother's drowning, her mother's death, and her father's death, which—in a way that turns out to be spurious—sets her free. After Lionel dies, Rosa drifts away from the world of political action in which she has been involved and goes to live with her lover, an alienated, cynical, disaffected hippie named Conrad. In the schematic terms the novel simultaneously invites and refuses, Conrad represents the antithesis of the faithful, who defer all thoughts of present gratification for a future that may well be an illusion. Like the skeptical, deracinated characters in the novels of his namesake, Joseph Conrad, Gordimer's Conrad believes that he is without illusions and derides the activists' commitment to their cause.[9] When Conrad tells Rosa that she has grown up through other people, he means that she has never had an authentic emotional life. Among the "illusions" he punctures is Rosa's feeling for Noel de Witt, the "fiancé" she visited in prison, may have fallen in love with, and hoped to follow out of the country. But in undermining Rosa, Conrad serves the ends of the state, whether wittingly or not—again, like the characters of his namesake—and he therefore calls into question the idea of a personal realm untainted by politics. The entire first part of Rosa's narrative is a rejoinder to Conrad, a text whose pretext is his version of bourgeois individualism. At one point, Rosa answers Conrad by imagining her father's thoughts: "Lionel Burger probably saw in you the closed circuit of self; for him, such a life must be in need of a conduit toward meaning, which posited: outside self. That's where the tension that makes it possible to live lay, for him; between self and others; between the present and creation of something called the future" (86).

Are we to believe that because Rosa's response to Conrad is her version of Lionel's response she is not free, still subject to the authority of her father? (Consider Woolf's Lily Briscoe, who does not complete her painting until she dispatches Mr. and Mrs. Ramsay and sees things for herself.) On one hand, Rosa is not yet free, still mourning the deaths of her brother and parents; on the other hand, the outcome of the novel endorses Lionel's view—and Rosa's—and therefore calls in question the convention whereby freedom, maturity, or development—*Bildung*—is marked by the protagonist's superseding, transcending, or displacing paternal authority.

In other ways, too, Rosa's relationship with Conrad suggests the limits of private life. She uses it to separate herself from the faithful and their ongoing political activity. It is infantile and virtually incestuous: it repeats Rosa's relationship with Tony, the brother who drowned, and with Baasie, a black boy who came to live with the Burgers when his father was jailed and who was brought up as Rosa's brother. (When Rosa's parents are imprisoned in the 1957 treason trial, she goes to stay with relatives, and Baasie is sent away.) In other words, private life or the personal, which is here portrayed as the working out of a repetitive compulsion, is no more authentic than the political commitment of the faithful to a future they are trying to bring into being.

Eventually, Rosa does leave South Africa. After witnessing two events that her father's theories cannot account for—she observes a drunk die on a park bench and watches in horror as a black man viciously beats his donkey on a deserted road between a black "location" and Johannesburg—she feels politically impotent and attempts to "defect," to exile herself from "Lionel's country" (210). Rosa goes to the south of France to stay with Katya, Madame Bagnelli, her father's first wife. There, she falls in love with a married French academic named Bernard Chabalier. With Chabalier, Rosa seems for the first time to have an authentic emotional—sexual and personal—life, and she comes to believe that "it's possible to live within the ambit of a person, not a country. . . . There's nothing more private and personal than the life of a mistress, is there?" (302–4). Chabalier, then, represents romantic love as a version of personal liberation: his name, after all, has the same etymology as *chivalry* and *chevalier.* But in these echoes we can see (hear) the regressive undertones of romantic love, for the chivalric order is feudal, a step backward from the bourgeois order ironically named by Rosa's father, Lionel *Burger (Die Burger* is also the name of a leading Afrikaans newspaper), and from the socialist future represented by Rosa Luxemburg, for whom, along with his mother, Rosemarie Burger, Lionel Burger names his daughter.[10] (Significantly, we are never told definitively whether Rosa is named for either, neither, or both. Katya's friends call Rosa *Rose,* a name that identifies her with the object of the [male] romantic quest. Equally important, as a person "named" by the regime, Rosa is prohibited from participation in public life.) One could argue, of course, that the concept of progress which defines the bourgeois order as more advanced than the feudal order does not take women into account. Or, conversely, one could argue that romantic love is an ideology of male dominance, rendering women as vassals subject to men.[11] Gordimer is not so much asserting one position or the other as suggesting the double-edged character of romantic love, as of other Western/European versions of personal liberation. This point is underscored by the way the love affair of Rosa and Chabalier, the apotheosis of the personal, is punctuated by their discussion of languages—English, Afrikaans, French, and Langue d'Oc—as records of political struggle (267–75). The doubled-edgedness, the progression that is also a regression is worked out not only for Rosa's sexual life but also in the way she is represented as a daughter in relation to two mothers.

Rosa's affair with Chabalier coincides with her visit with Katya, who takes her in and mothers her. In other words, Rosa's sexual awakening is enabled by her (re)discovery of her mother, a (re)discovery that, like her affair with Chabalier, is both a progression and a regression. That the (re)discovery of mother is more important than the love affair is implicit in the choice of Katya, not Chabalier, as the narratee in part two. Katya offers a contrast with Rosa's actual mother, Cathy Jansen Burger. Katya comes from an English-speaking family, whereas Cathy's family are Afrikaners: Rosa's two mothers evoke the two mother tongues she tells Chabalier she grew up speaking (267). Mother tongues for Rosa, these languages are *lingue franche* for black South Africans (315). But language is not the main difference between the two mothers, for Cathy is a committed activist and Katya resisted the discipline that tied the faithful together and eventually "defected" to Europe: thus she suggests the seductions of Euro-

pean culture, and her original name—she was born Colette Swan—
evokes the two most important mothers in modern French literature. The
allusions to Proust and Colette reinforce the identification of Katya with
the idealized mother of the family romance or pre-Oedipal fantasy (Garner et al., 20–24): Katya, fully realized in descriptions both by Rosa and by
the third-person narrator, displaces the somewhat shadowy Cathy as a
maternal presence. (There are two other fully realized maternal figures in
the novel: Lionel, in Rosa's memory of snuggling up to his breast with
Baasie and Tony as he taught them to swim, and Marisa Kgosana, a black
activist whose maternal relationship with Rosa becomes one of sisterhood.) Thus, as in other modern novels about young women's loss of in-
nocence (Elizabeth Bowen's *The Death of the Heart*, for example), Rosa's
sexual awakening is associated with a return to mother. But the family romance is not the whole story, for though Katya represents the fantasy of
the nurturing or sustaining mother, she is also limited in/by the individualism that defines her—a bohemian version more attractive than Conrad's
or even Chabalier's, but one that is limiting nonetheless. And in this respect, Katya and all she stands for represent an interlude in Rosa's life, a
stage in her development.

Under Katya's tutelage, and Bernard's, Rosa undergoes an aesthetic as
well as a sexual awakening. Katya introduces her to modern art, for example, and one night she takes her to hear nightingales sing. Listening, the
two women experience an ecstasy both like and unlike the one Keats describes in his "Ode to a Nightingale":

> Katya's breathing touched her as pine-needles did. All around the two
> women a kind of piercingly sweet ringing was on the limit of being audible.
> A new perception was picking up the utmost ring of waves whose centre
> must be unreachable ecstasy. The thrilling of the darkness intensified with-
> out coming closer. She gave a stir, questioning; the shape of Katya's face
> turned to stay her. The vibrating glass in which they were held shattered
> into song. The sensation of receiving the song kept changing; now it was a
> skyslope on which they planed, tipped, sailed, twirled to earth; then it was a
> breath stopped at the point of blackout and passing beyond it to a pitch hit,
> ravishingly, again, again, again. (261)

This passage, viscerally descriptive of female orgasm, epitomizes the way
Gordimer evokes a *locus classicus* of European culture to point to the difference made by both the female and the African contexts. As a fable of literary production, Keats's ode suggests that the poet makes his poem as a way
of recreating the solitary ecstasy he experiences in listening to the bird:

"Away! Away! for I will fly to thee, / Not charioted by Bacchus and his pards, / But on the viewless wings of poesy." Keats's nightingale is both the occasion and the sign of the poet's affirmation of his vocation. The episode in *Burger's Daughter* has a different valence. The moment of ecstasy is sexual as well as aesthetic, not solitary but shared by a mother and daughter. Nor is this episode a fable of literary production: it is reported not by Rosa, who in any case does not write an ode, but by an omniscient narrator. And though it embraces both the aesthetic and the sexual/maternal dimensions of Rosa's relationship with Katya, it also marks what Rosa leaves behind when she leaves Katya: the maternal locus, Europe, the life of aesthetic pleasure.

Rosa does leave Katya. She goes to London, where she falls in with a group of South African exiles and soon encounters the man she knew as Baasie. The name means "Little Boss" in Afrikaans, as he now reminds her when he tells her the name his father gave him, Zwelinzima, which in his language means "suffering land." In a late-night phone call, Zwelinzima taunts her: "Whatever you whites touch, it's a take-over" (321). But the eventual result of this phone call is Rosa's return to South Africa: "I've heard all the black clichés before. I am aware that, like the ones the faithful use, they are an attempt to habituate ordinary communication to overwhelming meanings in human existence. They rap out the mechanical chunter of a telex; the message has to be picked up and read. They become enormous lies incarcerating enormous truths, still extant, somewhere" (328).

Rosa's response to Zwelinzima has at least a double significance. Rosa accepts the arbitrariness of language, the inability of language and especially politicized language to arrive at truth. But the instability that results from the dismantling of a master code does not lead her, like Conrad or Katya, to defect or remain in exile. Nor, conversely, does it make her believe that the rift between herself and Zwelinzima, suffering land, can be easily healed: although Gordimer flirts with allegory, she does not sink to sentimentalism. Rather, Rosa recognizes that "no one can defect" (332),[12] and the novel endorses this recognition. This passage occurs at the beginning of part 3, which is headed by the ANC slogan and addressed by Rosa to Lionel Burger. The passage announces Rosa's recommitment to political struggle, which leads her not only to resume her work as a physical therapist and reaffirm her relationship to her father but also to occupy his and her mother's place.

Burger's Daughter ends where it began, with a group waiting to bring parcels to the detained persons in prison. Rosa is now among those inside,

detained for her participation in the movement now (1977) led by the
Soweto students. (This movement began as a protest against instruction in
Afrikaans.) Resistance is signaled, as before, in the use of domestic codes to
convey messages among the faithful, both inside and outside the prison.
A friend who visits Rosa remarks, "We joke a lot. . . . After all, why
shouldn't family matters be funny? They're boring enough. You only realize how boring when you have to try to make them metaphors for something else" (360). But the friend does not have the last word: it is deleted by
prison censors from a letter that Rosa sends to Katya: "There was a reference to a watermark of light that came into the cell at sundown every
evening, reflected from some west-facing surface outside; something
Lionel Burger had once mentioned. But the line had been deleted by the
prison censor. Madame Bagnelli had never been able to make it out" (361).
Rosa has taken her father's place; earlier, Lionel described the sun's appearance in prison only as the reflection of shadows (64). Moreover, Rosa's
situation is like that of Plato's cave dweller who sees only shadows of images (*Republic*, book 7). But here again, Gordimer at once recalls and recasts
the European tradition: Rosa does not emerge like Plato's cave dweller into
the light of truth, of pure forms, and in this respect the novel's ending apparently repudiates European cultural hegemony in the guise of the logo-
centrism symbolized by Plato. In addition, Gordimer subverts the hierar-
chical vision that underlies the cave analogy: while Plato's philosopher
returns to the cave to educate those left in the darkness below,[13] Rosa's relationship with the other prisoners is one of equality, solidarity, and sorority. More important, the ending insists on the importance of the African
context: it signals Gordimer's continuing opposition to apartheid, for the
specific agent of her revision of European cultural traditions is, of course,
the prison censor, whose action inscribes apartheid as absence. To this action, the novel is a counteraction that makes apartheid visible at least in its
effects. In putting both these positions into play, *Burger's Daughter* partners a
deconstructive poetics—a destabilizing of the discourses and especially the
novelistic codes that inscribe European cultural hegemony—with a politics of opposition to apartheid and its regime.

    This ending appears to assert that the African context takes primacy
over the female one, that the exigency of abolishing apartheid overrides
the concerns of gender, but it actually reenacts (reiterates) the novel's
both/and vision and forces us once again to reconceive the meaning of
exile. At the end of the novel, Rosa's position darkly echoes that of Woolf's
walker down Whitehall. She has left Europe, and she is simultaneously inside and outside the "civilization" she inhabits, exiled in the prison (inside)

and exiled from the Afrikaner regime against which she struggles, alien and critical, a victim and an opponent. Because Rosa is incarcerated in the prison where her father died, her exile in prison marks a (re)turn to her father that seems to exile her and with her the novel from a feminist tradition that conceives *Bildung* as transcendence or displacement of paternal authority. But though the (re)turn to father appears to privilege the filial relationship that designates Rosa as Burger's daughter—her visitor reports, for example, that she looks like a little girl (360)—return is not identified with regression, for Rosa's life in prison is also governed by her sisterhood with her fellow prisoners. This experience of sisterhood—a sisterhood that transcends race—is made possible by Rosa's memory of "something sublime" in Lionel, the "sweet lucidity" and "elation" he shared with the black children in revolt against the regime (349). In other words, Rosa discovers herself in finding the father whose commitment to ending apartheid shapes her experience of sisterhood. *Burger's Daughter*, then, refuses a closure that privileges any one reading or reinstitutes a novelistic master code. Indeed, though the last scene finds Rosa occupying her father's place in prison, it ends not with Rosa or Lionel but with Katya, whose presence in the novel evokes the question of gender and especially gender and the personal as/and exile from Africa. Rosa, Lionel, Katya, censor: the refusal of closure here reinforces the both/and vision. That the last word, if there is a last word, belongs to Katya, who almost displaces Lionel in the narrative, suggests that although the struggle against apartheid takes precedence over sexual liberation or personal fulfillment, the issue of gender cannot be exiled from women's texts.

Notes

I thank my British Women Novelists class for provoking me to think about *Burger's Daughter*; Virginia Anderson, Mimi Doorga, Nasryne Matin, and Amy Tompkins of New Horizons Daycare Center for child care that freed me to think and write; Jean Herskovits for sharing with me her knowledge of African history; and Celeste Schenck, Deirdre David, Angela Ingram, Jane Marcus, Ronnie Scharfman, and Bob Stein for helpful comments on earlier versions of this essay and for encouragement that made me feel unlike an exile.

1. Gordimer notes in a 1982 interview that in South Africa color is the crucial issue. The interview ends at this point, and six months later it resumes with Gordimer asserting that when white oppression of black ceases, black women will fight against their oppression by black men ("Conversation," 20).

2. Gordimer assumes an audience familiar with South African history and not in need of having the particulars spelled out. The killing of blacks protesting at Sharpeville against the Pass Laws (1960) ended the possibility of change through nonviolent protest; subsequently, there was an increase in underground and armed activity, including the founding of the armed wing of the ANC, Umkhonto we Sizwe (Spear of the Nation) and, concomitantly, an increase in the banning, detention, and imprisonment of opponents of the regime. The Communist Party, banned in 1950, continued as an underground organization, its members banned and jailed. I thank Jean Herskovits for clarifying this chronology for me.

3. Joseph Lelyveld points out that South African whites literally arrange not to see blacks: the policy of forced resettlement of blacks in "homelands" or black locations ensures that apartheid is invisible to whites (7).

4. The model of narration I am relying on is the dialogical paradigm of Mikhail Bakhtin in "Discourse in the Novel" (261–63).

5. Boyers (72), Newman, Cooke, and Clingman all comment on the articulation of public and private in the novel.

6. Thus Gordimer's narrative style is secular in the sense intended by Said (16–42), a structure of affiliation not filiation.

7. According to Stephen Clingman (175), "the family" was a code name for the SACP when it was underground.

8. Barbara Harlow makes a similar point about Third World women's prison narratives, which, she argues (505), challenge the literary conventions of autobiography.

9. Susan Greenstein regards Conrad as a "debilitated version of his namesake" (234).

10. Rosa Luxemburg serves as a model for Rosa's commitment to political struggle in *Burger's Daughter.* Because Luxemburg defines a social democratic—that is, Communist—politics that is not identical to Lenin's, she also signifies the complicated relationship of South African Communist opponents of apartheid to Soviet-inspired Communist parties and politics. Particularly germane to Lionel Burger's politics and the activism of South African Communists (and Communists) generally is Luxemburg's notion that the particular program of "social democracy" is less important than the way that program is "interpreted in action" (Luxemburg, 380).

11. Feminist historians and theorists have argued the case both ways. For an interrogation of the concept of progress, see Kelly (both titles); for critiques of romantic love, see de Beauvoir and Rich. Rachel DuPlessis articulates the critique of romance with narrative theory in her notion of the romance plot as a trope for the sex/gender system (*Writing beyond the Ending,* 5).

12. Here Rosa recalls Joseph Conrad's Marlow. For both, praxis—work for

Marlow, political action for Rosa, narrative for both—compensates for the loss of meaning, for the fact that lies incarcerate truth, that meaning is not "inside like a kernel but outside, enveloping the tale which brought it out only as a glow brings out a haze" (Conrad, 68).

13. I thank Morris Kaplan for bringing this to my attention.

Works Cited

Abel, Elizabeth, Marianne Hirsch, and Elizabeth Langland. Introduction to *The Voyage In: Fictions of Female Development,* edited by Elizabeth Abel, Marianne Hirsch, and Elizabeth Langland, 3–19. Hanover, N.H.: University Press of New England, 1983.

Bakhtin, Mikhail M. "Discourse in the Novel." In *The Dialogic Imagination,* translated by Caryl Emerson and Michael Holquist, edited by Michael Holquist, 259–422. Austin: Texas University Press, 1981.

Beauvoir, Simone de. *The Second Sex.* Translated and edited by H. M. Parshley. New York: Bantam, 1961.

Boyers, Robert. "Public and Private: On *Burger's Daughter.*" *Salmagundi* 62 (1984): 62–92.

Buckley, Jerome Hamilton. *Season of Youth: The Bildungsroman from Dickens to Golding.* Cambridge, Mass.: Harvard University Press, 1974.

Clingman, Stephen. *The Novels of Nadine Gordimer: History from the Inside.* London: Allen and Unwin; 1986.

Conrad, Joseph. *Heart of Darkness.* 1899. Reprint. New York: Signet, 1950.

Cooke, John. *The Novels of Nadine Gordimer: Private Lives/Public Landscapes.* Baton Rouge: Louisiana State University Press, 1985.

DuPlessis, Rachel Blau. *Writing beyond the Ending: Narrative Strategies of Twentieth-Century Women Writers.* Bloomington: Indiana University Press, 1985.

DuPlessis, Rachel Blau, and Members of Workshop 9. "For the Etruscans: Sexual Difference and Artistic Production: The Debate over a Female Aesthetic." In *The Future of Difference,* edited by Hester Eisenstein and Alice Jardine, 128–56. Boston: Hall, 1980.

Garner, Shirley, Claire Kahane, and Madelon Sprengnether. Introduction to *The (M)other Tongue: Essays in Feminist Psychoanalytic Interpretation,* edited by Shirley Garner, Claire Kahane, and Madelon Sprengnether, 15–29. Ithaca, N.Y.: Cornell University Press, 1985.

Gordimer, Nadine. *Burger's Daughter.* New York: Penguin, 1980.

———. "A Conversation with Nadine Gordimer." *Salmagundi* 62 (1984): 3–31.

———. "A Writer in South Africa." *London Magazine,* n.s., 5 (May 1965): 21–30.

Greenstein, Susan M. "Miranda's Story: Nadine Gordimer and the Literature of Empire." *Novel* 18 (1984–85): 227–42.

Harlow, Barbara. "From the Women's Prison: Third-World Women's Narratives of Prison." *Feminist Studies* 12 (1986): 501–24.

Kelly, Joan. "Did Women Have a Renaissance?" In *Becoming Visible: Women in European History,* edited by Renate Bridenthal and Claudia Koonz, 137–64. Boston: Houghton Mifflin, 1977.

———. "The Doubled Vision of Feminist Theory: A Postscript to the Women and Power Conference." *Feminist Studies* 4 (1979): 216–27.

Lelyveld, Joseph. *Move Your Shadow: South Africa, Black and White.* New York: New York Times Books, 1985.

Luxemburg, Rosa. "Our Program and the Political Situation." In *Selected Political Writings of Rosa Luxemburg,* edited by Richard Howard, 377–408. New York: Monthly Review, 1971.

Nadine Gordimer: Politics and the Order of Art. Salmagundi 62 (1984).

Newman, Judie. "Prospero's Complex: Race and Sex in Nadine Gordimer's *Burger's Daughter." Journal of Commonwealth Literature* 20 (1985): 81–99.

Rich, Adrienne. "Compulsory Heterosexuality and Lesbian Existence." In *Blood, Bread, and Poetry,* 23–75. New York: Norton, 1986.

Said, Edward W. "Secular Criticism." In *The World, the Text, and the Critic,* 16–42. Cambridge, Mass.: Harvard University Press, 1983.

Woolf, Virginia. *A Room of One's Own.* New York: Harcourt, Brace and World, 1929.

Suggested Reading

Attridge, Derek, and Rosemary Jolly, eds. *Writing South Africa: Literature, Apartheid and Democracy, 1970–1995*. Cambridge: Cambridge University Press, 1998.

Barnouw, Dagmar. "Nadine Gordimer: Dark Times, Interior Worlds, and the Obscurities of Difference." *Contemporary Literature* 35, no. 2 (1994): 252–80.

Bazin, Nancy Topping, and Marilyn Dallman Seymour, eds. *Conversations with Nadine Gordimer*. Jackson: University of Mississippi Press, 1990.

Boyers, Robert. "Nadine Gordimer: Politics and the Order of Art," *Salmagundi* 62 (Winter 1984): 62–92.

Brown, Duncan, and van Dyk, Bruno, eds. *Exchanges: South African Writing in Transition*. Pietermaritzburg, South Africa: University of Natal Press, 1991.

Clayton, Cherry. "White Writing and Postcolonial Politics," *Ariel* 25, no. 4 (Oct. 1994): 153–67.

Clingman, Stephen R. *Bram Fischer: Afrikaner Revolutionary*. Amherst: University of Massachusetts Press, 1998.

———. *The Novels of Nadine Gordimer: History from the Inside*. London: Allen and Unwin, 1986.

Coetzee, J. M. *White Writing: On the Culture of Letters in South Africa*. New Haven, Conn.: Yale University Press, 1988.

Cooke, John. *The Novels of Nadine Gordimer: Private Lives/Public Landscapes*. Baton Rouge: Louisiana State University Press, 1985.

Daymond, M. J., J. U. Jacobs, and M. Lenta, eds. *Momentum: On Recent South African Writing*. Pietermaritzburg: University of Natal Press, 1984.

Driver, Dorothy, et al. *Nadine Gordimer: A Bibliography of Primary and Secondary Sources, 1937–1992*. Oxford: Zell, 1993.

Driver, Dorothy. "Nadine Gordimer: The Politicisation of Women," *English in Africa* 10, no. 2 (1983): 29–54.

Engle, Lars. "The Political Uncanny: The Novels of Nadine Gordimer," *Yale Journal of Criticism*, 2, no. 2 (1989): 101–27.

Ettin, Andrew V. *Betrayals of the Body Politic: The Literary Commitments of Nadine Gordimer.* Charlottesville: University Press of Virginia, 1993.

Glenn, Ian. "Nadine Gordimer, J. M. Coetzee and the Politics of Interpretation," *South Atlantic Quarterly* 93, no. 1 (1994): 11–32.

Gordimer, Nadine. *The Essential Gesture: Writing, Politics and Places*, edited by Stephen Clingman. New York: Penguin, 1989.

———. "The Fischer Case," *London Magazine* 5, no. 12 (Mar. 1966): 21–30.

———. "Why Did Bram Fischer Choose Jail?" *New York Times Magazine*, 14 Aug. 1966, pp. 30–31, 80–81, 84.

Green, Robert. "From *The Lying Days* to *July's People*: The Novels of Nadine Gordimer," *Journal of Modern Literature* 14, no. 4 (1988): 543–65.

Greenstein, Susan. "Miranda's Story: Nadine Gordimer and the Literature of Empire," *Novel*, 18, no. 3 (Spring 1985): 227–42.

Guide to the Nadine Gordimer Papers in the Lilly Library, rev. ed. Bloomington: Indiana University, 2001.

Haarhoff, Dorian. "Two Cheers for Socialism: Nadine Gordimer and E. M. Forster," *English in Africa* 9, no. 1 (1982): 55–64.

Haugh, Robert F. *Nadine Gordimer.* New York: Twayne, 1974.

Head, Dominic. *Nadine Gordimer*. Cambridge: Cambridge University Press, 1994.

Holland, Heidi. *The Struggle: A History of the African National Congress*. London: Grafton, 1989.

Holland, Roy. "The Critical Writing of Nadine Gordimer," *Communiqué* 7, no. 2 (1982): 7–33.

Johnson, Karen Ramsay. "'What the Name Will Make Happen': Strategies of Naming in Nadine Gordimer's Novels," *Ariel* 26, no. 3 (1995): 117–37.

King, Bruce, ed. *The Later Fiction of Nadine Gordimer.* London: Macmillan, 1993.

http://landow. stg.brown.edu/post/gordimer/gordimerov.html

Laurence, John. *The Seeds of Disaster.* London: Gollancz, 1968.

Leeuwenburg, Rina. "Nadine Gordimer's *Burger's Daughter*: Why Does Rosa Go Back?" *New Literature Review* 14 (1985): 23–31.

Martin, Richard G. "Narrative, History, Ideology: A Study of *Waiting for the Barbarians* and *Burger's Daughter*," *Ariel* 17, no. 3 (1986): 3–21.

Nadine Gordimer Special Issue. Ariel 19, no. 4 (Oct. 1988).

Ndebele, Njabulo. *Rediscovery of the Ordinary*. Manchester, England: Manchester University Press, 1991.

Newman, Judie. *Nadine Gordimer*. London: Routledge, 1988.

Oliphant, Andries Walter. *A Writing Life: Celebrating Nadine Gordimer*. London: Viking, 1998.

Peck, Richard. "Condemned to Choose, But What? Existentialism in Selected Works by Fugard, Brink and Gordimer." *Research in African Literatures* 23, no. 3 (Fall 1992): 67–84.

———. "One Foot before the Other into an Unknown Future: The Dialectic in Nadine Gordimer's *Burger's Daughter*," *World Literature Written in English* 29, no. 1 (1989): 26–43.

Pettersson, Rose. *Nadine Gordimer's One Story of a State Apart*. Stockholm, Sweden: Almqvist and Wiksell, 1995.

Rich, Paul. "Tradition and Revolt in South African Fiction: The Novels of André Brink, Nadine Gordimer and J. M. Coetzee," *Journal of Southern African Studies* 9, no. 1 (1982): 54–73.

Roberts, Sheila. "South African Censorship and the Case of Burger's Daughter," *World Literature Written in English* 20 (1981): 41–48.

Smith, Rowland, "Living for the Future: Nadine Gordimer's *Burger's Daughter*," *World Literature Written in English* 19 (1980): 163–73.

Smith, Rowland, ed. *Critical Essays on Nadine Gordimer*. Boston: Hall, 1990.

Temple-Thurston, Barbara. *Nadine Gordimer Revisited*. New York: Twayne, 1999.

Thompson, Leonard. *A History of South Africa*. New Haven, Conn.: Yale University Press, 1995.

Trump, Martin, ed. *Rendering Things Visible: Essays on South African Literary Culture*. Johannesburg, South Africa: Ravan, 1990.

Van Onselen, Charles. *Studies in the Social and Economic History of the Witwatersrand*. London: Longman, 1982.

Visel, Robin. "A Half-Colonization: The Problem of the White Colonial Woman Reader," *Kunapipi* 10, no. 3 (1988): 39–45.

———. "Othering the Self: Nadine Gordimer's Colonial Heroines," *Ariel* 19, no. 4 Oct. 1988): 33–42.

Wade, Michael. *Nadine Gordimer*. London: Evans, 1978.

———. *White on Black in South Africa: A Study of English-Language Inscriptions of Skin Color*. New York: St. Martin's, 1993.

Wagner, Kathrin. *Re-reading Nadine Gordimer: Text and Subtext in the Novels*. Bloomington: Indiana University Press, 1994.

Ward, David. *Chronicles of Darkness*. London: Routledge, 1989.

Wettenhall, Irene. "Liberalism and Radicalism in South Africa since 1948: Nadine Gordimer's Fiction," *New Literature Review* 8 (1980): 36–44.

White, Jonathan. *Recasting the World: Writing after Colonialism.* Baltimore, Md.: Johns Hopkins University Press, 1993.

White, Landeg, and Tim Couzens, eds. *Literature and Society in South Africa.* London: Longman, 1984.

Yelin, Louise. *From the Margins of Empire: Christina Stead, Doris Lessing, Nadine Gordimer.* Ithaca, N.Y.: Cornell University Press, 1998.

———. "Problems of Gordimer's Poetics: Dialogue in *Burger's Daughter*," in *Feminism, Bakhtin and the Dialogic*, ed. Dale M. Bauer and Susan Janet McKinstry, 219–38. Albany: State University of New York Press, 1991.